GLOBAL SECURITY WATCH
INDIA

INDIA

Amit Gupta

PRAEGER

AN IMPRINT OF ABC-CLIO, LLC
Santa Barbara, California • Denver, Colorado • Oxford, England

Library of Congress Cataloging-in-Publication Data

Gupta, Amit, 1958–
   Global security watch—India / Amit Gupta.
      p. cm. — (Global security watch)
   Includes bibliographical references and index.
   ISBN 978-0-313-39586-4 (hardcopy : alk. paper) — ISBN 978-0-313-39587-1 (e-book)
  1. India—Foreign relations. 2. National security—India. I. Title.
   DS449.G87   2012
   355'.033054—dc23   2012020976

ISBN: 978-0-313-39586-4
EISBN: 978-0-313-39587-1

16 15 14 13 12   1 2 3 4 5

This book is also available on the World Wide Web as an eBook.
Visit www.abc-clio.com for details.

Praeger
An Imprint of ABC-CLIO, LLC

ABC-CLIO, LLC
130 Cremona Drive, P.O. Box 1911
Santa Barbara, California 93116-1911

This book is printed on acid-free paper ∞

Manufactured in the United States of America

Contents

Preface

International observers looking into the future see China, the United States, and India as the world's largest economies, and these analysts assume that with the rise of India and China there will be a corresponding growth in these countries' military capabilities and their foreign policy interests. India's rise to power, however, is dependent on its ability to resolve its internal challenges as well as its willingness to participate as a stakeholder in the international system—particularly in what has been described as the Indo-Pacific region.

Internally, India will have to create an economy that is sound enough to successfully absorb the large mass of youth that comprise more than 50 percent of the nation's population. In part, this absorption will require genuinely effective poverty reduction programs that can lift more than 300 million Indians out of abject poverty. The other part is to continue policies that educate young Indians and successfully integrate them into the global economy. Both of these steps will require overhauling the education system to train a working-age population that can meet the requirements of a rapidly evolving global economy. Additionally, India will have to continue the policies that encourage market reforms and lead to an economy that is increasingly innovative and globally competitive. In a globalized world, moreover, the economic development of India rests on reshaping or modifying its bilateral relationships with several nations as well as creating opportunities in an increasingly complex and integrated international system. For India, its most important relationships are with Pakistan, China, the United States, and, primarily from a military perspective, Russia.

Pakistan remains a security concern for India because of its ability to carry out nonstate violence in India through various terrorist groups, and there remain doubts about the stability of the nuclear balance in South Asia. For India, the security dilemma remains how to convince Pakistan to not support terrorist groups and to work toward stabilizing the nuclear balance without conceding significant concessions on the Kashmir issue. It has been argued that India will, in fact, be unable to play a major role in international affairs unless it is able to successfully move its relationship with Pakistan to a less hostile one. While this author disagrees with that belief, the fact remains that Indian policymakers remain concerned about Pakistan and make it a central focus of the nation's foreign and security policy.

While Pakistan continues to create problems for India, it is China that is emerging as the major challenger to New Delhi in the international system. A nearly 50-year-old territorial dispute, the arming of Pakistan (which includes the transfer of nuclear and missile technology), concerns about China locking down energy supplies globally and preventing India from accessing them, and China's reluctance to support India's accession to permanent membership of the United Nations Security Council are among the reasons India believes that China will not allow India to achieve its rightful place as a major power in Asia. India's options for dealing with China are either to engage in a costly arms race that allows it to match Beijing's military prowess or to seek alliances that help India to balance off China. Indian developmental priorities will not permit the first, while residual Indian worries about violating its nonaligned position as well as a real concern that it would anger China and precipitate action by Beijing make the second option difficult. Yet, if India has to continue with its economic development and reinforce its security, it will have to make this hard choice. The third alternative is one where the two countries can resolve their security differences as well as their contradictory worldviews to cement their bourgeoning economic relationship. The fact that both countries have a rapidly growing trade relationship and are cooperating in multilateral forums like the BRICs summits are examples of the future basis for a political relationship. Foreign policy optimists in India believe that such an accommodation of interests is possible, while the more pessimistic would suggest it will likely make India into a state that is subordinate to China.

Given the need to balance China, the United States becomes the most logical partner for future Indian foreign policy endeavors. Similar values, increasingly common perspectives on international security issues, worries about future Chinese intentions, and the need for U.S. technology to forward Indian developmental and defense efforts make it likely that the India–U.S. relationship will flourish in the coming decades, leading perhaps to a true strategic partnership. Many within the Indian polity, foreign policy circles, and academia, however, view such an alliance as constraining Indian autonomy in the international system and making India into a junior partner of the United States. How to increase the density of the relationship while maintaining autonomy is, from an Indian perspective, the major challenge to the evolution of the relationship. India is working through increased military contacts and the procurement of certain types of weaponry to improve its ability to plug and play with the United States in the area of military operations. At the same time, the foreign policy concept of a strategic partnership is fluid enough to allow both countries to pick and chose where and when they seek to work with each other to achieve certain security outcomes. What issues they seek to work together on remain to be seen.

While the United States is becoming a significant supplier of weapons systems to India and a new political partner, Russia remains a major arms supplier but a diminished political ally to New Delhi. Russia has transformed the India–Russia military relationship from a political alliance into a cash-and-carry economic transaction, and to hold on to the Indian market, as well as safeguard its own industry, Moscow has agreed to transfer systems to India that it would not give to other nations—including the leasing of two Akula nuclear submarines. Yet, despite such significant arms sales, India–Russia bilateral trade was under $9 billion in 2011 and will never touch the volume that exists between India and the more economically dynamic regions of the world. Politically, a diminished Russia does not fit into New Delhi's future plans for regional order in the Indo-Pacific region.

Given these facts, where does Indian foreign policy stand? To summarize its problems, it has to neutralize Pakistan, gain respect from China, have closer ties with the United States yet not appear to be a puppet, and continue the military relationship with Russia. The first three issues are central to the Indian foreign policy dilemma. Closer ties with the United States, for example, require reorienting some of India's major relationships like the one it has with Iran, something that India, for both external and domestic political reasons, has been unwilling to do. Neutralizing Pakistan is difficult, given the presence of nuclear weapons in Islamabad's arsenal and the Indian inability to effectively counter terrorist actions emanating from Pakistani soil.

Gaining China's respect is central to India's preservation of its own territorial integrity, given a disputed border with China, but also to its own emergence as a major power. Unless China makes the accommodations that India requires, which include support for permanent membership of the United Nations Security Council, a great power status would be difficult if not impossible. How India goes about gaining such a Chinese accommodation will be a central part of its foreign policy efforts.

If India is able to successfully resolve its foreign policy dilemmas, the question remains whether India has the will to be a major stakeholder in the international system. So far, the record in this area has been poor. Indian leaders have been obsessed with internal political and developmental issues and have been reluctant to focus their nation's energies abroad. Secondly, India faces a demographic chasm where the country's leading politicians are sexagenarians and septuagenarians, while the overwhelming majority of the country comprises young people. While the young are innovative, energetic, and globalized in their outlook, the old are cautious in the exercise of military power and limited in their worldview.

Till a demographic transition takes place in the ranks of political authority, we are unlikely to see a major shift in India's will to project power. This could include an unanticipated border conflict between India and China that is sparked by miscommunications or domestic political posturing. In that case, India would successfully militarize and become far more proactive extraregionally, as it seeks to counterbalance China. This was certainly the case after the 1962 India–China war when India responded by militarizing. Which way India goes will be determined, therefore, by time circumstances.

This book, therefore, examines why India's foreign and security policy is configured in its current manner and where it is headed in the short to medium term. It does this by looking at India's central interactions as well as its foreign policy actions in adjacent areas like Southwest and Southeast Asia. It then goes on to look at where the Indian government is headed in the future within the Indo-Pacific region, a geographical and political region best described by Secretary of State Hillary Clinton.

The views expressed in this book are those of the author and not necessarily those of the U.S. Department of Defense or the United States Air Force.

Acknowledgments

Like all academic books, this one was made possible by the help given by friends and institutions. In India, the Institute for Peace and Conflict Studies has been my watering hole for several years now, and my sincere thanks to General Dipankar Banerjee, Mr. P. R. Chari, Suba Chandran, and Mallika Joesph for all their help over the last few years.

In the United States, the USAF Air War College has been a generous and patient employer.

No book of mine can be completed, however, without thanking my mother Ambika Gupta and my sister Ira who helped in this case by making my trips to India more successful.

Finally, this book is dedicated to my dear friend Siri Skare who was killed in the line of duty in Afghanistan in April 2011. Lieutenant Colonel Skare of the Royal Norwegian Air Force went on a second tour of Afghanistan, by choice, as a member of the United Nations force to help the people of Afghanistan. When a close-minded preacher in the United States burnt a copy of the Koran, she was one of the innocent victims brutally murdered by an equally close-minded mob in Mazar-e-sharif, Afghanistan, that sought to avenge the desecration of the Muslim holy book.

Siri was a good friend and a thoughtful human being. My last conversation with her was about the women who worked in the compound where she was staying. These women had been sacked, and she was working hard to find them alternative employment because they were the breadwinners of their families—as they say, the good die young. Her death is mourned by her family, friends, and colleagues.

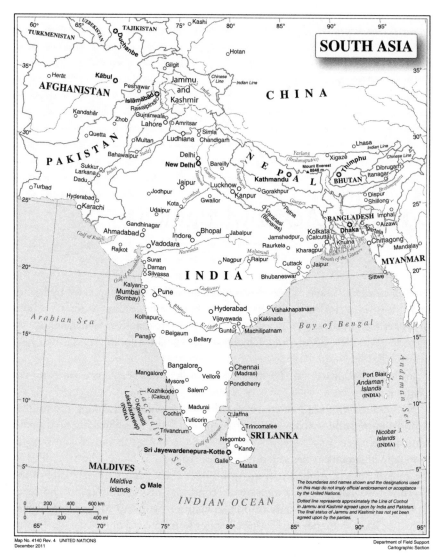

India Map: (South Asia, Map 4140 Rev. December 4, 2011,
UN Cartographic Section)

CHAPTER 1

India: Domestic and International Considerations in an Age of Globalization

In recent times, external observers as well as Indians themselves have spoken of the emergence of India as a global power. Thus, the Mckinsey Corporation spoke of the Indian economy as a "bird of gold" that was ready to take flight.[1] India's Bharatiya Janata Party (BJP)—the Indian People's Party—in its 2004 election campaign went with the slogan, India Shining, which included everything from high growth rates and market reforms to the successful test of nuclear weapons. Both external and internal cheerleaders are basing their analysis on an examination of the Indian political, social, and economic process. What this chapter does, therefore, is to examine the domestic trends that are shaping India in the short to medium term and use them to lay the basis for a discussion of Indian power capabilities and foreign policy objectives. Before doing this, however, it is necessary to lay the background for what the fundamentals of Indian foreign policy are and how they have changed in the decades since independence.

BACKGROUND

The characteristics of Indian foreign policy emerged from India's historical experience, the worldview of its leadership, and the global environment of the Cold War into which the newly independent India was thrust in 1947. While a colony, India underwent large-scale political mobilization on both sides of the political spectrum. Pre-independence India thus had a range of opinions on foreign policy issues ranging from the Indian Communists who saw the world in terms of revolution and class struggle to right-wing political groups that sought to recreate an ancient Indian empire that extended from India to Southeast Asia. Within the center, there were groups like the now-defunct Swatantra Party that sought to follow a pro-American foreign policy with a liberalized economy. This range of views led to lively debates in the Indian parliament as described by Werner Levi:

> It was a heated debate and innumerable proposals were made. M. R. Masani, at one extreme, advocated the closest possible cooperation with the West. Brajeshwar Prasad, at the other extreme, suggested a Moscow-Peking-Delhi axis. Wandering in between, as Nehru expressed it, were all the others advertising their particular schemes: a stronger United Nations, a federal world government, a third force, a series of non-aggression pacts, an Indian-Japanese-Indonesian Union, a better British Commonwealth, withdrawal from the British Commonwealth. The great variety of plans indicated the indecision and doubt now prevailing in India and the split personality of many Indian leaders between Westernization and the "Asia for the Asians" complex. Underlying all suggestions was an urgent sense of the need for a more positive policy. In the end, no one suggestion received enough support to be accepted. The government's policy was approved without a dissenting vote.[2]

Levi's comments show the range of political opinions existing in a new and fragile Indian political system, and, therefore, it was perhaps natural that the policy that emerged was one that sought to include all these shades of opinion in a broad-based national consensus. This policy, conceived by the Indian prime minister Jawaharlal Nehru and his advisors, was one of nonalignment in external affairs.

In 1947, independent India faced a bleak foreign policy environment. Although recognized by the major nations of the world, none of the powers were welcoming of the newly independent country. Stalin's Soviet Union accepted an ambassador from India, but Stalin never met the ambassador—Nehru's sister Vijaylaxmi Pandit—during her tenure. The Soviet Union also had no problems supporting the Communist Party of India, which in 1948–1949 sought to wage an armed insurrection against the government in parts of India.[3] As for the United States, the feeling in New Delhi, even among the non-Communist elites, was that the United States was not willing to see India achieve its rightful place in the international system and that Washington resented India for not being able to impose the type of international order that Cold War rivalries demanded. In the Chinese case, while Indians were concerned about the challenge posed by Indian communism, they welcomed Chinese communism for its nationalist and anticolonial aspects and in the early years Mao reciprocated in what has been called the golden years of the Sino-Indian relationship.

Nehru subsequently sought to create a foreign policy that would allow India to use the goodwill of both emerging global power blocs to help in the advancement of India. What followed was the policy of nonalignment that he saw as permitting India to have good relations with both blocs and thereby to benefit economically and politically from such arrangements. Nehru's foreign policy was based on the premise that while India was a poor country it was a great one that had the right to be a prominent actor in international affairs. It was with this in mind that Nehru sought to participate actively in the affairs of the United Nations, and subsequently India was to play a prominent role in the negotiations over the termination of the Korean War; India was invited to the 1954 Geneva Peace Conference on Korea. In fact, till the India-China war of 1962, Nehru, using the platform of nonalignment, was able to give India far greater prominence in international affairs than merited by the country's then modest military and economic status.

Nonalignment as perceived by Nehru was not Swiss style neutrality but rather a policy where countries like India sided with either of the superpowers based on the merits of the issue. In actual practice this did not work that well. While India got rave reviews in the developing world for its condemnation of the Anglo-French-Israeli invasion of the Suez Canal in 1956, Nehru's silence over the Soviet invasion of Hungary in the same year left outside observers accusing him of double standards (the point usually made is that India had to maintain diplomatic silence since it had recently signed an agreement with the Soviet Union to acquire a steel mill).

The second plank of Nehru's foreign policy, and again another one that was to help get the country prominence in the international stage, was to push for global disarmament and the reduction of tensions between the great powers. While usually dismissed as an Indian attempt to confuse foreign policy with Indian traditions of nonviolence and Gandhianism, it was actually based on an understanding of the realities of the international system. Nehru felt that the world being turned into two armed camps made it an exceedingly dangerous place and by building a nonaligned movement it created a geographical space that was insulated from Cold War politics and, therefore, helped reduce tensions between the two superpowers. The Indian prime minister believed that if global disarmament would take place, it would permit nations to move resources away from militarization to tackling the problems of poverty and underdevelopment in the non-Western world, which, in the long run, would be perhaps the greatest challenges to international peace. Given the wars and strife that beset the non-Western world, and the impact these had on global security with the involvement of the great powers, this was not an unrealistic assumption on Nehru's part. While Nehru sought to create a foreign policy that would give India greater prominence in regional affairs, his regional policy was based on the continuation of British policies in the South Asian region. Further, the creation of the state of Pakistan had brought about a new set of security challenges that made it difficult for India to have a calm neighborhood that promoted regional development.

Yet, while Nehru's global policies were liberal internationalist, his policies in the South Asian region were pragmatic and hard-core realist. To quote Levi again, "In the region surrounding India, foreign policy has been neither neutral nor easily compatible with the high moral principles Nehru insists on seeing applied on the world scene. Here, Nehru is neither the 'dreamer' nor the 'idealist' but very much the realist who knows that in a sovereign nation-state system national survival is the primary aim of foreign policy. 'I am on my side and nobody else's,' he said during the recent debate."[4] There Nehru essentially took on the British security policy and adopted the position that should be a cordon sanitaire around South Asia and that India's borders were unalterable; the latter position was to lead to disastrous consequences in the relationship with China. By 1962, the India-China border dispute escalated into a war that saw China overrun the Indian positions. Beijing then imposed a unilateral cease-fire. Fifty years later, the border remains a disputed issue between the two countries and a sore spot in the Indian psyche. More importantly, the border war exposed the weaknesses of Nehru's foreign and domestic policies as the country was unable to defend itself.

THE INDIRA GANDHI PERIOD

Nehru died in 1964, and his successor, Lal Bahadur Shastri, had a short tenure only to die during the India-Pakistan peace talks in Tashkent (following the war of 1965) and was succeeded by Nehru's daughter Indira Gandhi. Mrs. Gandhi inherited an India that was plagued by economic and social tensions. In the late 1960s, the country faced the Bihar famines, which forced the Indian government to ask for American largesse in grain supplies. This period was also marked by the start of the first major rebellion in the Bengali district of Naxalbari. At the same time, the Indian economy had started to show the limitations posed by a socialist policy of overdependence on state-led development. Unlike her father, therefore, Mrs. Gandhi's foreign policy was more consumed by regional and domestic matters.

International and regional events, however, improved Mrs. Gandhi's fortunes and allowed India to improve its foreign policy position and its security status in South Asia. By 1969, the open military clashes between China and the Soviet Union along the Ussuri and Amur rivers led to a clearly visible split in the Communist world—one which was exploited by India in 1971 when it signed a peace and friendship treaty with Moscow. The other shift was the disintegrating political situation in East Pakistan.

Since independence, Pakistan had posed as India's major security and foreign policy challenge with the two countries fighting wars in 1947–1948 and 1965. In both wars, action had primarily been along the borders with West Pakistan. By 1970, however, the political situation in East Pakistan had started to deteriorate as Bengali nationalists demanded greater autonomy for their province. In the Pakistani elections of March 1971, Sheikh Mujibur Rehman, leader of the Awami League party, won the elections and given his party's majority should have been allowed to form the government in Islamabad. Instead, Pakistan's military overturned the election results, leading to a civil war in East Pakistan. East Pakistani refugees flowed into India, and the Indian government, in December 1971, launched a full-scale assault on the eastern flank of Pakistan. What followed after a brief war was the dismemberment of Pakistan.

The creation of Bangladesh left India without a strategic competitor in South Asia, but at the same time it sowed the seeds for long-term problems with Islamabad. India cemented its position of predominance in South Asia by testing a nuclear device in 1974. These actions while stabilizing India's position in the short term created long-term security problems for the country. Pakistan reacted to the loss of East Pakistan by actively seeking nuclear weapons and then supporting terrorism in Indian Punjab in the 1980s and sending in jihadis as well as supporting the domestic insurgency in Kashmir in the 1990s.

Faced with increasing domestic opposition and civil unrest, Mrs. Gandhi imposed an authoritarian government on the country in 1975 and snuffed out all political dissent till 1977 when she called for a snap election. Mrs. Gandhi, however, underestimated the opposition to her authoritarian rule, particularly the attempt in northern India to carry out forced sterilizations. She lost the elections, and the octogenarian Morarji Desai led a coalition of parties to power. Unlike Mrs. Gandhi, Desai was staunchly antinuclear. He was also in favor of improving relations with the country's neighbors, which saw a period of cordiality in the region. The policy emanating from New Delhi suggested that New Delhi was willing to go with a reduced security in favor of improved relations. Desai's government fell due to political infighting, and Mrs. Gandhi returned with a majority in 1980.

By the time Mrs. Gandhi came back to power, the Soviet Union had invaded Afghanistan, and India, which was by then tied to the hip with Moscow, ended up supporting the Soviet action. Indian nonalignment had by then lost credibility that was not to be regained until after the end of the Cold War. New Delhi's compulsions stemmed from the fact that by the 1980s the Soviet Union had become a major trading partner, a security guarantor, and the largest arms supplier to India—providing perhaps 70 percent of India's weaponry. What consumed Mrs. Gandhi's attention, however, was the crisis in Punjab where Sikh extremists, with support from Pakistan, had started a campaign of violence and terror. The Sikh terror campaign ultimately claimed Mrs. Gandhi's life as she was gunned down by her Sikh bodyguards in revenge for the Indian Army's attack on the Golden Temple—the holiest site of the Sikhs that was taken over by the leader of the extremists, Jarnail Singh Bhindranwale.

Mrs. Gandhi's tenure as prime minister had been marked by triumph but also by putting India into an economic stagnation as socialistic practices weakened the economy and encouraged corruption. India, by the 1980s, had fallen behind Southeast and East Asia, which were by then labeled as dynamic economic tigers. Politically, with the renewal of the Cold War, after the Afghan invasion, India was marginalized because it no longer could play the role of maneuvering between the major powers.

Rajiv Gandhi

Mrs. Gandhi was replaced by her son Rajiv Gandhi who sought both economic reforms as well as to put military teeth to India's foreign policy. Gandhi introduced the first set of economic reforms that permitted the entry of multinationals into the country. The Indian consumer, starved of options for nearly 40 years, was suddenly inundated with cars, televisions, and other consumer goods thus making the economy boom. Gandhi also sought to build up the Indian military capability, particularly the nuclear weapons program. The program, that had been essentially moribund since the 1970s, was now given teeth as India started to invest in producing credible delivery systems and in attempting to make the Indian nuclear deterrent more credible. Gandhi, in 1987, also agreed to send troops to Sri Lanka to try and bring about peace between the warring factions. The Indian intervention ended disastrously as it did not lead to peace in the country, and Indian troops ended up fighting the Tamil rebels (who India had trained and armed earlier). Rajiv Gandhi lost the 1989 elections and before the 1991 election results could be announced was assassinated by the Tamil Tigers.

Narasimha Rao and Reforms

The Congress party turned to the veteran politician Narasimha Rao to be prime minister, and he chose the technocrat Manmohan Singh as his finance minister. The Narasimha Rao government was forced to make major shifts in Indian foreign and economic policies because of the changed international environment due to the Cold War as well as a crisis in the domestic economy. By 1991, the Indian economy had run aground, and the country was on the verge of not being able to pay for its imports. Under the guidance of Manmohan Singh, the country instituted far-reaching economic reforms to make India more competitive and to attract foreign investments.

The other major problem faced by the Indian government came from the collapse of the Soviet Union. The death of the Soviet Union left India with several hard choices. It now faced an international environment where it no longer had a superpower backer and was required to reformulate its approach to the new constellation of power in the international system. In effect this meant working out a new relationship with the remaining superpower, the United States. The Rao government's economic reforms had far-reaching consequences for the country, moving it from a nation stuck in economic stagnation into an economy that is reckoned to become the third largest economy in the world by 2030. More importantly, the Narasimha Rao government worked to operationalize the nuclear weapons program to the extent of contemplating a nuclear test, although the decision was made not to test because:

> He [Rao] said there was no consensus on the test. There were divisions not only among the economists and administrators but also among the scientists themselves. He felt that he would conduct the test if he came back to office.[5]

Rao was also under considerable pressure from the United States, but the decision to not test may indeed have been because Indian scientists may not have been ready to carry out a range of tests with any certainty.

Rao's government was followed by coalition governments led most prominently by Inder Gujral who put forth the Gujral doctrine that called for improving relations with India's neighbors. The real shift in Indian foreign and security policy came with the coming to power of the BJP in 1998.

Led by Atal Bihari Vajpayee, after a gap of 24 years, the BJP moved ahead to test a new group of nuclear weapons, and this was after giving U.S. officials an assurance that no tests were forthcoming. India's tests were marked by sanctions by all the Western nations except France, but the BJP was pro-American, and its active diplomacy gradually persuaded the United States to adopt a more nuanced approach in dealing with New Delhi.[6] The other major event of the Vajpayee government's time in rule was the emergence of India as an information technology powerhouse even though the government had little to do directly with the emergence of this industry. The Vajpayee years were marked by the rise of India from being a poor backward nation to being considered as not only an emerging economy but also a major political player in the world. Vajpayee's rule was marred by the tragic 2002 Hindu-Muslim riots in Gujarat where the state's BJP government sat back and let Hindu mobs rampage Muslim neighborhoods, leading to the death of more than 2,000 people, mostly Muslims. The riots were India's first globalized riots since they were broadcast worldwide by the media, and the international community reacted adversely to the widespread killings. The long-term repercussions of the riots were that India's Muslim population turned irrevocably against the BJP perhaps hurting its chances for ever returning to power in New Delhi.

Thus, in 2004, the BJP launched its Shining India campaign that projected India as a modern nation of information technology, nuclear weapons, a booming stock market, and a globalized economy, but in a surprising turn of events the BJP lost and the Congress party was returned to power. The party appointed the technocrat Manmohan Singh as the prime minister, and he faced a globalized world where the characteristics of globalization now impacted heavily on the making and implementation of Indian foreign policy.

GLOBALIZATION AND INDIA

Globalization can take on multiple meanings, but for the purposes of this book we are viewing it as the globalized flow of wealth and investments, technologies, ideas, and labor. Wealth and investment flows are obvious as nations and individual investors seek, at the stroke of an electronic keyboard, to send investment flows across the world for greater profits. Thus, the rise of foreign direct investment (FDI) and foreign institutional investment (FII) have raised or lowered the futures of countries across the world. Technologies, especially information technologies, have acted as levelers in the quest of nations to compete globally. We are also seeing a situation where techno-nationalism, which is a nation's pursuit of indigenously developing technologies, is being replaced by techno-globalism, where nations collaborate across borders to improve their products and technologies.

Ideas that have gained root in a globalized world are those of democracy and good governance, and perhaps, more importantly, they have been spread by the language of globalization, which is English. Francis Fukuyama[7] was partially correct in his essay on the end of history in that nations are now either democratic or making excuses for why they are not following the democratic path. And such is the power of English that it has become the language that conveys these ideas across the world, and it is, therefore, viewed as the language of modernity. For India the rise of democracy and the global spread of English are natural advantages since India, despite its flaws, remains a functioning democracy, and its large pool of English speakers have given it a major advantage in terms of competing economically in a globalized world.

Lastly, the spread of globalization has been marked by the flow of intellectual and professional labor. In a globalized world, Ben Wildavsky points out that all nations are eagerly competing to attract the best brains from other countries in the form of students since this import of intellectual labor strengthens a nation's educational institutions, technological capability, and knowledge-based economy.[8] For India, the flow of intellectual labor out of the country has created a highly affluent Indian diaspora, which now plays a significant role in boosting the country's economic fortunes. Further, the flow of investments out of India, as well as the new opportunities created by global trade linkages, has allowed India to tap into civilian and military sectors of other nations to boost both its economy and its military capabilities. While globalization has boosted the country's economy, several internal factors may create potential long-term problems for India. A good way of looking at these issues is within a 15-year time lens since this takes us from the short to the medium term in making an analysis of Indian capabilities.

2010–2025

If we view the period 2010–2025 as a short- to medium-term period, then what are the major characteristics of the India that is likely to emerge at the end of this time frame? First, India will remain a very young country. Its current median age is 25, and by 2025, according to the United Nations Population Report, it will rise to 29.7.[9] This young population is likely to be better educated, with a larger number of students going on to college and seeking an English language education. The attempts by various Indian governments in the past to try and push Indian languages are now being replaced by a belief among the Indian educational consumer that English is going to be central to any child's success in the Indian economy of the 21st century.

Yet, this youth bulge, as a recent Rand Corporation report argues, cannot provide an optimized performance unless it is linked to an improved infrastructure, better communications technology, and the creation of an increasing number of jobs so as to harness this youth-based economic potential.[10] If it is not harnessed successfully then the alternative scenario exists where large numbers of discontent youth revert to violence.

This is also a young population that is caught in a fundamental age divide. The people who rule India are septuagenarians while the largest group of people in India is the young. India's prime minister, Manmohan Singh, and his leading advisors like Pranab Mukherjee are in their seventies as is the leader of the largest opposition party, the BJP, Lal Krishna Advani. The septuagenarians are not in tune with the new Indian population that is emerging because they, the older generation, are essentially a holdover from the days of a newly independent India. Thus, the septuagenarians are the generation that saw the greatest value in a policy of nonalignment even though the policy has outlived its usefulness in the post–Cold War world. Further, the older generation is the one that implemented Jawaharlal Nehru's vision of a socialistic society, even though it was the current prime minister, Dr. Manmohan Singh, who carried out large-scale market reforms in 1991.

The septuagenarians are also tied down by a worldview that comes from regional and national instability. Their foreign policy mindset is one that emerges from dealing with a neighborhood in which the surrounding states have consistently been politically fragile and where India, by its size and stature, should have a natural role to play in directing the future of the region. Yet, at the same time, this remains a generation that was traumatized by the loss of the 1962 war to China. Since then, India's political elite, while vocal in its criticism of China and concerned about its long-range ambitions in Asia, has been one where the government has been very careful to not antagonize Beijing.

How this interplay between the old and young in India plays out, therefore, will be an interesting one since it will decide the shape of India's economy and political drive. If the old manage to hold on then creeping economic reforms, a timidity in foreign policy, and the inability to think in truly global terms will continue. If the young begin to assert themselves in the country's economic and political system, one may see a vibrant, outwardly oriented policy. The reason for this is that India's younger generation is better educated, has global aspirations, and is not hindered by the baggage of colonialism and the economic and military crises that India faced in the immediate years after independence.

Second, unless there are major discoveries of oil or other energy resources, India will remain a natural resource poor nation that will be dependent on the international energy market. The long-term repercussions of this energy dependency will be felt both in terms of economic development and in terms of the country's international strategy. India, at present, has serious energy production deficiencies, and when coupled with the dependence on other countries for natural gas and oil, the long-term energy problem becomes more acute.

At the international level, the Indian government is concerned about its energy dependence since China has effectively shut out India in its bids to secure oil supplies around the world. On several occasions, in Angola, Nigeria, and Ecuador, India was outbid by Chinese firms and thus ended up unable to lock down long-term energy contracts or the development of energy fields in different regions of the world.[11] Indian analysts thus fear a long-term situation where China has effectively blocked India's access to global energy supplies and thus constrained the country's long-term developmental plans. Yet, energy is going to be vital to India's developmental efforts, and its recent 7–9 percent growth rate has been achieved despite a 20 percent power deficit. This deficit is only likely to grow in the future.

Attempts at harnessing alternative energies have been ongoing in India since the 1990s when the country, in an attempt to improve air quality levels, moved its public transport fleet and its taxis and motor scooters to natural gas. In the short term this move led to a reduction in pollution levels in Indian cities, but with the boom in middle class car sales the advantage of this shift has been lost. For India to aggressively develop, it, even more so perhaps than China, will have to focus on the development of alternative energies and on efficient public transportation.

Another serious constraint, unless addressed, will be the water shortage that the entire South Asian region is likely to face. Environmental changes and a growing population are going to push the country toward severe water shortages in the medium term. With India's population expected to peak at 1.6 billion, Pakistan's population at 335 million, and Bangladesh's at more than 200 million, water shortages become crucial to the survival and future economic and social health of all these states. What makes the water issue more complex is the fact that China has started building dams that will divert the waters of the Brahma-putra away from their natural flow into the Bay of Bengal, thus depriving both Indian and Bangladeshi populations of much needed water supplies.[12]

Fourth, India is a nation with deep ethno-religious divisions that will have to be addressed with developmental, social, and public policy tools. It is a country with more than 177 million Muslims, making it the third largest Muslim coun-try in the world after Indonesia and Pakistan and (depending on whose numbers you look at) the second or third largest Shia country in the world. Estimates vary on whether Pakistan or India is the second largest Shia country. By 2030, the Pew Foundation estimates that India will have a population of 236 million Muslims.[13]

A Muslim population of 177 million cannot be called a statistical minority and is, in fact, a country within a country. India's Muslims, therefore, have the advantage of sheer numbers but do, at the same time, have the problem of being dwarfed by a Hindu population that is economically and educationally more ad-vanced. Within this context there are both positive and negative aspects of the status of Indian Muslims. Electorally, their sheer numbers make them a popula-tion group that cannot be ignored by any of the political parties in the country. The right-wing Hindu nationalist party, the BJP, has sought to position itself in Indian politics as a political grouping that did not require the electoral assistance of the Muslims, but this has backfired electorally at the national level where the number of Muslims makes it difficult for a party with an overtly Hindu nation-alist, and therefore anti-Muslim, agenda to succeed. At the same time, Indian Muslims face the challenges of a dispossessed minority. They complain about ha-rassment by law enforcement authorities and of job discrimination. Further, un-like India's former untouchable population, now referred to as Scheduled Castes, they do not have affirmative action policies working in their favor at the federal level to help push a young generation of Muslims into the white-collar work-place. The Muslim community also complains that when it comes to investigat-ing acts of terror, the government is far more ready to look at Muslim actions and less likely to examine the acts of Hindu extremist groups[14] (although the Indian government has implicated a right-wing Hindu terrorist group in the bombing of the Samjhauta Express train from Pakistan to India, in which 53 Pakistanis were killed).

Worse, there remain continued feelings of insecurity in the Muslim commu-nity about the possible outbreak of sectarian violence—a phenomenon that has plagued India from pre-independence times. The danger, as analysts see it, is of an increasingly alienated Muslim population that feels the need to turn to vio-lence or terrorism in order to press its legitimate demands and/or to ensure the community's security.

The other internal problem that has plagued India in recent years has been the rise of a Maoist insurgency that has cut through the middle of India, working its way into remote areas and getting recruits from the poorest sections of Indian society. The Indian government has adopted a policy it has developed over decades of carrying out police and counterinsurgency operations in the country. The country's paramilitary has been deployed against the Maoists, belatedly developmental efforts have been targeted toward the affected areas, and, more recently, the Indian government has decided to use aerial surveillance to gather intelligence against the insurgents.[15] Unless effective developmental measures are taken, however, this insurgency can be a detriment to the Indian state's capacity to effectively modernize the nation.

Fifth, India lives in a region that is relatively unstable and will continue to be so in the short to medium term. For India, Pakistan continues to be the central regional concern, though Pakistan no longer poses as a challenger to India for regional supremacy. Instead, Pakistan now poses a problem because of its internal instability and its ability to still support terrorist activities in India. Its internal instability leads to fears ranging from the breakup of the Pakistani state—which most Indian analysts consider less likely—to the takeover of the state by a hardline fundamentalist regime that seeks to carry out jihad in India and has the nuclear weapons to back up its action. The propensity to carry on terrorist activities in India—as witnessed by the 2008 Mumbai attacks that left 166 people dead—is now magnified by the existence of a robust and active Indian media that highlights these issues, much to the embarrassment of the state and union governments in the country.

The other countries in the region have similar problems in terms of their stability levels. Bangladesh remains the primary source of illegal immigration into India and, Indian security analysts claim, a source of terrorist activities. Nepal has been in turmoil since the emergence of the insurgency, and even though the Maoists have successfully entered parliament and the country's monarchy has been deposed, the country remains an economic basket case that heavily depends on exporting labor to India.[16] Sri Lanka has successfully destroyed the Tamil Tiger insurgency but will have to take meaningful long-term steps to reintegrate its alienated Tamil minority into the country's body politic.[17]

India, therefore, is surrounded by neighbors who have their own internal political, economic, and security issues, and these do impact adversely India's own domestic security. The Mumbai terror attacks, for example, were conducted by less than a dozen men but brought to a standstill India's most vibrant city and scared tourism away from it. A state system in Pakistan that sees the need to encourage jihadi activities is, therefore, of serious concern to India.

At the military-strategic level, two factors are important while discussing the Indian capacity to engage as a serious world power. The first is India's own military enterprise and how it contributes to the accumulation of an Indian power capability. The other is the political will of the Indian elite to become a great power.

Since independence, India has sought to develop an indigenous arms production capability and has met with mixed results. Its quest to develop conventional weaponry has been met with cost overruns, lengthy delays, political and military-institutional interference, poor quality, and rapid obsolescence. As a consequence, India has had to largely rely on external suppliers for its military supplies, and this has led to an arsenal that is an odd mix of weapons systems from different countries—which has led to both supply and maintenance nightmares. It also has an arsenal that has, at times, been unable to meet the demands of the armed services to combat existing threats capably.

Thus, despite investing in indigenous arms production since the 1950s, the country has had a lackluster record of developing conventional weapons systems and, instead, has been repeatedly forced to seek alternative systems from abroad. What makes this worse, from an Indian standpoint, is that the Indian arms industry has sought to develop state-of-the-art weapons systems while ignoring feasible and practical systems that are in some ways more critical to the immediate success in a conflict. Thus, in the 1999 Kargil conflict, the Indian Army ran out of howitzer shells and had to import them from Israel, even though India had purchased the 155 mm howitzer in the 1980s and its ordnance factories had been producing ammunition since before independence.

Similarly, India has sought to build fighter aircraft and tanks, but its security forces have, till recently, had to soldier along with obsolete small arms (while terrorists and insurgents operating against the state have automatic and semiautomatic weapons). During the November 26 Mumbai terror attacks, one televised scene that brought home the misplaced priorities and failed procurement strategies of the Indian government was the sight of a policeman with a World War II (WWII) vintage bolt-action rifle taking on an AK-47-wielding terrorist. Even more critical, perhaps, was the fact that police officers going into battle against the terrorists had poor quality bulletproof vests and helmets that did little to stop bullets. Thus, India has ended up with a military production capability that squanders resources on producing weaponry that either is of poor quality or is rendered obsolete by the time it is ready for service.

The inability of the arms industry to meet the basic requirements of the armed services has led to a situation where India has to depend on external suppliers for building its military arsenal. In the past, this dependence was constrained by the lack of hard currency resources and the lack of willingness of an external supplier to provide the needed systems. In the past decade, as the economy has boomed, cost is no longer the issue as the government now has the financial resources to pay for the weaponry that its services require. At the same time, the end of the Cold War and the growing burden of maintaining a military force in the Western world have led the major arms-producing nations to open their arms cupboards to India with none of the geo-political restrictions and few of the technological restrictions that existed during the bipolar international system. In fact, the future of several Western weapons programs could well depend on the ability to find markets in non-Western countries like India. France's Dassault, for example, has been saved by getting the Indian Medium Multirole Combat Aircraft deal because the Rafale fighter has yet to find an external buyer.[18] Thus, what we are witnessing in India is a real expansion of the armed forces to meet future threats, with the focus being increasingly on China.

Yet, at the same time, there remains a lack of political will in India to make India a militarily viable global power. The Indian political elite's worldview has changed since the Cold War, reflecting the opening up of new spaces for the country to exercise influence in the international system. Also, the loss of the Soviet Union as an ally forced India to be more regionally proactive in an effort to establish its interests. India thus sought to support the Northern Alliance against the Taliban and to establish a presence at the Ayni airfield in Tajikistan. Additionally, India's move to participate in the global economy has meant that the country's government had to be concerned about protecting its new global assets.

At the same time, the general thrust of Indian politicians remains focused on the local—on their constituencies, their states, and the highly profitable positions in the central cabinet in New Delhi. Thus, while India does take a proactive view on issues like proliferation, climate change, and intellectual property rights (some would say it, in fact, plays the role of a spoiler), it remains a nation that is unwilling to participate in extraregional military operations. As this author was told at a meeting with military officials in New Delhi, the word "expeditionary" is taboo in Indian political circles.

Yet, its economic and security compulsions are making it play an increasingly important role in world affairs. Its energy dependency on external suppliers now makes India worried about the Persian Gulf crisis and the disruption of the free flow of oil from there. This has led to a growing set of naval exercises with other countries in the Indian Ocean region. It has also led to broader patrolling by the Indian Navy as it seeks to prevent piracy and the flow of weaponry across the Indian Ocean region.

Coupled with the growing economic imperatives has been the expansion of China into the Indian Ocean region. While the Chinese claim that their intentions are benign and that New Delhi is overreacting to what is essentially an expansion of Chinese economic interests, India remains worried that China is gradually creating a ring of naval bases to encircle it. Thus, China's presence in the Cocos Islands, Myanmar, Sri Lanka, and Pakistan is seen as an effort to throw a naval ring of containment around India.

India has started to respond to this perceived encirclement by developing its own naval and air power capabilities. The problem for India is that it is moving perhaps far too slowly against a Chinese juggernaut that has bigger economic resources, has a perceived long-term strategic plan, and is committing its resources to the development of a 21st-century military capability. Thus, China's push to develop missile technology, its successful testing of an antisatellite weapon, its plans to build a blue-water navy, its move to build a fifth-generation fighter, and its rapid expansion of infrastructure in the Tibetan region are viewed with grave concern by New Delhi.

The problems for India in its attempts to respond to the Chinese challenge are threefold. First, China has successfully built up Pakistan to the extent that it provides Beijing with deterrence on the cheap vis-à-vis India. Pakistan's nuclear weapons technology was provided by China and Beijing has continued to provide weaponry to Islamabad when other external suppliers have shut it off. Second, India is a latecomer to the game of economic globalization and, as such, is playing catch up to a China which has been pursuing economic reform and modernization for the past 30 years. It finds itself, therefore, lacking the economic resources to compete with China in global markets. Yet, if India is unable to capture some of these markets in the short term, it is likely to find itself shut out by China when it, India, seeks to propel itself toward long-term economic development. Third, India, unlike China, is constrained by the challenge of being a democracy where every policy decision has to be negotiated at length and then may be contested by different interest groups in the Indian public. While China has been able to make spectacular progress due to its totalitarian government, India has faced challenges on issues such as granting companies and public sector corporations land or mining rights because it has involved displacing people who have legal rights and who go to the courts to enforce them.[19] Thus, the Tata Corporation's Nano car project had to be pulled from West Bengal, where the company's acquisition of land was met by a grassroots agitation, and moved to Gujarat, where the big business-friendly chief minister, Narendra Modi, welcomed the entry of the company and its iconic product. Attempts to build dams, expand railways, and allow corporations to explore mineral rights run into environmental concerns, political agitations, and legal challenges, making the sort of growth and progress that China has achieved difficult to replicate within a democratic framework.[20]

Lastly, there is the issue of resolving governance, preventing democratic gridlock, and rooting out corruption in India. Like other democracies around the world, India has been plagued with the problem of gridlock. In the Indian case, this has emerged both from the coalitional politics that have driven the country for the past 15 odd years and from the compulsions of electioneering that make parties become intransigent in an election year, thus bringing about policy paralysis.

India's recent governments have all been based on coalitions, with the smaller members of the groupings using their clout to halt proposed programs or investigations that are viewed as being unfavorable to their power base. The recent controversy over permitting Walmart into the country is a case in point, where coalition members of the Congress party (and elements within the party itself) along with significant public opposition have been reluctant to allow the mega-retailer into the country because it was seen as hurting their power base.[21]

Political calculations during an election year have also seen Indian political groups seek to work against foreign policy and national security measures. With their eye on the 2009 elections, several political groups, including the left parties that supported the Congress government, sought to defeat the government on a resolution to accept the India–U.S. nuclear agreement that would serve as the basis for making India's civilian nuclear program sanctions-free.

Corruption is the other problem that debilitates both democracy and economic development in India. By 2011, foreign corporations, tired of paying bribes to unreliable politicians and bureaucrats, had cut back quite dramatically on FDI into India. The backlash was felt domestically as well, as Anna Hazare launched a Gandhian protest campaign against the government for its inability to reduce corruption and to pass a tough anticorruption bill in parliament.[22] The problem with corruption in India is that it impacts on the general public in the form of micro-corruption as people are harassed by bureaucrats and the police for bribes. It also catches the public eye as India's thriving media unearths scandals of mega-corruption, as in the 2G phone scandal where nearly $31 billion was lost in government revenues.[23]

The net result of such bickering is to create the image of an India that is difficult to do business with and has a chaotic governance process. Unless India is able to improve this image, it will have trouble making the kind of economic leaps it requires to move a large section of its people from poverty into the middle class. More importantly, unless corruption is brought within control in India, not only will it be an unattractive venue for external investment, but it will also start to decay the competencies that have maintained Indian society since independence. Within an environment of corruption, India has institutions that work well and have been the spine of Indian society. Institutions like the Election Commission that has conducted fair and free elections in the world's largest democracy, the Indian armed forces that maintain high levels of professionalism, the Reserve Bank of India that maintains control over monetary policy, and the Indian Institutes of Technology that provide a world-class education in engineering are examples of such islands of efficiency in a corrupt environment. Yet, under constant pressure from the corruption that plagues broader Indian society, these institutions may not be able to successfully survive the strains imposed on them. If that happens, then India is in a real societal crisis that may be impossible to break out of.

STRUCTURE OF THE BOOK

The book examines Indian foreign and security policies within the context of a globalized international system. Within such a system, the Indian government has to try and reconcile between the competing forces of economic integration and national sovereignty. The former is seeing the creation of strong economic connections between India and the rest of the world including hitherto untapped markets like China. On the other hand, there are very real security imperatives that are forcing India to build a more extensive military and take a more proactive and extraregional role in international affairs. The book, therefore, first examines the development of India's indigenous military capabilities because this will be central to its emergence as a great power. It then looks at India's relations with the countries in which it has the greatest interests: the United States, China, Russia, and Pakistan. In the chapter on United States, the role of the Indian American diaspora that may emerge as a key link between the two countries is discussed. The book goes on to examine how India is responding through its economic and military policies to the region that is now defined as the Indo-Pacific. This region is the one that is going to be the area of principal interaction for India in the coming decades and, therefore, merits detailed examination. The volume concludes with a discussion of the future challenges to India in the coming decades.

NOTES

1. Jonathan Ablett, et al., *The "Bird of Gold": The Rise of India's Consumer Market* (San Francisco, CA: Mckinsey Global Institute, 2007), p. 19.

2. Werner Levi, "India Debates Foreign Policy," *Far Eastern Survey* 20, no. 5 (1951): pp. 49–50.

3. M. R. Masani, "The Communist Party of India," *Pacific Affairs* 24, no. 1 (1951): pp. 27–28.

4. Levi, "India Debates Foreign Policy," p. 50.

5. K. Subrahmanyam, "Narasimha Rao and the Bomb," *Strategic Analysis* 28, no. 4 (2004), p. 593.

6. See C. Raja Mohan, *Impossible Allies: Nuclear India, the United States, and Global Order* (New Delhi: India Research Press, 2006).

7. Francis Fukuyama, The End of History and the Last Man, (New York: Free Press, 2006).

8. Ben Wildavsky, *The Great Brain Race: How Global Universities Are Reshaping the World* (Princeton, NJ: Princeton University Press, 2010).

9. *World Population Prospects: The 2010 Revision*, http://esa.un.org/wpp/Excel-Data/population.htm.

10. Charles Wolf Jr, et al., *China and India, 2025. A Comparative Assessment* (Santa Monica, CA: Rand Corporation, 2011), p. 23.

11. Vibhuti Hate, "India's Energy Dilemma," *South Asia Monitor*, no. 98 (2006), p. 4.

12. Sachin Parashar, "Drought Hit China to Divert Brahmaputra?" *The Times of India*, June 13, 2011.

13. *The Future of the Global Muslim Population, 2010–2030, Pew Templeton Global Religious Futures Project, Washington, D.C., 2011*, p. 11.

14. These issues are discussed in the Sachar Committee Report, *Social, Economic, and Educational Status of the Muslim Community in India*, Prime Minister's High Level Committee, Government of India, New Delhi, November 2006, pp. 11–15.

15. "Maoist Insurgents in India: More Bloody and Defiant," *The Economist,* vol. 396, issue 8692, July 24, 2010.

16. See *Nepal's Peace Process: The Endgame Nears, Asia Briefing No. 131,* International Crisis Group, Brussels, December 13, 2011.

17. See *Reconciliation in Sri Lanka: Harder than Ever, Asia Report No. 209,* International Crisis Group, Brussels, July 18, 2011.

18. K. P. Nayar, "Why India Chose the Rafale," *The Telegraph,* Kolkata, India, February 6, 2012.

19. Runa Sarkar, "Overview of the Report," in Nirmal Mohanty, Runa Sarkar, and Ajay Pandey (eds.), *India Infrastructure Report 2009* (New Delhi: Oxford University Press, 2009), p. 1.

20. Vikas Bajaj, "India Approves Long Delayed Steel Mill Project," *The New York Times,* January 31, 2011.

21. Kanya D'Almeida, "India's Stores on Big-Box Frontier," *Asia Times,* February 2, 2012.

22. Ranjit Devraj, "India Fighting for a Less Corrupt Year," *Asia Times,* January 4, 2012.

23. Ibid.

CHAPTER 2

Indian Arms Acquisition and Production

As India moves toward achieving a greater prominence in international affairs, the role of its military industry comes into focus as it seeks to make its force structure more capable and more autonomous to external pressures. Central to acquiring greater autonomy has been the desire of India's political and scientific elites to design and develop weaponry at home, and since the early years of independence, the Indian government has encouraged scientific endeavor in this area. What this chapter establishes is that the structural flaws that have existed in the Indian arms production industry since the onset of the independent Indian state continue to plague Indian arms production efforts. Coupled with India's mixed record with arms acquisition from external sources, it has led to the development of a force structure that has not been able to fully match India's security requirements nor can it meet future threats.

DEFENSE PRODUCTION IN INDIA

India today has a comprehensive arms industry comprising 52 defense research laboratories, 41 ordnance factories, and 8 defense public sector undertakings. These defense production establishments both license produce and independently develop a range of weapons systems for the three branches of India's armed forces. The indigenous production efforts include the Tejas Light Combat Aircraft (LCA), the Arjun main battle tank (MBT), the Integrated Guided Missile Development Program (IGMDP), as well as a nuclear submarine program. More recent projects include the Sitara Intermediate Jet Trainer (IJT), the Advanced Medium Combat Aircraft (AMCA), a multirole transport aircraft, an aircraft carrier program, and an ambitious shipbuilding program. Further, the Indian space program, with its increasingly impressive record of launches, allows India to improve both its surveillance and missile delivery capabilities.

Such indigenous programs are supposed to help boost Indian military capability that is expected to grow significantly in the coming decades. By 2022, the Indian Navy plans to have a 160 ship force with 3 aircraft carriers and up to 400 combat and support aircraft. The coast guard will have from 76 to 217 ships and from 45 to 74 aircraft.[1] The Indian Air Force (IAF) will similarly be seeking to build up its fully sanctioned capacity of 48 combat squadrons. In all these purchases, the Indian government would like to see a greater input from the domestic arms production companies and, in fact, aims to help make these corporations more productive. The government changed its rules, permitting up to a 26 percent stake by foreign direct investment.[2]

Despite such progress, however, the Indian arms industry remains constrained by some of the problems that have beset it since independence. There is a continued reliance on external suppliers, both for technological components and complete systems. There are lengthy delays in the production of indigenously developed systems and, consequently, the arms industry is unable to secure some of the basic requirements of the Indian armed services. In times of war, India has had to look elsewhere for ammunition and on other occasions has had to undertake expensive imports of less advanced systems that could have been produced at home.

Thus, despite positive changes in the past decade, the Indian arms industry continues to display patterns of selecting weapons production programs that come from the country's economic strategy during the era of state-sponsored socialism. Consequently, not only is the country's defense preparedness affected, but so too is the viability of the nation's defense industries. While recent Indian arms production policy has sought to remove some of these deficiencies, the government will have to take steps to move the arms industry away from wasteful and lengthy projects to ones that can not only be successfully completed but will also find a ready market among the country's armed services—as the Agni and Prithvi series of ballistic missiles from the IGMDP have.

This may require giving up some of the expensive and prestigious projects that are ongoing and, instead, focus on producing what cannot be acquired from external suppliers. Further, the pursuit of joint ventures and the development of noncompetitive systems will help the Indian arms industry to be competitive and satisfy the country's defense requirements.

PAST ARMS PRODUCTION POLICY

After India attained independence, the Indian government invited the British scientist, P.M.S. Blackett, to write a report on Indian defense requirements, including any future attempts to initiate indigenous weapons production efforts. Blackett's most important suggestion, taking into account the state of Indian defense science and the general level of Indian industrialization, was that India develop noncompetitive weapons systems. These were weapons that would not become obsolete because of the development of competing and more advanced systems in the industrialized world and ones where the relative quality of the system did not matter. Blackett recommended that India develop antiaircraft guns and transport vehicles, and set the grounds for an aircraft industry by designing and developing trainer aircraft.[3]

Indian defense production, however, did not take this path. In the 1950s, Jawaharlal Nehru took the decision to both cut back military expenditure and use existing defense production facilities to encourage broad-based industrialization in the country. Indian ordnance factories used surplus capacity to produce coffee percolators and sewing machines. At the same time, the Nehru government authorized the development of a supersonic combat aircraft, the HF-24 Marut, the logic being that it would help India develop a modern aircraft industry.

Indian arms production efforts, therefore, followed the country's broader economic strategy. Arms production was state owned and directed and aimed not only at achieving autonomy in military policy, but also in helping to further national economic development. The result was that the country followed a twofold path to weapons development. Ignoring Blackett's advice, the Indian government sought to develop expensive and ambitious projects like the HF-24 Marut. It also invested in the licensed production of conventional weaponry, taking the decision in the early 1960s to license-produce the Soviet MiG-21 and later the Vickers Vijayanta tank. The belief was that developing what were then advanced weapons systems would help the broader industrialization of the nation and help build its scientific base.

DEVELOPMENTAL CONSTRAINTS

Indian defense production efforts were constrained, however, by developmental delays, the existence of threats that needed to be countered, and the bureaucratic agendas of the military and the arms production units. As a late-industrializing country, India found it difficult to develop weapons in a reasonable time frame or to match the superior systems produced in the industrialized countries. The Marut program, for instance, was started at a time when India lacked both the industrial infrastructure and the scientific personnel to carry out such an ambitious program. The emphasis on self-reliance and indigenization, which was integral to Nehru's strategy of state-driven industrialization, led to India wasting scarce resources on reinventing the wheel. Thus, Indian weapons programs were marked by lengthy delays and outright failures or, when weapons finally became available, they were considered obsolescent and the armed forces preferred to import better and more reliable systems—as was the fate of the Marut.[4]

The immediacy of threats has also forced India to import weapons rather than permit the lengthy developmental periods required for indigenously developed weaponry. In the modern-day context, for example, IAF requirements led to the purchase of Sukhoi-30 and Mirage 2000 fighters, while the indigenously de-signed Tejas continued to go through test flights. In the 1980s, India purchased the Bofors howitzer because it found that Pakistan had outgunned it by buy-ing 155 mm howitzers.[5] More recently, the IAF has acquired Airborne Early Warning Systems from Russia because of the lengthy delay in the indigenous sys-tem being developed by the domestic arms industry.

Similarly, the Arjun MBT, which has been under development since 1974—giving it the unflattering title of the world's longest-running tank program—became a lower priority because of the purchase of Russian T-72 and T-90 tanks. In 2004, the Indian Army received its first batch of Arjun tanks and complaints soon emerged about the weight of the tank as well as its fire control system, lead-ing to criticism that the tank should be written off.[6] In 2010, the Army reluc-tantly agreed to purchase another 124 Arjun MBTs even though it saw the tank as reaching obsolescence and wanted to begin the search for a futuristic armored vehicle.[7] The Heavy Vehicle Factory was hoping for an order in the 500–600 range but had to be content with the Army purchase, arguing that it would permit keeping the production line open.

On the naval front, India has manufactured its own nuclear submarine, which is undergoing sea trials, while at the same time leasing two Akula class boats from Russia. The more troubling procurement has been of the modified Kiev Class carrier, the *Admiral Gorshkov* (renamed *Vikramaditya*), that has seen delays and a ballooning in costs. In addition, the configuration of a ski jump for takeoffs and arrestor wires for landing has led to a dependence on the Russian MiG-29K as the combat aircraft to man the carrier since no other currently available naval aircraft has the capability to perform these types of takeoffs and landings. The marine version of the F-35 Lightning Joint Strike Fighter would fit the Indian Navy's requirements, but it is still at the developmental stage and plagued with problems.

From an Indian perspective, the purchase of Russian naval equipment fits nicely into the plan to develop a strategic navy in the coming years. Such a navy would be able to project power around the Indian Ocean littoral and deter Chinese expansion into the area. Given the problems domestic programs have run into, the procurement of Russian nuclear submarines and long-range bombers would give India a quick and ready nuclear strike force. In fact, India's former navy chief Admiral Arun Prakash also called for the country to quickly firm up the Scorpene conventional submarine deal with France and reiterated the Navy's "desperate desire to acquire nuclear submarines but said it was for the government to take decisions."[8]

While threats have constrained the indigenous development of weapons systems, bureaucratic agendas have pushed the Indian government to agree to continue funding programs, both to keep scientists employed and to help in the overall development of the economy—the old argument of defense aiding development. This resulted in the 1980s in several major programs getting government funding—the IGMDP, the Dhruv advanced light helicopter (ALH), the Tejas LCA, and the Arjun MBT.[9]

The Indian armed services, however, were operating in a global military environment and, therefore, comparing their weapons requirements and doctrines with those of Western militaries. In the 1960s, the Indian Navy, for example, drew up a requirement for four aircraft carriers because it wanted to assume the role recently relinquished by the Royal Navy in the Indian Ocean.[10] The IAF, in the 1980s, while drawing up requirements for the LCA based them to a large extent on the 1970s U.S. Light Weight Fighter program that produced the F-16.

The armed forces, therefore, came up with technological requirements that given the state of Indian technological development were difficult to achieve. They also changed their requirements midway through a program—as was the case with the original LCA program and with the earlier Ajeet fighter program.[11] This made the task of bringing the program to fruition even more difficult since changes in specifications led to design and developmental delays. Moreover, when it became possible to purchase weapons from abroad, the armed services preferred to acquire proven imported systems rather than rely on untested indigenous weaponry.

The Indian government, however, has been committed to creating and sustaining a defense science base within the country, and this led India's defense scientists to propose that state-of-the-art weapons systems be designed as opposed to realistic programs that are easily deliverable and do not tend toward obsolescence. Thus, in the 1980s, the Indian government, at the insistence of the defense science establishment, agreed to fund the development of the LCA and an MBT. At that point in time, the IAF was pressing for a new trainer aircraft for its fleet, and the plane it wanted was to be imported from the United Kingdom. When I asked V. S. Arunachalam, the then-head of India's Defence Research and Development Organization, why the country was building an LCA (now named Tejas) that was technologically ambitious and prone to obsolescence rather than build a technologically feasible jet trainer, he replied that building a jet trainer was subjecting the country to technological colonialism.[12] In the broader context of national technological development, Arunachalam's objection made sense. But the arms industry did not have the track record of delivering such systems.

The Tejas LCA has had a troubled history and the plane is finally entering into the inventory of the IAF while development continues of the navalized version that is to take off from carriers.[13] Moreover, the indigenously built Kaveri engine remains in the developmental stage and, therefore, cannot be tested on the aircraft—the latest reports suggest that the engine will not be used on the Tejas but, instead, will be used on Hindustan Aeronautics' future fighter program, the Advanced Medium Combat Aircraft.[14] In the meantime, the naval variant has run into delays, causing the Indian Navy to order more MiG-29Ks for its aircraft carrier fleet.[15]

At the same time, the lure of purchasing foreign aircraft will further hurt the LCA's chances of becoming a mass-produced and successful frontline combat aircraft. India is already license-producing the Sukhoi-30MKI—a far more capable aircraft—and keeps increasing the number it procures from Russia. Moreover, the IAF has decided to purchase the Rafale as a Medium Multirole Combat Aircraft (MMRCA) and has entered into the codevelopment of a fifth-generation fighter aircraft (FGFA) with Russia. Given that each of these airframes offers a significant upgrade in capabilities, it brings into question whether the IAF would be willing to keep pumping resources into the far less capable Tejas.

The issue was again raised during the MMRCA fighter competition when Sweden brought in the Gripen combat aircraft as a competitor. While the Gripen was not shortlisted by the IAF, there were suggestions that if the Tejas program was scrapped, the Gripen would make an impressive substitute for the indigenously built fighter:

> In fact, the Gripen is so light, relative to the competition, that the IAF would be better served by purchasing it in place of its own Tejas LCA, which is growing in weight, does not have the combat capabilities anywhere close to the Gripen's, and lacks both the information fusing and the human engineering factors that distinguish the Swedish aircraft.[16]

The history of the Tejas LCA is perhaps instructive of the structural problems within the Indian weapons production system. The designers and developers face demands for state-of-the-art equipment from the services, and their own scientific egos lead to a willingness to try and implement complex and expensive weapons projects. Consequently, these projects are marked by lengthy delays as not only does Indian defense science seek to reinvent the wheel but has to face significant problems when dealing with new technological approaches. In the case of the Tejas, the Arjun tank, and the Dhruv helicopter, the Indian defense industry drew heavily on externally manufactured systems as well as foreign developmental assistance, but even this more pragmatic approach created developmental delays. In the aftermath of the Indian nuclear tests of 1998, the U.S. government cut off all defense science assistance to India and this was to adversely affect the Tejas program.

Yet, while India continues to invest in technologically advanced and ambitious weapons programs, it runs up a not insignificant tab by purchasing less advanced weapons systems that can be produced domestically, from abroad. Two clear cases of this phenomenon are the purchase of basic and advanced trainers for the IAF where the Indian government ended up buying the British Aerospace Hawk Advanced Jet Trainer (AJT) and has now purchased the Pilatus PC-7 II as a basic trainer. In both cases, the national exchequer would have saved large amounts of money by building the systems indigenously and it would have provided long-term employment at the defense science and defense production base.

The AJT was an advanced trainer that did not require the expensive avionics package and powerful engine that the LCA needed. It would, therefore, be easier to design and develop. Nor would it be obsolescent by the time it entered service since its mission was to train advanced pilots. Building the systems indigenously, would have led to a multibillion dollar savings in hard currency that the 2004 decision to purchase the British Aerospace Hawk would not permit. It would have given the Indian aeronautical community a proven aircraft to show their political masters and it would have also allowed India to enter an admittedly crowded export market for such type of aircraft. Neither project was pursued.

Almost two decades after the decision to make the Tejas, the arms industry agreed to make a Sitara Intermediate Jet Trainer (IJT) for the IAF, and the technological path chosen as well as the progress made on the program is instructive. The decision was taken to use as many off-the-shelf components as possible to facilitate rapid development. To integrate the plane with the training and missions of the IAF, the same mission computer is used for the plane as the one that has been fitted in the Su-30 MKI and the Tejas. A realistic appraisal of technological capabilities and mission requirements led to the IJT being developed in three years—a heartening development for the arms industry that has had few indigenous successes. Although the plane has subsequently met with developmental delays.[17]

What makes the arms industry's indigenous development of weapons systems difficult is the attitude of the government to such programs once initiated. While supporting the development of such programs, the government has not provided the monetary support to make the Indian weapons systems economically viable and internationally marketable. When it does, the success of a program is more likely. A good case in point is the Dhruv helicopter. The Dhruv was built as a multimission helicopter that would fulfill the requirements of the Army, Navy, Air Force, and Coast Guard for their medium lift requirements. It was also seen as being used in a civilian market. The Dhruv program has been successfully completed and Hindustan Aeronautics Limited (HAL) has produced a working helicopter that, while not technologically advanced, can carry out a range of missions for the armed forces and find a civilian and external market; the Dhruv has been exported to Ecuador, Suriname, Myanmar, Mauritius, and Nepal while one aircraft was gifted to the Maldives for search and rescue operations.[18] The Indian government is making the Dhruv a commercially viable product by helping sell it to the domestic civil aviation industry and by using it for both the central and state governments. Turkey and Peru have purchased the aircraft for civilian use. This will, potentially, make it an attractive product for foreign customers.

In the country's arms production efforts, the Indian government has in fact allowed financial imperatives to override considerations of technological advancement and national security. In that context, its approach has been similar to that of West European governments that have repeatedly cut weapons programs when they have been viewed as being financially exorbitant or when, quite rightly, the threat environment has changed, thereby reducing the need for further development of a particular type of weapons system.

The fate of these programs shows the course Indian arms production has taken and the factors that have constrained it. The missile program succeeded in delivering a series of ballistic missiles that made India's nuclear deterrent a credible one because sanctions prevented the import of comparable systems. On the other hand, both the Tejas and the Arjun suffered from developmental delays and, in the case of the Arjun, there was the Indian Army's reluctance to accept the system into service. The Tejas is being delivered to the IAF in 2012 with an engine and avionics suite from the late 1980s, thus making the plane obsolescent by the time it is inducted into the IAF. The IAF may well decide, therefore, to commit its resources to the more versatile Sukhoi-30 MKI that is being license-produced in India or to ask for an import to replace the airplane. The fact of the matter is that the first generation of Tejas has not met the standards demanded by the IAF, but the first planes will be delivered to the IAF regardless but in far fewer numbers than envisaged by the plane's producers.[19]

Indian arms production policy has at times adversely affected the country's defense preparedness and its long-term military capability. The emphasis on major projects has led to the more basic requirements of the Indian armed forces being ignored. During the 1999 Kargil conflict with Pakistan, for instance, India, despite its large defense production base, was unable to supply artillery and mortar shells to the army. The Indian government had to make an emergency purchase of 40,000 artillery shells and 30,000 mortar shells from Israel so as to continue the bombardment of Pakistani positions in Indian Kashmir.[20] Thus, one of the major shifts in arms production may be to develop what is appropriate rather than what is advanced. For Indian soldiers fighting in the mountainous terrain of Kashmir, it is important that they have suitable light weapons, night vision equipment, and adequate supplies of ammunition to combat both insurgents and the Pakistani armed forces. In the Siachen glacier region, a simple change like using GPS-guided pallets can ensure that supply drops reach their intended recipients and do not fall in the hands of the adversary.

While conventional systems have faced opposition from domestic constituencies, as well as subsequent delays, nonconventional systems have been successfully brought to production and induction in the Indian armed services. The development and production of the Prithvi and Agni missiles was possible because there was a need for nuclear-capable delivery systems and these systems could not be purchased from external suppliers. Coupled with the unavailability of external suppliers was the fact that the missiles were not prone to technological obsolescence. Further, neither of India's rivals—Pakistan and China—had (or are likely to have) ballistic missile defenses. Thus, a combination of existing threats, the inability to purchase systems externally, and continued technological relevance made it possible to shield the Agni and Prithvi programs from bureaucratic pressure that might otherwise have led to their termination. A more recent case is of the Indian nuclear submarine, the Arihant.

The Arihant is the first of a series of nuclear submarines that are expected to emerge from a program that began in 1974 after India's nuclear tests. It is conjectured that the Arihant is based on a Russian design, though commentators differ on whether it is a Russian boat of the Victor/Akula generation or is based on an earlier Charlie class design.[21] More critically, the reactor was developed with some Russian assistance, thereby permitting a completion of the project.[22] The submarine is expected to carry 12 ballistic missiles when it enters service.

The nuclear submarine program is another example of the ability of the Indian arms industry to bring projects to fruition when not faced with the pressure of competing with external suppliers or being asked to constantly upgrade systems to match comparable weaponry from foreign suppliers. From the perspective of Indian defense industries, what is required, therefore, is a greater governmental commitment to programs that can be pursued without fear of termination or of being hindered by constant organizational infighting.

CURRENT STRATEGY

In the past decade, Indian arms production policy has shifted to pursue a multipronged strategy for weapons production. While the government continues to support big-ticket items and licensed production, it has cautiously moved to allow private Indian companies to produce weaponry. It has also invested in joint ventures and decided to produce noncompetitive weapons systems. Joint ventures are currently being pursued with Israel and Russia (and potentially the United States), and these collaborative efforts reflect the changing international environment.

India established diplomatic relations with Israel in 1992 and since then has forged a mutually beneficial military relationship with that country. Israel has now become India's second largest supplier of military hardware, and New Delhi has worked the new relationship to its advantage in several ways. India has gained access to newer technologies and has been able to modify its existing weapons systems, as well as newly purchased ones, with improved Israeli systems. Thus, India's MiG-21 fleet is being upgraded with Israeli assistance and its Russian Sukhoi-30 MKI has Russian, French, Israeli, and Indian avionics and computers integrated into it.

The linkage with Israel also serves an important political function as some analysts view it as an alliance between two democracies that is aimed at achieving complementary foreign policy goals. For the Israelis, India has emerged as a lucrative market that helps sustain Jerusalem's military–industrial complex. Israel has sold India the Phalcon airborne warning and control system.[23] India would also like to purchase the Israeli Arrow 2 antiballistic missile to help establish a missile defense grid (the United States, however, has reportedly vetoed the sale). The ties with India are also viewed as lessening Israeli isolation in the non-Western world (as well as moving an important country away from what was, till the 1990s, a very pro-Arab foreign policy).

THE MILITARY RELATIONSHIP WITH RUSSIA

The Indo-Russian arms production relationship has been revived because Moscow recognized its economic and strategic value. After the fall of the Soviet Union, Russia followed a pro-Western policy and terminated most of its old links with India. In the early 1990s, India found it difficult to find spare parts for its large inventory of Soviet weapons. By the mid-1990s, however, the Russian leadership, strapped for hard currency and facing the rapid implosion of the country's military–industrial complex, renewed its arms sales relationship with India.[24] Russia, disappointed with its initial overtures to the West, also viewed India as an important strategic partner. It once again threw open the arms cupboard and New Delhi negotiated the purchase of aircraft carriers and the leasing of nuclear submarines. In return, India helped fund the development of the Sukhoi-30 and invested in the joint production and development of a supersonic cruise missile, the Brahmos company's PJ-10.[25] The two countries have also entered into an agreement to jointly develop an FGFA, and HAL was reportedly considering investing in the Irkutsk Aviation Production Organization.

In 2010, India and Russia signed a $5.5 billion deal for the development of an FGFA. The Indian rationale for entering into the project was both to have access to a fifth-generation fighter and to help advance the domestic aircraft industry. While India and Russia have different needs, India expects to have between 250 and 300 such aircraft in its arsenal.[26] The FGFA deal was preceded by the joint development of the Brahmos Missile that can be air, land, sea, and subsurface launched, thus providing a missile commonality to the different branches of the armed services. India and Russia have also entered into the codevelopment of the multirole medium transport aircraft.

The India–Russia arms design, development, and production relationship is mutually beneficial for it has led to a much-needed monetary transfusion into the cash-strapped Russian weapons industry while giving India the technological boost for its own indigenous industry. Given that the Western nations have till recently placed restrictions on technology transfers to India—both out of restraints on India's nuclear program and the general worry about India's reliability as a partner—the Russian connection has worked to give India a step up the technological ladder in arms production that it has always desired. More importantly, the Russian connection in both civilian and military programs has allowed India to pursue the autonomy it requires. This is most apparent in the Indian space program, which has benefited from Russian scientific and technological assistance.

At the same time, Moscow's tardiness in providing spare parts to India and the delays in Russian projects that are meant for India, like the *Vikramaditya* aircraft carrier and the multirole transport aircraft, have led to calls in India for diversifying India's weapons procurement activities.[27] Concerned about the quality of Russian equipment, Moscow's tardiness as a supplier of spares, and the unwillingness of Russia to give friendship prices, the Indian parliament recommended that the government move away from its dependence on Russian arms and, instead, increase imports from other, more reliable suppliers.[28] Given India's ambitious military plans, however, it is unlikely that the country can significantly reduce its military dependence on Russian systems. For political and security reasons, the West will not provide the type of strategic systems that India requires. Supplier restrictions remain on providing India with the dual-use and military technologies that it requires. Further, the broader Western concern about India's growing nuclear capability has also led to restrictions on the transfer of sensitive Western technologies.

ENTER THE UNITED STATES

India gained an additional option when Prime Minister Manmohan Singh and President George W. Bush signed an agreement for the transfer of conventional weapons systems and, more importantly, permitting the sale of civilian nuclear technology to India. The decision to do so was hailed as a pragmatic one since it accepted India as a de facto nuclear weapons state and allowed India to separate its civil and military nuclear programs and place only the former under international safeguards.[29] Further, as part of the new Indo-U.S. defense agreement, both countries agreed that they would

in the context of our strategic relationship, expand two-way defense trade between our countries. The United States and India will work to conclude defense transactions, not solely as ends in and of themselves, but as a means to strengthen our countries' security, reinforce our strategic partnership, achieve greater interaction between our armed forces, and build greater understanding between our defense establishments.[30]

Thus, it seemed likely that there would be greater U.S.–Indian military cooperation in the future because the agreement discussed the possibility of joint military operations, enhancing the capability to prevent the proliferation of weapons of mass destruction, and to promote the capabilities of both militaries to enhance security and defeat terrorism. Such coordinated efforts would, it was assumed, require a greater integration of Indian and American weapons systems and communications technologies, thus leading the United States to build up India's military capability. Former U.S. ambassador to India, Robert Blackwill, explained the American rationale for seeking to build up India's military capability:

> Of course we should sell advanced weaponry to India. The million-man Indian army actually fights, unlike the post-modern militaries of many of our European allies. Given the strategic challenges ahead, the United States should want the Indian armed forces to be equipped with the best weapons systems, and that often means buying American. To make this happen, the United States must become a reliable long-term supplier through co-production and licensed-manufacture arrangements and end its previous inclination to interrupt defense supplies to India in a crisis.[31]

From a broader perspective, joint ventures, such as those proposed to be undertaken with the United States, have worked to India's advantage because they made Indian arms procurement and production more efficient and cost effective, they have helped India gain access to a range of new technologies, and they have helped firm up relationships with strategically important countries. The use of private corporations and universities to develop weapons systems has worked quite well, particularly in the case of the IGMDP.

NONCOMPETITIVE SYSTEMS

Finally, the Indian government has also gone in for the production of noncompetitive systems that will not be obsolescent and will, therefore, find markets at home and, potentially, abroad. Two such systems are the ALH and the IJT. The ALH was designed and developed with German assistance, and its components come from both France and Germany. The aircraft was never meant to be a state-of-the-art helicopter but, instead, was meant to be a workhorse that could be used in the civilian and military sectors.

This emphasis on building a reliable and workable helicopter has led to HAL getting orders from the Indian military and civilian sectors for 300 aircraft. Given the needs of the various Indian state governments and those of its paramilitaries to conduct border patrols and surveillance, the ALH should be a genuine commercial success for the Indian arms industry.

The IJT, similarly, is on the right track since it fulfills a need of the air force and could potentially save the Indian exchequer the cost of importing comparable systems. The IJT was commissioned in 1999 and the first flight took place in 2003—a timely completion that was supposed to help the plane's domestic marketability. The IJT is expected to replace the IAF's Kiran basic trainer and, Indian aerospace analysts claim, a version with a more powerful engine could serve the need for a follow-on to the AJT. Like all Indian programs, the IJT has been plagued with difficulties that have delayed the completion of the project and putting the aircraft into serial production.

The shift in arms production strategy should produce definite benefits for India, but in the long run it will have to forgo the development of expensive state-of-the-art weaponry, increase joint ventures, and make more noncompetitive systems. The Arjun tank, for example, is an expensive project that will not fulfill the requirements of the Indian Army that is aiming now for a futuristic vehicle. The proposed plan to develop an Advanced Medium Combat Aircraft (AMCA), as a follow-on to the Tejas, is also ambitious given that the developmental costs will be prohibitive and India will be license-producing the versatile Su-30 that can have its avionics modernized at a much cheaper cost than initiating a new project. The expected completion date for the AMCA of 2018 is also unrealistic given the problems that have continued to beset the Tejas project. Further, such projects, where the armed forces have the alternative to buy abroad, will always flounder because they have lengthy developmental processes that do not fit the immediate needs of the armed services, and the question of matching the quality of imported systems will pose an additional stumbling block.

Further, while projects are being delayed, technology continues to develop. Thus, by the time a system is available, it may be obsolescent or the armed service might want a technological upgrade. This further delays the weapons induction and condemns it to failure. India should, therefore, not build such systems but instead focus on the development of systems that cannot be procured externally because of technological restrictions. A case in point was the successful development of the Prithvi and the Agni series of missiles that took place only because sanctions prevented the purchase of such missiles from external suppliers.

The indigenous development of an aircraft carrier program was another correct step in this direction given India's unhappy experience with the procurement of the *Vikramaditya* from Russia. The costs of the *Vikramaditya* doubled as the Russians demanded a significantly larger amount to complete the retrofit and then delayed the work on the carrier to the extent that the carrier is only expected to be delivered to India in 2013. (The *Vikramaditya* deal was signed in 2004 and the carrier was to be delivered to India in 2008.)

The production of noncompetitive weaponry must also be expanded to meet the most basic needs of the military. Light arms, ammunition, and field artillery are some examples of the type of noncompetitive weapons that can be produced domestically. In conventional wars and low-level conflicts, it is precisely such weaponry that sees the most use. Domestic production, therefore, ensures a steady supply of such hardware in wars and removes the need to seek emergency suppliers who may not always be as generous and prompt as the Israelis were during the Kargil conflict.

In an era of globalization, the Indian arms industry has shifted to successfully integrate some of the key elements of transnational weapons production. What is now needed is a realistic appraisal of ongoing projects to see which will actually survive and prosper in a global arms market where new avenues have opened to India and put pressure on the Indian arms industry to change its production policies. To sum up, you cannot go it alone in a globalized world.

WEAPONS ACQUISITION

Indian weapons acquisition used to be constrained by the lack of hard currency resources as the country, trapped in its socialistic economy, could never fully develop the economy to the point where it would have been able to purchase weaponry of its choice. Thus, only when hard currency resources were available was India able to make purchases from Western suppliers. The other constraint came from the willingness of suppliers to provide only certain types of weaponry to India. Thus, while the former Soviet Union was willing to engage in a Rupee–Rouble trade that obviated the need for hard currency, it did lead to a large trade imbalance for India and ensured that by the end of the Cold War period the Indian armed forces were heavily dependent on Soviet weaponry, which, by some estimates, by then made up to nearly 70 percent of the Indian arsenal. The Soviet, and subsequently Russian, relationship was problematic since India had a problem with the supply of spares and the quality of some of the systems delivered was questionable.

On the other hand, the Indians were able to build a sizeable military capability by integrating systems from other nations onto the platform provided by the Soviets. India also felt comfortable about the reliability of the Soviet Union as an arms supplier in contrast to Pakistan's bitter experiences with American weapons embargos in the 1960s, 1970s, and the 1990s.

The problem with these two constraints was that it led to the creation of a military inventory that had far too many types of weapons, leading to a logistical and maintenance nightmare. Additionally, the Indian propensity to buy big-ticket items and not focus on the smaller, less glamorous, yet vital weapons and support systems led to a force that had high-quality weaponry but lacked some of the more necessary systems to forge an effective defense. The lack of unmanned aerial vehicles, for example, left a coastline that was unguarded and permitted the Mumbai terror attack of November 26, 2008. Worse, the lack of modern rifles, other light armaments, and Kevlar led to a situation where a small group of terrorists had outgunned the Mumbai police.

Procurement has changed as India has envisaged a broader role for itself in the Indian Ocean region. While the idea of expeditionary conflicts is still taboo in Indian official circles, India has sought to purchase the systems that would provide for an extraregional reach. Thus, the IAF has acquired aerial refueling aircraft and in the Su-30 MKI a versatile long-range platform. The Indian Navy has leased nuclear attack submarines from Russia and is on course to acquire a carrier fleet—although, as discussed in this chapter, the transfer of the *Admiral Gorshkov* has not been without a host of associated problems. India has also profited from the opening of the U.S.–India military relationship.

The U.S.–India military relationship has led to the induction of weapons that not only permit the enhancement of an Indian extraregional capability but also potentially allow for greater interoperability with the United States in the future. As discussed in the chapter on the Indo-Pacific, the shift in the thinking of nations in the region has been toward creating strategic partnerships that allow for the discussion of security issues, of how to balance different nations in the international system, and for greater military cooperation. Moreover, all this can happen without the restrictions of an alliance system or the confrontational symbolism that an alliance may bring—after all, an alliance, by its very definition, has to be targeted against someone or some entity. In such circumstances, the infusion of systems like the C-17 transport aircraft (India wants to buy 10 but may go up to 16) and the P-8 maritime reconnaissance aircraft not only gives India the extra regional reach it desires but also allows for greater synergy with the United States and its allies in the event of regional multinational operations.

For India, the acquisition of long-range systems, somewhat paradoxically, opens up its options with regard to operations in the Indo-Pacific region. Long-range transport aircraft facilitate the kind of military operations other than war that we saw when India, along with Japan, Australia, and the United States, participated in the Tsumani relief efforts in 2004. In actual fact, these operations are the ones that the Indian political leadership is most comfortable with in terms of expanding the Indian footprint across the region. Another good weapons system in this context would be the U.S. Global Hawk UAV, which with its long loiter time provides an excellent reconnaissance vehicle that can be linked to other regional militaries to provide information on the movements of pirates, tracking WMD transfers, and other perceived maritime crises. The United States has cleared the Global Hawk for sale to India and it will be up to the Indian government to decide whether it wants to acquire the system to beef up its intelligence, surveillance, and reconnaissance capability.

But the key shift India will have to make in terms of acquisitions is in upgrading the capability of its internal security forces. India has traditionally kept the capabilities of its internal security forces at a lower standard than that of the military for a variety of reasons. The internal security forces were, and are, poorly trained, thus integrating them with more advanced systems is not an easy thing to do. Cost factors negated the effort to modernize the internal security forces and there was also the need to maintain a clear distinction between the military and the internal security forces; one way to do so was to keep a qualitative distinction between the technological capabilities of the two forces.

In the new Indian domestic landscape, however, retaining a poorly armed and poor trained internal security force makes little sense given the continued threat posed by terrorist groups and internal insurgencies, as witnessed by the rise of the Maoist rebellion in parts of rural India. To upgrade domestic capability, the Indian police and paramilitary forces will have to be better armed and will require better intelligence, surveillance, and reconnaissance capabilities. Additionally, the Indian security forces will require better training and an understanding of what constitutes antiterrorist and anti-insurgency techniques. The reason for this is that both the terrorist and insurgent groups are likely to be better armed and more motivated than the Indian security forces. The terrorist strike on Mumbai in 2008 saw terrorists using AK-47s and communicating with their masterminds in Pakistan with voice over internet protocol. Had the Mumbai police been better armed and better trained, they might have been able to deal with the terrorists before the latter were able to inflict a high level of casualties.

To sum up, India continues to invest in both an indigenous weapons production capability and the expensive import of weaponry from abroad. The domestic production system, at least in this author's view, needs to be reshaped to design and produce those weapons systems that are not available from external suppliers. Next, it has to produce noncompetitive systems that save the country hard currency resources and also provide the continued basis for employment in the domestic arms industry. Lastly, it has to produce those basic requirements that can aid a war effort, like ammunition.

Even some of the low-technology weapons like guns and rifles are perhaps best license-produced or bought outright given the contrast between the long developmental times and the rather rapid need for countering escalating threats like those posed by indigenous terror groups.

As far as acquisitions are concerned, India's emerging foreign policy is likely to shape the acquisition process. The purchase of weapons systems, apart from the need to counter threats, will also take place to forge political alliances both within and outside Asia. The MMRCA deal shortlisted the Rafale and the Eurofighter, and one of the rationales given for this decision was that it would lead to a stronger political and economic relationship with the nations of the European Union (the contract was eventually won by Dassault). Within Asia, procurement of particular weapons platforms has the potential to create synergies with other nations that share similar worldviews as India. Purchasing the C-17, for example, allows for greater interoperability with both the United States and Australia. Potentially making arms purchases from Japan allows for a similar outcome. India will have to start thinking in these terms given its goals to maintain a broader presence in the Indo-Pacific region, to work with other Asian and extraregional powers to maintain regional stability, and to serve notice to China that it is willing to work to counter Beijing's influences in the region. Carefully considered weapons procurement would help to further all three objectives.

NOTES

1. Radhakrishna Rao, "Boosting India's Defense Production Base," *Military Technology,* November 2010.

2. Ibid.

3. Amit Gupta, *Building an Arsenal: The Evolution of Regional Power Force Structures* (London and Westport, CT: Praeger, 1997), p 33.

4. Thomas W. Graham, "India," in James Everett Katz (ed.), *Arms Production in the Third World* (Lexington: Lexington Books, 1984), p. 170.

5. Ravi Rikhye, *The Militarisation of Mother India* (New Delhi: Chanakya, 1990), p. 38.

6. Anantha Krishnan, "Tank Buy, Missile Test Give Indian DRDO a Boost," *Aerospace Daily & Defense Report,* May 20, 2010.

7. "Indian Army Places Order for 124 Arjun Tanks," Press Trust of India, May 17, 2010.

8. "Seal Scorpene Deal Fast: Navy Chief," *The Times of India,* August 12, 2004.

9. Gupta, *Building an Arsenal,* pp. 54–55.

10. Gupta, "Determining India's Force Structure and Military Doctrine: I Want My M-i-G," *Asian Survey* 35, no. 5 (1995): p. 445.

11. Rajendra Prabhu, "Misgivings over LCA Plan Changes," *The Hindustan Times,* January 24, 1987 and Raj Chengappa, "LCA Project: A Testing Time," *India Today,* August 31, 1988.

12. Interview with V. S. Arunachalam, New Delhi, August 9, 1991.

13. "Battling the Naysayers," *Flight International,* February 1, 2011.

14. "It's Would-Be Engine," *Aviation Week and Space Technology,* vol. 173, issue 3, January 17, 2011, p. 27.

15. "India Orders More Mig-29s as Tejas Naval Fighter Slips Again India Adds More MiG-29s to Carrier Fleet," *Flight International,* March 23, 2010.

16. Ashley J. Tellis, *Dogfight! India's Medium Multi-Role Combat Aircraft Decision* (Washington, DC: Carnegie Endowment for International Peace, 2011), p. 110.

17. C. Manmohan Reddy, "Making Haste, Slowly," *The Hindu,* December 26, 2002.

18. "Indian Dhruv Helicopter Falls under the Scanner as Ecuador Expresses Dissatisfaction," *Defence Now,* July 29, 2011, http://www.defencenow.com/news/255/india%E2%80%99s%E2%80%98dhruv%E2%80%99helicopterfallsunderthescannerasecuadorexpressesdissatisfaction.html.

19. Chethan Kumar, "Tejas Flies, but IAF Dithers," *Deccan Herald,* January 10, 2012.

20. Rahul Bedi, "Moving Closer to Israel," *Frontline,* vol. 20, issue 4, February 15–28, 2003.

21. Rahul Bedi, "India Finally Launches ATV," *Jane's Defence Weekly,* August 5, 2009.

22. Ravi Velloor, "India Extends Reach with N-Sub Launch," *The Straits Times,* July 27, 2009.

23. "Indian AWACS Moving Forward on Two Fronts," *Defense Industry Daily,* November 9, 2011, http://www.defenseindustrydaily.com/Indian-AWACS-Moving-Forward-on-2-Fronts-04855/.

24. For a discussion of the ongoing problems of the Russian military–industrial complex, see R. G. Gidadhubli, "Refurbishing the Military Industrial Complex," *Economic and Political Weekly,* August 23, 2003, pp. 3546–50.

25. "The Seventh Flight of BrahMos," *Frontline,* vol. 21, issue 13, June 19–July 2, 2004.

26. "India Russia Sign Deal for Fifth Generation Fighter Aircraft," *The Hindu,* December 21, 2010.

27. Jyotsna Bakshi, "India–Russia Defence Cooperation," *Strategic Analysis* 30, no. 2 (2006): pp. 453–54.

28. V. Raghuvanshi, "Report Urges India to Widen Contracting Process," *Defense News,* April 30, 2001, p. 6.

29. For an opinion on how the nuclear deal benefited India, see C. Raja Mohan, "Ending Our Nuclear Winter," *The Indian Express,* July 26, 2005. For criticisms of the agreement by India's political parties, see John Cherian, "Deals and Doubts," *Frontline,* vol. 22, issue 16, July 30–August 12, 2005.

30. See, "New Framework for the U.S.–INDIA Defense Relationship," Washington, DC, June 28, 2005, http://www.indianembassy.org/pressrelease/2005/June/31.htm.

31. "The India Imperative: A Conversation with Robert D. Blackwill," *The National Interest,* no. 80 (Summer 2005): p. 11.

CHAPTER 3

India and Pakistan: The Enduring Conflict

Six decades after the creation of both countries, India and Pakistan remain locked in an enduring conflict. Both sides have nuclearized, and their primary targets remain each other's homelands and military facilities. Pakistan supports, both diplomatically and practically, the Kashmiri insurgency in India, and Pakistani groups, with the support of official and unofficial elements in Pakistan, carry out terrorist operations in India—the most spectacular of which was the November 2008 assault on the city of Mumbai by a commando unit of the Lashkar-e-Taiba group. What further complicates the matter are issues of competing models of nationalism, sectarian tensions, divergent political and economic paths, and the quest for riparian resources. For India, the stakes are high since any attempt to become a major power in the international system will require stabilizing its own neighborhood. Otherwise, New Delhi will continue to be bogged down by a conflict relationship that drains its resources and saps its diplomatic and political energies. Resolving the dispute with Pakistan is also important since South Asia is an interconnected geographical and economic region, and to continue a hostile relationship with Pakistan only takes away the economic opportunities provided by regional proximity—development of both the Asian Road and the Rail Networks comes to a screeching halt the moment these two networks hit the tangled hostilities of South Asia.

BACKGROUND

The decision to create Pakistan was based on the idea that Hindus and Muslims were two separate entities that could not survive within one sovereign space—the

so-called two-nation theory. In fact, more recent literature suggests that the decision to create Pakistan was taken primarily to protect the socioeconomic interests of Muslims who were likely to fall behind Hindus in a post-independence
India. Recent scholarship revives a point that has been made before that Mohammed
Ali Jinnah, the founder of Pakistan, wanted a moderate Muslim state where people of all religions were free to practice their own faiths.[1] In essence, Pakistan remained a moderate Muslim state till the 1980s, when its then dictator, General
Zia ul-Haq, transformed the politics of the country toward a more radical brand
of Islam.[2] In the 1940s and 1950s, however, the challenge for Pakistan's security
came not from the bitter memories of partition or the sectarian tensions of Muslim Pakistan versus Hindu India but from the more basic problems of realpolitik.
Pakistan, as the Indian scholar Sisir Gupta pointed out, was not a small country
but was surrounded by the two largest countries in the world, India and China.
Given the huge population disparities, Pakistan became a small state. As the Pakistani scholar Aslam Siddiqui argued in 1948, when a small country borders a
larger country, it is bound to face pressures of dominance from the larger nation
and it is logical, therefore, for the smaller country to resist.[3] Siddiqui viewed religion as the barrier that would prevent Indian domination, but at the more secular level it was necessary for the young Pakistani state to put together a military
capability to stop India from taking it over. The fear of an aggressive India that
would seek to undo partition or at the very least want a weak and pliable Pakistan
in the South Asian region has led Pakistan's leadership to first (in the 1950s and
1960s) seek conventional military parity with India, and then, since the 1970s,
develop a nuclear deterrent. Pakistanis still point out that in 1947 India actually
stopped the flow of water into Pakistan as an example of how New Delhi sought
to weaken the Pakistani state.

The second direct challenge to Pakistan came through the competing identities
of India and Pakistan. India, under the leadership of Jawaharlal Nehru and the
framers of the Indian Constitution, sought to develop a secular and democratic
nation-state.[4] Pakistan's attempts to create a democracy failed as the country was
unable to bring about true democratic elections and, by 1958, succumbed to the
first of several military leaderships. Unable to put together the building blocks of
a modern nation-state on secular or democratic grounds and ruled by a military
that lacked trust in politicians, national unity and control were sought by projecting India as the major threat to the survival of Pakistan. Such methods could not,
however, prevent the internal contradictions of a geographically and culturally
separated East and West Pakistan from emerging. By 1971, Pakistan was involved
in a civil war as the Eastern wing sought to secede from the West.

The 1971 India–Pakistan war saw the emergence of an independent Bangladesh and the worsening of Pakistan's security dilemma vis-à-vis India. The war
had left India the predominant power in the region and left Pakistan's elites fear-
ing the further breakup of their country—a fear that was not exaggerated because

by 1973 Pakistan faced a second insurgency in Balochistan. The military was able to crush the insurgency, but the fragility of the nation-state was once again exposed to the rest of the world and perhaps, more importantly, to the Pakistani elite.

The birth of India and Pakistan had been marked by sectarian violence culminating in the mass movement of refugees from both countries and the ensuing bloodbath that took place. Conservative estimates place the number of deaths at more than a million and the scars remain etched in the memory of the people of both sides. For several years after independence, a sectarian riot in one country would be marked by a reprisal in the other. It took the Nehru–Liaquat pact in 1951, where both countries agreed to look after and provide security to their minorities, to ease the tension on this issue. Neither government, however, was that effective at halting sectarian tensions, with India having its last major incident in 2002 with the Gujarat riots. The impact of such violence has been etched in the psyche of both countries' elderly leadership. Lal Krishna Advani, the Bharatiya Janata Party leader and one-time prime ministerial candidate, was born in Pakistan, and this colored his thinking on that country. Pervez Musharraf was born in India and in his autobiography recounts the tension and fear as his family moved from Delhi to Pakistan. His subsequent views on India must in part be attributed to his early childhood experiences.

Sectarian tensions still complicate matters between the two countries since they provide the incentive for recruitment to jihadi groups in Pakistan. Such behavior in turn has spawned Hindu terror groups in India who have committed violent acts, most notably the bombing of the Samjhauta Express train service.

The third problem stems from divergent social and economic agendas. India has pursued market reforms since the early 1990s, when its hard currency reserves fell precipitously and the economy was on the brink of collapse. This has led to an India which grows at fairly impressive rates and one which was somewhat impervious to the global economic recession of 2008–2009. The Indian economy slowed but did not go into a recession, and in 2010 the economy grew at a healthy 8.9 percent. In this new India, which is also demographically young, the old sectarian tensions may be fading away as market pressures make for different and more secular social and economic dynamics in the country.

In contrast, Pakistan remains a partially feudal economy and one that is dependent on the export of cotton and leather goods, thus not having progressed toward becoming a 21st-century knowledge economy. In this system, there is little incentive to look for a growing mass of educated workers who can propel a modern economy and, consequently, there does not exist the type of educated and globalized middle class that would want changes in the Pakistani political system, its global status, and its relationship with India. Such a change is likely to come only when Pakistan moves from being an economic basket case that survives on international monetary bailouts and moves to achieve its potential as a country that is one of the 10 largest nations in the world. But perhaps the two most contentious issues for India and Pakistan remain Kashmir and the demand for riparian resources by both nations.

Kashmir is viewed in Pakistan as the unsettled business from partition, and both countries view the state as central to their national identities. For Pakistan, the large Muslim-majority state should be an integral part of Pakistan and, in fact, was allowed to become a contentious issue due to British perfidy and Nehru's influence on Lord Mountbatten. India, on the other hand, views Kashmir as an integral part of India's secular identity. If the Muslim-majority state were to become part of Pakistan, or become independent, it would not only mark the failure of the Indian secular experiment, but it would also precipitate further secessionist pressures within the country. Kashmir's strategic value, in terms of terrain and the border with China, further ups the stakes for the government in New Delhi.

Added to this is the problem of ceding territory and the consequent impact on the domestic political situation and the perceived balance of power with both Pakistan and China. Ceding land to Pakistan would make it near impossible for India to retain its territorial claims on the land that New Delhi argues China captured in 1962.

Finally, there is the problem of water resources. With India's population expected to peak at about 1.6 billion and Pakistan's at 335 million, the demand for water in the South Asian region will double and this makes control of the riparian resources a crucial matter for both states. Kashmir would be a key part of any water sharing plan between the two countries, so both sides would like to be in a position of territorial advantage when dealing with the issue of water resources. As things stand, India and Pakistan's sharing of water resources is governed by the 1960 Indus Waters Treaty that divided up the waters of the two countries between them. Guaranteed by the World Bank, the treaty has survived two major wars and a limited conflict between India and Pakistan and is seen as one of the rare instances where both nations have been able to put aside their differences and cooperate. The treaty also expects both sides to work toward developing the water resources of the Indus waters system to their mutual advantage, but little has been done to carry out the latter part of the agenda.

Yet, water will be the crucial issue of the future for both countries and unless they are able to sit down and work out more effective ways of sharing and building on their water resources, we are likely to see serious conflicts emerge between India and Pakistan on this issue.

THE MODERN RIVALRY

The modern rivalry between India and Pakistan begins in the aftermath of the 1971 war, which saw the dismemberment of Pakistan and the creation of

Bangladesh. For Pakistan's politicians and military, the issue was no longer one of balancing India but, instead, one of ensuring the survival of the nation. The fear was that India would be tempted to take away further parts of Pakistan and leave it weakened and incapable of survival. It was this belief that led Pakistan's then prime minister, Zulfiqar Ali Bhutto, to seek a nuclear weapons capability. Yet, for India, the 1970s were not a problematic period in terms of South Asian politics. With the dismemberment of Pakistan, India had achieved preponderance in the region and, more importantly, the United States—which had supplied Pakistan with military hardware and political support in the 1950s and 1960s—was now preoccupied with events in South East and West Asia and, therefore, lost interest in the South Asian region. Further, China, by the early 1970s, was a less compelling threat to India. The Chinese had by 1969 engaged in armed clashes with the Soviets along the Ussuri and Amur rivers and were more concerned with their principal rivals and with building a more productive relationship with the United States.

The Indian decision to test a nuclear device in 1974, however, further exacerbated the Pakistani security dilemma. The decision to go nuclear was not a response to immediate security concerns but, as has been argued, an attempt to quell domestic opposition to Mrs. Indira Gandhi's rule and perhaps to satisfy India's scientific community, which had been pressing for the test to take place. Instead, it did have the effect of furthering scaring an already paranoid Pakistani security establishment. In the 1970s, therefore, Islamabad embarked on a program to rapidly develop a nuclear capability—one that saw it acquire technology through both overt and covert means and, eventually, a working bomb design from China. By 1987, Pakistan had gone nuclear, and it was to start using its newfound nuclear capability to engage in a serious effort to promote the insurgency in Kashmir.

The unrest in Kashmir cannot be solely laid at Pakistan's doorstep, although Islamabad was certainly an important agent in promoting and sustaining the effort of Kashmiri groups to challenge the Indian state. In 1987, the Indian federal government permitted the rigging of state elections in Kashmir, and in the resultant backlash a homegrown insurgency was born in the state. There were deep-rooted causes of poverty, alienation, and corruption that led to discontent against the Indian state, but it was the election that provided the catalyst to stoke an insurgency against India.

Pakistan saw an opportunity in the crisis and began to provide training, weapons, and support to the insurgents. Its Inter Services Intelligence (ISI) also set up jihadi groups that were under its control and patronage to carry the fight into India. Pakistan's newfound capability did not prevent India from attempting to coerce Islamabad. In 1990, 1999, and 2001–2002, India either placed its troops on the border in a show of force or, as in the case of 1999, actually fought a limited war with Pakistan.[5] India also went on to develop a military doctrine that was meant to allow the use of conventional force against Pakistan while not provoking it to use nuclear weapons—the Cold Start doctrine. The net effect of Pakistan's going nuclear was, however, that it dissuaded the Indian political leadership from using conventional military power to challenge Pakistan's use of insurgents in India since New Delhi seemed to recognize that the cost–benefit calculus of using force did not favor it.

Pakistan's problem with fueling extremism in India is that it has come at a heavy cost to the government itself because it has fueled extremism in Pakistan, which creates serious problems for the ruling elite and its grasp on power. Yet, at the same time, it is a weapon that the Pakistani security establishment cannot walk away from since it allows that country the extra instrument with which to put pressure on India and maintain Pakistan's own security.

The 2002 standoff led to yet another freeze in India–Pakistan relations that was gradually broken. By 2004, both countries agreed to once again start talking, and a series of discussions took place on a range of issues, most notably Kashmir. Under Pervez Musharraf, Pakistan put aside some of its long-standing positions and, instead, began discussing a Kashmir settlement that included no real shift in boundaries and the free movement of people.[6] Negotiations between India and Pakistan move at a glacial pace and are likely to be stalled by the slightest of pressures. In this case, two events worked to push the negotiations off track. First, internal opposition to Pervez Musharraf gained momentum with the lawyers' agitation that called for his dismissal. India was unwilling to deal with a weakened Musharraf since New Delhi felt that he would lack the credibility to persuade the Pakistani public and security elite to accept an agreement. The second problem was the attack on Mumbai by the commandos of the Lashkar-e-Taiba terrorist group.

The peace talks between India and Pakistan led to discussions about resolving the status of Kashmir, the status of the Siachen glacier, and other contentious issues between the two countries, but they were slowed down by the agitation against Pervez Musharraf, which eventually led to his dismissal. But what derailed the talks was the Mumbai terror attack of November 2008. Broadcast on all the major Indian channels and from there sent globally, the attacks put an end to the attempted rapprochement between the two countries. Instead, India was able to put the last surviving terrorist up on trial and use it to implicate the Pakistan-based terrorist group Lashkar-e-Taiba in the attack. The prime ministers of both countries met in Sharm el-Sheikh in July of 2009 and issued a joint statement condemning terrorism, but the Indian government walked away with little satisfaction from the interaction since Pakistan neither took responsibility for the Mumbai attacks nor took any substantive measures against Pakistan-based anti-Indian groups in the country. So, where does that leave the India–Pakistan relationship now?

The India–Pakistan relationship now resides around several issues, none of which are easy to resolve in the short to medium term. They include the nuclear relationship, the issue of terrorism, Kashmir, Pakistan's fear of a growing India, the water issue, and the continuing role of India in Afghanistan.

THE NUCLEAR ISSUE

Since both India and Pakistan went overtly nuclear in 1998, the two countries have fought a limited war in Kargil (1999), engaged in a military standoff along the border (2001–2002), and had their budding peace process destroyed by the Mumbai terror attack (2008). The nuclear issue is interconnected to the issue of jihadi terrorism and the Pakistani case for Kashmir. For Pakistan, nuclearization not only provided deterrence vis-à-vis a conventionally superior Indian military force, but it also gave Islamabad the opportunity to use the nuclear capability as the shield that permitted the use of jihadi violence in India—which is used as an instrument to keep alive the Kashmir issue. Both in 2001 following the attack by jihadis on the Indian parliament and in 2008 following the Mumbai attack, there were calls in India for a military strike on Pakistan. In each case, the Indian government did not opt for the military option, although the rationale for doing so varies, depending on whom you talk to. Pakistan's leadership believes that its nuclear deterrent worked, while some Western observers believed that the Indians blinked. The Indian leadership claims that the 2001–2002 military standoff was an exercise in coercive diplomacy that worked because Pervez Musharraf made the commitment to not support jihadi activities in India. In the case of the 2008 attacks, the Mumbai Police's capture of Ajmal Kasab, the surviving terrorist, gave India a useful bargaining chip with which to get the Western nations to put pressure on Pakistan and someone to put on trial, and put Pakistan-based terrorist groups on the defensive. The problem for India is that it can expect to have more jihadi violence on its soil given that it has no real way to counter the Pakistani nuclear deterrent with conventional military power.

In an attempt to make its conventional forces relevant in such a scenario, India resorted to the Cold Start doctrine,[7] which called for using available forces in forward areas to conduct a retaliatory attack on Pakistan and allow reinforcements to follow. The problem with this doctrine was that it was based on the assumption that Indian forces would not cross a red line that invited Pakistani nuclear retaliation, but Pakistani nuclear doctrine is deliberately vague on what constitutes the crossing of an irrevocable red line. More importantly, there were genuine concerns about whether India could sustain such an assault, for a U.S. Embassy in New Delhi assessment concluded that:

India "would likely encounter very mixed results" if it ever went ahead. "Indian forces could have significant problems consolidating initial gains due to logistical difficulties and slow reinforcement," it said. To implement the plan in any form would be to "roll the nuclear dice," the cable warned. "Indian leaders no doubt realise that, although Cold

Start is designed to punish Pakistan in a limited manner without triggering a nuclear response, they cannot be sure whether Pakistani leaders will in fact refrain from such a response."[8]

India has since disclaimed the Cold Start doctrine, but it still leaves the problem of how to engage Pakistan when a future terror attack takes place. None of the options provide satisfactory outcomes that would help improve India's security situation. India could retaliate by sponsoring terrorism in Pakistan but this, at the very least, would be embarrassing if discovered (Pakistan already charges India with fomenting insurgency and terrorism in Balochistan) and would make the Indian government liable under international law. More problematically, it would then remove all internal and external restraints from Pakistan to retaliate in kind. If such tit-for-tat retaliation took place, it would only be detrimental to India's long-term interests because, unlike Pakistan, India has become a true part of the global economy. India's economic growth is based on its linkages with foreign companies that have made the country the back office for all their activities, and terror strikes would only serve to scare away such investors and commercial partners.

Another avenue that the Indian government has explored is to try and get the United States—as one of the three countries that funds Pakistan—to try and reduce or eliminate its jihadi activities. In New Delhi, the belief has always been that Washington could do far more to rein in Islamabad's support to anti-Indian groups. In Washington, the response has always been that the United States, despite the large doses of foreign and military aid that it provides Islamabad with, has far less influence in shaping Pakistani policy than New Delhi believes. Indeed, the U.S.–Pakistan relationship since September 11, 2001, has been described as a bad marriage, with both sides accusing the other of bad faith and not following through in both the letter and the spirit of the agreement between the two countries. The United States has accused Pakistan of not doing enough to check the activities of anti-U.S. terrorists and jihadi forces in Pakistan or to take on the Haqqani group. The killing of Osama bin Laden on May 1, 2011, in Abbotabad, Pakistan—just 35 miles from Islamabad—only adds to the suspicion that the ISI is not to be trusted and cannot deliver on what Pakistan promises.[9] Pakistan accuses the United States of carrying out an excessive number of drone attacks in the tribal regions of western Pakistan and thus infuriating Pakistani public opinion. Islamabad also argues that Washington does not recognize the sacrifice and contribution that Pakistan makes to the global war on terror or its legitimate concerns about Indian hegemony in the region. Islamabad, says Bruce Riedel, would like to go back to the Reagan rules of the Cold War where the Saudis and the Central Intelligence Agency (CIA) provided ISI with money but the CIA adopted a largely hands-off policy vis-à-vis the operations of its Pakistani counterpart—something which is impossible to do in a post–Cold War world where the focus is on terrorism.[10] The net result has been that Pakistan has cooperated with the United States where its national interest is not harmed and has given lukewarm assurances on dealing with the issue of jihad in India.

What will be interesting to see, in this context, is how the U.S.–Pakistan relationship unfolds following the killing of bin Laden. Does the United States now feel that it can exert more pressure on Pakistan? Will Islamabad be more amenable to acceding to American wishes, which would include lowering tensions with India? Or, will we continue to see what Michael O'Hanlon calls a bad marriage between Pakistan and the United States,[11] in which the problems between the two countries continue to grow, yet they remain tied to each other because of wider political and military goals.

In the year since the bin Laden killing, there have been multiple instances of trouble emerging in the U.S.–Pakistan relationship. The problem over drone attacks by the United States on terrorists operating out of Pakistani territory, the impasse on allowing NATO supply trucks to transit through Pakistan, the U.S. refusal to apologize for the killing of 24 Pakistani soldiers through friendly fire, are all symptomatic of the mutual distrust that has bubbled out since the killing of bin Laden. It has led Islamabad to think in terms of "resetting" the relationship between the two countries by seeking a stronger relationship with China and there have even been some conciliatory gestures to India. The development to watch, therefore, is what path the relationship between Washington and Islamabad takes after the U.S. troop pullout from Afghanistan in 2014. If a reset takes place then Washington will have even less leverage over Islamabad as the former tries to use stronger measures to make the latter pursue acceptable policies.

Given the troubled nature of the U.S.–Pakistan relationship, the more likely alternative for combating Pakistan-based jihadi activities is what India has been doing since the Mumbai attacks—strengthening its antiterrorist capabilities to ensure that future attacks are either deterred or quickly stopped. Such a defensive approach does not satisfy those in the Indian public who are tired of Pakistani attacks on civilian targets, but it does have the advantage of giving India the moral high ground in the court of international public opinion and it does narrow Pakistan's options.

Pakistan's problem lies in the fact that it has used the jihad weapon but potentially lost control over it. When asked about the 2001 attack on the Indian parliament, Pervez Musharraf is reported to have said it is a "dirty business," which commentators have taken to mean that either he was not informed about the attack or that ISI had lost control over its operatives.[12] Similarly, the Mumbai attack was supposed to have been carried out under the instructions of mid-level ISI operatives, thus absolving the senior leadership of blame. Bob Woodward, in his book *Obama's Wars*, suggests that it was the evidence that pointed to the mid-level management of the attack that helped reduced tensions with India.[13] The problem that emerges from this lack of oversight over jihadi activities is twofold. First, it means that the jihadis are loose cannons who once unleashed go after targets that are not in Pakistan's interests—as an attack on the Indian parliament certainly was not—and can lead to a rapid escalation of tensions between the two nuclear neighbors. The Mumbai attacks, similarly, targeted foreigners and took away the fig leaf that Islamabad and Washington had always used on the issue of terrorism in India, in that it was only aimed at Indians. The Mumbai attacks particularly targeted foreigners, and there was no attempt to even try and restrict casualties; with Hindus, Muslims, Christians, and Jews being targeted, it was equal-opportunity killing. The sheer scale of the Mumbai attack created a nightmare for every urban law enforcement agency in the world since it was the template for future terrorist attacks. But the danger of Mumbai for Pakistan, apart from the fact that it cannot control its cadres, is that for groups like Lashkar-e-Taiba, which is credited with staging the attack, the future now requires even more daring and bloodthirsty attacks. The argument made is that Lashkar staged the attack because its cadres were leaving the organization, so its leadership sought to do something spectacular to bring the group to the forefront of the jihadi process. It also had the secondary effect of essentially killing off promising India–Pakistan peace talks. The problem it created, however, is that Lashkar and other terrorist groups operating in India will now have to stage even more spectacular attacks with high body counts in order to attract the attention of the global media. After Mumbai, killing security forces in Kashmir is no longer headline grabbing. And anything with impact on global media poses a major problem for Pakistan since such an attack would put incredible international pressure on the government in Islamabad. As other countries' citizens get killed, something that is likely to happen in a globalized India now brimming with multinational corporations, they will be the ones putting the diplomatic and economic pressures on Pakistan to halt such activities and to bring the perpetrators to justice. Of course, this does not mean that such consequences have been thought through in Pakistan and are likely to serve as a deterrent to potential future action. From an Indian perspective, therefore, the best approach may be to follow a defensive approach based on good antiterrorism strategies and intelligence gathering rather than coercive diplomacy vis-à-vis Pakistan.

The other part of the nuclear issue is that of the security of Pakistan's nuclear weapons, something that raises concerns in Western capitals. After September 11, 2001, part of the U.S. engagement with Pakistan lay in securing the country's nuclear weapons from theft or seizure by radical forces. More recently, the concern has been about the rapidly expanding Pakistani nuclear force, which is expected to become the world's fifth largest nuclear arsenal. American analysts fear that this increases the threat of the theft of fissile material to build a dirty bomb and it also creates a possible future nightmare where Islamic radicals take over the state of Pakistan and then have access to these weapons. This has led, if Bob Woodward is correct, to the Obama administration coming up with the retribution plan where if there is a major al-Qaeda-led or inspired attack on the United States that originates from Pakistani soil then the United States will go after 150 targets in Pakistan, with no regard for collateral damage.[14] For India, these concerns do little to change its perspective on the nuclear situation in South Asia.

Indian policymakers and strategic analysts believe that their nuclear deterrent prevents a war with Pakistan and that if a dirty bomb were to be used in India it would probably be because the material was provided by groups within the Pakistani government. Thus, the growth of the arsenal per se does not increase the Indian threat calculus. What it does do is push India toward building more defensive systems like antiballistic missiles and refining its own missile program and air force to meet the challenge posed by such systems. It also lowers the threshold for a Pakistani nuclear strike on India since if the United States attacked Pakistan, either in response to an attack from Pakistani soil or because it sought to secure Pakistani nuclear weapons from falling in the wrong hands, it is possible that the Pakistanis would go in for a doomsday scenario that involved using the nuclear weapons rather than losing them—and this would mean an attack on India as well. It is not the number of weapons, therefore, that bothers people in New Delhi. It is the likelihood of their use. This becomes all the more important if one takes into account the growing economic, social, and educational disparity between the two nations.

Since India adopted market reforms in 1991, not only has its economy been growing, but it has increasingly been incorporated into the modern 21st-century post-industrial economy. A visit to Bangalore, Hyderabad, or Gurgaon shows the number of multinationals and cutting-edge information technology firms that have set up shop in these cities. And with it has come a synergy between Western and Indian businesses that would not have existed a decade ago. A few years ago, during a visit to the Bangalore offices of Cisco, this author was told that the IT giant now has two major offices in San Jose and Bangalore and that a seven-hour flight radius from each of these centers covers 70 percent of humanity. In contrast, investment in Pakistan is not coming from sunrise industries of the Western or non-Western world. Islamabad's economy survives on economic bailouts, debt forgiveness, and large-scale foreign assistance from the United States, Saudi Arabia, and China. The growing economic disparity between the two countries cannot be bridged by a Pakistan that is caught up in an internal struggle between radical forces and the government. Further, the educational disparity between India and Pakistan is only likely to widen as the Indian government seeks to improve primary, secondary, and tertiary education. The real danger for Pakistan lies in the fact that in the coming decades it may end up being economically insignificant to an India that is projected to become the third largest economy in the world, after China and the United States. For Pakistan to compete with India, therefore, economic growth remains a vital platform and the control of water resources is seen in Islamabad as being central to Pakistan's economic survival.

WATER

Analysts in Pakistan now feel that water will be one of the key conflict areas between India and Pakistan given the growing populations of both nations. The estimates are that by 2050 India's population will peak at about 1.6 billion people while Pakistan's will peak at around 335 million. And for the Indians in northwestern India there is a dependence on the waters of the Indus waters system—consisting of the Indus, Ravi, Beas, Sutlej, Jhelum, and Chenab rivers—for agriculture and potable water. Water, however, is not a new concern in the relations between the two countries. It has been an issue since the events following the partition of India in 1948 when the Indian state of east Punjab shut off the flow of water to Pakistan in a show of sovereignty. This act is still cited by Pakistanis as an example of Indian attempts to strangle the new state of Pakistan, and it made water security a central concern of the new state. Coupled with this is the dependence on both sides of the India–Pakistan border on the waters of the Indus River for irrigation and, increasingly, energy purposes. Pakistan depends on the Indus waters system for its irrigation and agriculture, while India's energy shortages require the building of hydroelectric power capacity along the Indus River system.

It was the mutual need for the Indus waters and the tensions that arose from the need to guarantee the continued flow of waters to Pakistan that led the two countries to enter into negotiations—at the behest of the World Bank—and, in 1960, sign the Indus Waters Treaty.[15] The treaty divided the waters between the two countries and did not allow India to build any facilities that would obstruct the flow of the waters. It did, however, allow building of infrastructure to exploit the hydroelectric potential of the rivers. The treaty was eventually guaranteed by the World Bank and all disputes between the two countries first went to it and then, if needed, to arbitration. The treaty is considered by Pakistanis to have outlived its usefulness because of the riparian pressures that it now faces, but the other side of the argument is that it has stood the test of time because the two countries have gone through two full-scale and one limited war, but the Indian government has never seriously considered turned off the taps.

The Pakistani security establishment has argued that water is vital to the nation's future security.[16] The issue has been compounded by calls in India for using water as a weapon to halt Pakistani support to jihadis. The argument runs that if India manipulated the water supply, it would make Pakistan reconsider its training and support to terrorist elements.[17] Some in Pakistan argue that if there is a threat to cut off the water supplies, the Pakistani armed forces would have to bomb Indian dams being built along the Indus waters system. Pakistan has in fact repeatedly objected to Indian building of dams on the Indus Rivers and took India to the World Bank for the building of the Baghliar dam, which Pakistan saw as violating the Indus Waters Treaty.

What is unfortunate about the entire water dispute is that cooperation between the two countries, as envisaged in the second part of the Indus Waters Treaty, is necessary for harnessing the water resources of the Indus to the fullest benefit of both countries. Decades of distrust, wars, and now terrorism have not allowed that to happen, and thus we have all the makings of a long-term crisis. If cooperation were to take place, the two countries could address the situation, as Steve Solomon has argued, and take measures at the domestic level, in the case of India, to preserve water and prevent the drying up of ground water that would lead to more sustainable water use.[18]

KASHMIR

The issue that is touted as being central to the India–Pakistan dispute, however, is Kashmir. The Indian stand on Kashmir remains that it acceded to the country in 1947 and is an integral part of the nation. Its multireligious character makes it a continuing testament of the success of Indian secularism and the future unity of the country. Pragmatic strategic and economic factors also drive the Indian concerns over Kashmir. Since partition, one of the Indian government's objectives during conflicts has been to not cede any territory to an aggressor nation, and the fact that both Pakistan and China have annexed parts of Kashmir, including a section that was given to China in a border settlement with Pakistan, goes against the nationalist narrative in India. Economically, the river waters flowing through the state remain vital to both countries and increase Indian claims to the state. The disputed claims of India and Pakistan over the state have led to three wars, a limited conflict in 1999, and jihadi attacks since the late 1980s on the Indian side of Kashmir.

Kashmir's multireligious character—being a Muslim majority state but having a large Hindu and Buddhist population—makes it a difficult piece of territory to split up along cleanly divided ethnic lines (and this is not something that India wants to do in the first place). As Sumantra Bose points out, there are three sets of loyalties and nationalisms in the Kashmiri population: those who seek independence, those who want a Kashmir that is a part of India, and those who want a Kashmir that is a part of Pakistan.[19] The first and the third, he writes, exist in Pakistan as well. Pro-independence and pro-Pakistani sentiments have waxed and waned in Indian Kashmir since independence but took the form of a serious insurgency only after the rigged state elections of 1987, which brought to power, once again, the unpopular and corrupt National Conference Party. In retaliation, an indigenous insurgency broke out that was subsequently provided with support from Pakistan—the initial insurgent group being the Jammu and

Kashmir Liberation Front (JKLF). When the JKLF seemed to be becoming more independent of Pakistani control, Pakistan decided to turn its support to more pro-Pakistan elements within the separatist/insurgency movement and gave support to the Lashkar-e-Taiba group, which largely consisted of west Punjabis.[20] Kashmir already had a large Indian military presence, but the insurgency led to a higher infusion of troops and with it came violence, human rights violations, and allegations of extrajudicial killings.

As mentioned earlier, in 2002, President Musharraf pledged to stop support for jihadi groups, and this lessened the flow of infiltrators across the border. The general easing of tensions then led to peace talks between the two countries that included discussions on what to do about Kashmir. As Steve Coll shows, the two sides actually came up with some meaningful proposals for resolving the issue, which included demilitarization, a soft border, and self-government for the Kashmiris. But these slow attempts toward settling the Kashmir issue were shelved following the departure of Pervez Musharraf from the Pakistani presidency and, more importantly, the Mumbai terror attacks of 2008. The capture of Ajmal Kasab and his link to Lashkar-e-Taiba led to the Indian government losing all incentives to pursue a peace negotiation with Pakistan. Instead, the focus became on getting Pakistan to hand over the chief of Lashkar as well as other terror suspects to India—something that Pakistan was never likely to do.

Yet, while externally aided terror was declining, with Pakistan embroiled in its own domestic issues of countering terrorism, what sprung up in Kashmir in 2009 were large-scale protests against human rights abuses. The Indian state reacted heavy handedly, and this only led to an escalation in public protests and violence. The protests raged through the summer of 2010 and may have been targeted to gain international attention since India was going to host the Commonwealth Games in October 2010 and President Obama was to visit the country at the end of the year. Large-scale protests would work to not only embarrass the government in New Delhi but also draw attention to the Kashmiri cause—much in the same way as the international protests by Tibetans, as the Olympic torch passed by, embarrassed Beijing in 2008 and once again drew attention to the Tibetan issue.

The question for India then lies in how to manage the Kashmir dispute without escalating tensions with Pakistan. At the international level, India has achieved some success by keeping the issue off the agenda in its dealings with most of the major powers—China being the one exception. When the Obama administration came to power, the plan was to make Richard Holbrooke the special representative for Afghanistan, Pakistan, and Kashmir. India successfully protested and Kashmir was taken off the agenda. In 2010, both Nicholas Sarkozy and David Cameron came to India and gave speeches that criticized Pakistan for its role in terrorism and neither leader brought up the Kashmir conflict.

In July 2010, when the British prime minister, David Cameron, visited India, he was extremely critical of Pakistan, "I choose my words very carefully. It is unacceptable for anything to happen within Pakistan that is about supporting terrorism elsewhere. It is well-documented that that has been the case in the past, and we have to make sure that the Pakistan authorities are not looking two ways. They must only look one way, and that is to a democratic and stable Pakistan."[21]

In his December visit to India, Sarkozy made similar comments when he said, "It is unacceptable for the world that terror attacks originate or are masterminded in Pakistan and terrorists are trained there." He continued, "France won't forget the martyred city of Mumbai. We will stand by India till justice is done."[22] He added that India had shown remarkable restraint after Mumbai. The French president had earlier stated that he supported India's bid to become a permanent member of the United Nations Security Council (UNSC). Barack Obama also did not comment on Kashmir and, instead, called for India to become a permanent member of the UNSC (although the American president was not critical of Pakistan in the way that the French and British leaders were).

The unwillingness of the three leaders to publicly criticize India on the Kashmir issue or to make the argument that Pakistan had a case in Kashmir is probably the best argument that India can make to Pakistan about the ineffectiveness of using jihadi forces to try and resolve the ongoing India–Pakistan dispute. While India gets criticized for human rights abuses in Kashmir, it is not getting the type of sustained international cynosure that would strengthen the Pakistani case. The reason for this is that the export of terrorism from Pakistan may not draw the type of international condemnation and punitive measures that India wants (in part at least because of Pakistan's continued utility in the Afghan conflict), but neither does it lead to any embarrassing show of sympathy for Pakistan.

For Pakistan to get diplomatic leverage on the Kashmir issue, it will probably have to permanently forgo the jihadi alternative since it has lost its utility in a world where Pakistan gets labeled as the epicenter of terrorism. This is particularly the case when one looks at how relations may shape between Pakistan and the Western nations in a post–bin Laden world. Vali Nasr has suggested that the fact that American forces could go deep into Pakistan to kill bin Laden may mean that not only can Islamabad no longer keep secrets from the United States but Washington may have a lesser need for Pakistan. He went on to say, "Since Islamabad can no longer protect its jihadist and Taliban assets, it should reassess its strategic calculus and abandon a foreign policy that relies on jihadist adventurism."[23] Nasr, however, concluded that Pakistan could not be relied on to make the right decision.

From an Indian perspective, the problem is that India has very few options in its diplomatic, military, or economic arsenal to deal with Pakistan. Diplomatically, its attempts to put pressure on Pakistan come from its ability to influence Western nations to put the heat on Islamabad. Militarily, a second-strike nuclear policy combined with a conventional military force that is large but not flexible enough or joint enough to wage the type of operations that the United States has carried out in Afghanistan make it difficult for India to apply coercive pressure on Pakistan. Nor does a strategy of the type that China pursues in its relations with India work in the Pakistani context. China has sought to build up its economic relationship with India (bilateral trade is expected to go up to $100 billion by 2015) and argued that the complicated and emotional border issue be handled at a later date. For India, a similar short- to medium-term strategy would be one of using its diplomacy in Western capitals to get Pakistan to talk about mutually beneficial issues like the transit of pipelines across Pakistani soil to India or about the development of a solid South Asian road and rail network that can help the region economically integrate to benefit all the nations of South Asia. The problem is that Pakistan's leadership, especially its military leadership, sees no quid pro quo in engaging India in a process of economic integration. A process of integration would lower tensions with India but this, paradoxically, would not be in the interests of the Pakistani military since it would lead to domestic calls for a reduction in military expenditure and even lowering the role of Pakistan's military in the governing process.

Which then leaves two options, and neither is a very satisfactory policy measure. One is to use the flow of river waters as a bargaining tool, but this is quite likely to both enrage public opinion in Pakistan and potentially cause precipitous military action by Pakistan. The latter would cause a conventional war, and in the mind of policymakers in New Delhi the possibility of escalation is quite high. For an India that is attempting to make itself a haven for investment and project itself as a globalized economy, getting into shooting wars over water makes little sense.

The other option lies in maintaining a much closer relationship with the United States since in some sense India has used Washington, and its ties with Islamabad, to apply pressure on Pakistan to refrain from its support to jihadi factions. The problem here is that a section of the Indian political elite remains wedded to the idea of pursuing a nonaligned foreign policy that would allow it to keep its distance from the United States. In policy terms, that means an India that will keep its distance from the United States and not take sides in the international system. The pragmatic counterargument to this is that, except for the United States, which country has the ability to influence Pakistan, and does India want to remain trapped in a South Asian security dilemma that makes it spend an unnecessarily large part of its time, resources, and energy on countering Islamabad? The Indian elite, as of now, is unwilling to make the hard choice to ally itself with the United States, and this means that an indigenous solution to dealing with Pakistan comes into play. An indigenous option could include an employable, coercive capability that offers three choices: changing India's nuclear doctrine from no first use to possible first use; building conventional forces that can carry out special forces types of operations; or employing a tit-for-tat policy of supporting insurgency movements and terrorism in Pakistan.

The last option is the easiest to dismiss because it would destroy India's international reputation, lead to an escalation of such attacks in India itself, and potentially harm future economic growth. In fact, the Indian prime minister was so confident about India's staying off this course that he agreed at Sharm el-Sheikh to a joint communiqué with Pakistan in which the internal conflict in Balochistan was mentioned, thereby suggesting Indian involvement in the conflict. Prime Minister Singh, however, pointed out, "Mr. Gilani raised the issue of Balochistan and said people say India is active [there]. I said our conduct is an open book and that we are willing to discuss anything. . . . If you have any evidence, we are willing to look at it. We are an open society."[24]

Removing the no first use clause from the nuclear doctrine may, however, be a more workable option. It is unlikely that anyone in the corridors of power in Islamabad actually believes that India has a second-use nuclear doctrine, so making a formal declaration would only add to the uncertainty of thinking in Pakistan of Indian use of the option. The counterargument is that it is unlikely to stop Pakistani indulgence and training of jihadi forces since Islamabad may be convinced that its nuclear deterrent will prevail. Similarly, after the special forces attack on the bin Laden compound in Abbotabad, there has been a lot of discussion in the Indian media about the ability of the Indian armed forces to carry out a similar action, with the leaders of the armed forces claiming it could be done if the political will existed.[25] More cautious voices, however, state that the Pakistani doctrine of first use and the fact that India, unlike the United States, lacks a joint special operations command make such talk more machismo than a coherent, utilizable, coercive instrument.[26]

The long-term option for India perhaps then lies in making Pakistan irrelevant to the country's future, which in one sense it already is. India's accelerating growth rate depends on it being a part of the global economy, improving its education levels, and building a world-class infrastructure to replace the ramshackle one it has created since achieving independence in 1947. For this, India has to focus its resources internally and assure investors that the country is a safe and productive place to invest in. Terrorism of the Mumbai attack style can put a damper on this, but other countries with high levels of internal threats and terror scares—Israel being a notable example—are capable of high growth rates and integrating their scientific and technological base into the global economy. What India needs to do, therefore, is focus on strengthening its domestic capabilities to combat terrorism. This would include improving the police force, building its intelligence capability, buying the right kind of firearms and surveillance equipment, and improving its linkages with law enforcement authorities of other countries. This would provide the Indian people with greater confidence and allow the economy to grow at the same time. As for Pakistan, the best thing India can do is deter that country militarily and engage in minimum but consistent levels of dialogue with it. The best defense and foreign policy against an unimaginative Pakistani elite will be an India that outstrips its neighbor to the point that Islamabad is marginal in world affairs, like North Korea. South Korea and its relationship with North Korea may then be the model for the two countries.

NOTES

1. Stanley Wolpert, *Shameful Flight: The Last Years of British Rule in India* (New York: Oxford University Press, 2006), p. 167.

2. See Anatol Lieven, *Pakistan: A Hard Country* (New York: Public Affairs, 2011), p. 23.

3. Aslam Siddiqui, *Pakistan Seeks Security* (Lahore: Longmans, Green and Co, 1960), p. 17.

4. The best recent discussion of this is provided in Ramchandra Guha, *India after Gandhi: The History of the World's Largest Democracy* (New Delhi: Picador, 2007), pp 127–50.

5. For a discussion of these crises and Indian behavior, see P. R. Chari, Pervaiz Iqbal Cheema, Stephen P. Cohen, *Four Crises and a Peace Process: American Engagement in South Asia* (Washington, DC: Brookings Institution Press, 2007).

6. See Steve Coll, "The Back Channel," *The New Yorker,* vol. 8, issue 3, March 2, 2009, pp. 38–44.

7. For a discussion of Cold Start, see Walter C. Ladwig III, "A Cold Start for Hot Wars: The Indian Army's New Limited War Doctrine," *International Security* 32, no. 3 (Winter 2007–2008): pp. 158–90.

8. Matt Wade, "Primed and Ready: One Misbeat from Nuclear War," *Sydney Morning Herald,* December 2, 2010.

9. Karen Brulliard and Debbie Wilgoren, "Failure to Discover bin Laden's Refuge Stirs Suspicion over Pakistan's Role," *The Washington Post,* May 2, 2011.

10. Bruce Riedel, "Pakistan Plays Hardball: Relations with Washington Are on the Skids," *Newsweek,* April 25, 2011.

11. See, Michael O'Hanlon, "U.S.–Pakistan: Bad Marriage, No Divorce," *Politico,* May 2, 2011, http://www.politico.com/news/stories/0511/54091.html

12. Bob Woodward, Obama's Wars, (New York, Simon and Schuster, 2010), p. 46.

13. Bruce Riedel, *Deadly Embrace: Pakistan, America, and the Future of the Global Jihad* (Washington, DC: The Brookings Institution Press, 2011), p. 69.

14. Robert Woodward, *Obama's Wars* (New York: Simon and Schuster, 2010), p. 46.

15. Sisir Gupta, "The Indus Waters Treaty 1960," *Foreign Affairs Report,* New Delhi, December 1960, pp. 155–56.

16. Noor ul Haq, "Pakistan's Water Concerns," *IPRI Factfile* 127, October 2010, pp. 3–6.

17. A possible Indian use of water as a weapon is discussed by Rajiv Sikri, *Challenge and Strategy: Rethinking India's Foreign Policy* (New Delhi: Sage, 2009), p. 51.

18. Steve Solomon, *Water: The Epic Struggle for Wealth, Power, and Civilization* (New York: HarperCollins, 2010), pp. 422–24.

19. Sumantra Bose, "Kashmir, 1990–2000: Reflections on Individual Voices in a Dirty War," *Development* 43, no. 3 (2000): p. 100.

20. Basharat Peer, "Tear Gas over Batamaloo," *The National Interest,* November/December 2010, p. 26.

21. Nicholas Watt and Vikram Dodd, "Cameron Sparks Diplomatic Row with Pakistan after 'Export of Terror' Remarks," *The Guardian,* July 28, 2010.

22. Vinaya Deshpande, "Curb Terrorism, Sarkozy Tells Pakistan," *The Hindu,* December 8, 2010.

23. Vali Nasr, "In Pakistan, No More secrets," *The Washington Post,* May 5, 2011.

24. Siddharth Varadarajan, "Joint Statement Flowed from Meeting of Prime Ministers," *The Hindu,* July 17, 2009.

25. Rahul Singh and Pramit Pal Chaudhuri, "Can India Pull Off a Covert Strike?" *The Hindustan Times,* May 6, 2011.

26. Ibid.

CHAPTER 4

China

The India–China relationship will be the central concern that shapes Indian foreign policy in the 21st century. While Pakistan may remain a security threat, it is not an existential security threat. The relationship with China, on the other hand, has the ability to either lead the two countries into an era of great prosperity or, if poorly managed, aggravate tensions and lead to an arms race between the two largest countries in the world. In this context, India faces the same dilemma that all Asian countries, and even the United States, now face. An open confrontation with China will kill the goose that lays the economic golden eggs that have spurred Asian growth over the last decade. On the other hand, India, like other Asian countries, fears that as China's economic and military power grows, it will not permit the legitimate growth of other nations to a higher power status and will consign India to a secondary status in Asia.

BACKGROUND

When Mao Zhe Dung came to power in 1949, India was the second country after the United Kingdom to recognize the new Chinese regime. The Indian position was not reciprocated by the new government in Beijing, for Mao dismissed Jawaharlal Nehru as the running dog of the imperialists and complained about the Indian consulate in Tibet. What changed the Chinese position on India was the Indian stance in the Korean War, where its role and diplomacy led the country to be invited to the final peace conference in Geneva. In the aftermath of the

Korean War, India–China relations improved to the point where the two countries signed the Panchashila or the Five Principles of Peaceful Coexistence agreement. But at the same time the issue of the border between the two countries remained unsettled.

The Indians, who had inherited the border drawn by the British (but rejected by the Nationalist Chinese and Tibetans in a conference in 1914), were unwilling to discuss modifications to the border since this would, among other things, have put pressure on New Delhi to engage in similar exchanges of territory with Pakistan over the issue of Kashmir. Repeated attempts by the Chinese to resolve the border dispute were not met with a like-minded approach in New Delhi, and this was at a time when China had annexed Tibet in 1950 and was by 1959 facing unrest in its new territory. What complicated matters further was that the Dalai Lama had fled Tibet and been accepted as a refugee by India. Tibetan refugees based in India participated in the revolt against the Chinese. Beijing was also concerned about securing its borders because, by 1959, there were cracks in the Sino-Soviet relationship, which made China concerned about the status of its Western borders.

Tensions between the two nations escalated as India sought to physically enforce its position along the border by putting troops in forward positions. This, coupled with the Tibetan rebellion that was being aided by Tibetan groups in India, led the Chinese, in October 1962, to launch an attack on the Indian forces and seize the disputed territories. Having achieved their objectives of repelling the Indian forces to the south of the MacMahon line and gaining territories in the west in the disputed Aksai Chin area, the Chinese imposed a unilateral cease-fire and withdrew. India's humiliation was complete and to a large extent the memory of this defeat still colors the way New Delhi looks at Beijing. The popular mythology in India is that the Chinese betrayed their friendship with India by waging a surprise attack on the nation to secure Beijing's territorial objectives. Western observers tend to ascribe the blame to India for failing to recognize the seriousness of the Chinese intentions, the legitimacy of Beijing's territorial claims, and the fact that India carried out a forward policy to reclaim land that was never under its control.

Post-1962, India–China relations stalled as China focused its energies on the Vietnam War in Southeast Asia and on the growing Sino-Soviet tensions, with the latter leading to armed clashes along the Ussuri and Amur rivers in 1969. India was also caught up in its own domestic problems as the country first faced a famine in the late 1960s and then internal political turmoil as the Congress party started to lose its grip over political power both at the state and central levels in India (and the country faced a violent Maoist challenge in the state of West Bengal). Even then, the looming shadow of China remained over South Asian matters because during the 1965 India–Pakistan war, New Delhi feared that China might intervene on the side of Pakistan.

The 1970s saw India in a more secure environment since not only was Pakistan a truncated state—with the creation of Bangladesh—but China was engaged in more pressing global affairs and viewed the India–China border as a resolved issue.

In the 1980s, with the advent of the Rajiv Doctrine, the Indian government decided to use coercive diplomacy to try and attain Indian strategic objectives. Thus, the Indian government decided to place troops on the border along both China and Pakistan to try and resolve outstanding foreign policy and security issues. In both cases, India backed down because with Pakistan there was the concern that it could escalate into a broader conflict while with China it became apparent that matching Chinese force levels along the entire border would be an extremely expensive effort.

The Indian government began the long thaw in its relationship with China with the 1989 visit of Prime Minister Rajiv Gandhi to Beijing. This was followed in 1993 by a Peace and Tranquility Agreement that actually lowered force levels along the India–China border. What it also did was to create the concept of a line of actual control along the border. While meant to be a confidence-building measure, the line has become the center of allegations by both sides of territorial violations.[1] So, in which direction does the Sino-Indian relationship now seem headed?

To understand this problem is to recognize that the relationship is headed along two divergent paths. At the economic level, the India–China relationship has followed the direction that Beijing has sought to create in all its bilateral relationships—that of increasing economic interdependence. India–China trade now runs at approximately $60 billion, and the Chinese project an expansion of this economic relationship to approximately $100 billion by 2015. These numbers are not overly optimistic since trade was projected to rise to $40 billion by 2010. If the upper number can be brought about, it would add an economic dynamic to the relationship that would be hard for the Indian government to ignore in its dealing with Beijing. India would have a major economic dependency on China, much in the same way that other countries of Asia and Oceania do, that would potentially be the basis of future prosperity. As other nations in Asia have found, this strong economic relationship leads to the need to adapt a foreign policy that is more accommodating of Chinese interests. In fact, as the Indian journalist Kingshuk Nag has pointed out, there is now a growing business lobby in India that would seek a much stronger economic relationship with China and seek to downplay the continuing political and military-strategic differences with that country.[2] The idea here is that a "Chindia" will emerge, wherein the two countries will be able to get over their differences, cooperate economically and politically, and emerge as a major force in international affairs.[3]

In part, this idea of a Chindia is based on the notion that the two economies will remain complementary, with India being a services giant and China an industrial giant. The metaphor usually used here is of a computer where the Chinese build the hardware and the Indians provide the software. As Yasheng Huang points out, however, "Inherent in the idea of complementarity is the implication that Chinese industry should remain anonymous contract producers in the face of a burgeoning Indian service sector, an implication that overlooks China's larger economic ambitions. China is eager to grab a share of the software business."[4] If, as Huang argues, China follows the more typical path of development and builds its services industry, while India seeks to catch up in the area of industrial production, even this temporary complementarity will go away very quickly. Instead, the more challenging political, military, and power transition problems will take a more prominent place in the relationship.

The South Korean author Chung min Lee has made the argument that while every country in Asia benefits economically from the rise of China, they all worry about Beijing's political and military forays as the country continues to increase its power potential.[5] Thus, it was China's stimulus package and its continued need for raw materials and other imports that allowed trade to boom in Asia and Oceania after the onset of the recession of 2007–2008. The economic lure of China now is such that traditional U.S. allies, like Australia, Japan, and South Korea, are all heavily dependent on trade with China for their continued economic prosperity. This has led to some concern that these traditional allies, in the time of crises, would not be enthusiastic partners in a U.S. move against China. At the same time, the growth of China's military capabilities and its increasing assertiveness in the Asian region—on the South China sea, in its disputes with Japan, and along the India–China border—raise the danger that China may increasingly be willing to use force to resolve these disputes.

India like every other Asian country worries about this contradiction. Increased trade with China can only be in India's long-term interests, and if, as expected, it reaches the range of $100 billion, then the possibility of a strong economic interdependence between the two countries arises. The optimistic picture then would be one where as interdependence increases, so too does Indian and Chinese cooperation on political and economic issues, particularly in international forums. The first indication of this was when India and China, along with Brazil and South Africa, went to Copenhagen for the climate change conference and essentially demanded a separate agreement since the one forged by the Europeans did not suit the developmental plans of these nations. In the case of the replacement for the disgraced head of the International Monetary Fund, Dominique Strauss-Kahn, both India and China voiced their opinion that a non-European candidate should get the position, but there was no coordinated effort by the two countries to seek a new candidate or to even play the role of the spoiler. While there are those in India who see the advantages of an India–China collaborative alliance, most analysts believe that China will pose as an economic, political, and military challenge in the coming years.

The main economic driver that may lead the two countries on a collision course is the fact that both will seek natural resources and trade zones to boost their rapidly growing economies. One of the complaints in India has been that China is seeking to lock down natural resources around the world, particularly energy resources, by overbidding for these assets. As Phillipa Malgrem points out, when a Chinese state-owned firm decides to acquire a foreign one, it is because the order comes from Beijing and "no deal is too risky and no price is too high to pay if Beijing has ordered it to happen."[6] This Chinese attitude to external investment has led to India being outbid in places like Angola where it sought to acquire rights to oil fields or oil exploration. China's diplomacy, its willingness to bid exorbitantly for assets, and the fact that it is more willing to take risks at the global level have created the fear in New Delhi that China will be able to undertake an energy lockdown that will squeeze India's own developmental efforts that also require a massive infusion of imported energy resources. Additionally, India complains about the adverse terms of trade with China.

The India–China trade relationship has grown significantly to the point that it reached $60 billion in 2010. Premier Wen's December 2010 visit to India led to the signing of an agreement to raise bilateral trade to $100 billion by 2015—and, if the rapid growth of the past is any indication, that figure might be crossed at an earlier date. Indian analysts, however, point out that trade flows are actually in China's advantage and the gap keeps widening. India largely exports commodities to China while it imports finished goods, and the trade deficit between the two countries keeps widening—from $2 billion in 2002 to $20 billion in 2010—with India claiming that the dumping of Chinese good in India is killing Indian manufacturing.[7]

The other major concern India has comes from the potential diversion of water resources by China for its own use. The Brahmaputra River, which flows through India and Bangladesh, has its origins in Tibet as the Yarlang Tsampo river, and the Chinese government is seeking to build six dams along the river to permit economic development of the region. For India, the free flow of the Brahmaputra is vital for the development of its eastern region and, therefore, there is cause for concern in India about Chinese intentions.[8] Premier Wen made the argument that China was aware of Indian concerns and was not going to divert water resources, but the argument has been met with skepticism in New Delhi since there are no formal institutional arrangements to support the Chinese claim.

The other irritant in the relationship remains the all-weather friendship between China and Pakistan, although in recent years the relationship between the two countries has started to shift in a direction that may not be to the long-term liking of Pakistan. In the past, China provided Pakistan with the technology and designs for a workable nuclear weapon and with missiles for delivery systems (subsequently, Pakistan obtained longer range missiles from North Korea in exchange for supplying Pyongyang with nuclear weapons technology). The transfer of weapons technology was a simple and cheap way for Beijing to deter the rise of India's own nuclear program since it ensured that New Delhi remained focused on the Pakistani threat. Additionally, China, since the 1960s, has been one of the two major suppliers of weaponry to Pakistan, and, in recent times, the quality and technological advancement of Chinese weapons systems have improved, making them more effective against Indian forces.

From New Delhi's perspective, therefore, China remains a supplier of weapons to Pakistan, a useful ally to Islamabad in international forums and, potentially, a country that could put pressure on India—even to the extent of opening a second front—in a future India–Pakistan conflict. India's own rise, as well as Pakistan's own internal problems, may have changed the nature of the relationship, however, to a situation where New Delhi has greater leverage with Beijing on this issue.

The growth of extremism within Pakistan and the use of jihadi forces to promote Pakistani foreign policy and security objectives have not been endorsed by China. Beijing called for India and Pakistan to resolve the Kashmir issue peacefully, and it has been reluctant to have a large footprint in the Afghanistan–Pakistan area for fear of antagonizing the United States. Thus, in Afghanistan, China has not sought to provide armed protection for its copper mine, depending instead on U.S. troops to perform security duties in the area. Nor has it sought to get involved in the Afghan insurgency as it has not been a supplier of weapons or cash to the Taliban forces.

In its relationship with Pakistan, China has committed itself to supporting Islamabad, but not in a way that would endanger long-term Chinese interests or put it in the position of maintaining a state that becomes an economic basket case. Thus, China has not offered large-scale emergency economic assistance to Pakistan, forcing the latter to go to the International Monetary Fund for its financial needs. Similarly, after the bin Laden killing, the Pakistani premier, in a bid to diplomatically and economically distance Islamabad from Washington, went to China and offered Beijing control of the Gwadar port in Balochistan. On returning from Beijing, Prime Minister Gilani stated that China had agreed to take over control of the port, but he was soon contradicted by the Chinese government, which stated that it had no intention of doing so. China also declined to build a naval base at Gwadar, recognizing that it would raise American suspicions.[9]

China's calculations are based on very pragmatic considerations. Balochistan is a remote area of Pakistan and continues to face a low-level insurgency. Moreover, a Chinese naval base would only lead the United States to ramp up its own naval presence in the area to counter what will be seen as an aggressive move by China.

What China is willing to do, however, is to help maintain the existence of the Pakistani state. It, therefore, agreed, in the wake of the bin Laden killing and the cooling of Pakistani relations with the United States, to rapidly transfer 50 JF-17 fighter aircraft to the Pakistan Air Force. It is unlikely to break its military linkage with Pakistan and will continue providing a steady supply of weapons to help Pakistan augment its conventional force levels vis-à-vis India. But at the same time, it would be less likely, unless severely provoked by India, to up the ante and provide Pakistan with more advanced weapons systems to counter India's advantage in this area. In this context, the Chinese string of pearls strategy needs to be closely examined.

The string of pearls strategy was first coined in a Booz Allen Hamilton 2005 report titled "Energy Futures in Asia," and it has since been developed by strategic thinkers. The strategy envisages China building a series of bases along the Indian Ocean littoral to defend its economic interests and, in doing so, providing the Chinese Navy with the means to contain India. India's buildup of its own air and naval capabilities has, at least in part, been due to this Chinese effort.

The other contentious issue remains permanent membership to the United Nations Security Council. China is now the only permanent member of the Security Council that does not favor Indian admittance into the Council as a permanent member. While China's concerns may have far less to do with India and far more to do with keeping out Japan, it is viewed in New Delhi as a general Chinese unwillingness to allow India to attain its natural position as a major Asian and world power.

Finally, there is also the issue of whether there is just a serious miscalculation on the part of China, as Minxin Pei would argue, about the role and status of India in the forthcoming world order. Pei argues that at the mass level in China knowledge about India is marked by ignorance and prejudice while at the elite level there is a rapidly growing interest in India. The Chinese elite recognize the potential for economic competition, the role India can play in Tibet, the unresolved border issue, and the rise in Indian military capabilities as a challenge to China.[10] Pei concludes:

Chinese ignorance, prejudice, and misperceptions, in and of themselves, would be unpleasant but not necessarily harmful. Unfortunately, when coupled with strategic distrust, they could reinforce the political dynamics for long-term enmity and rivalry. At the moment, mass and elite opinions inside China are converging to the view that India is moving ever closer to being part of a U.S.-designed strategic framework for containing China's rise. Part of the tensions between India and China in the past few years could be indirectly attributed to the underlying strategic distrust.

It is not too late to counter such dangerous dynamics. A hostile rivalry between Asia's two great powers is sure to derail their aspirations to sustain their economic development in peace. The Chinese and Indian scholarly communities in China, India, and the U.S. should do their part to prevent such a tragic outcome from becoming a reality. The least they can do is to promote candid and honest academic exchanges and help narrow the perception gap between the two societies.[11]

How inevitable is a Sino-Indian rivalry that ends up with a serious arms race between the two countries and escalating tensions, with the possibility of conflict emerging between them? A lot rests on the way the two countries conduct their growth to major power status. If they can accommodate each other's interests, then it will be a rise that could reshape international relations. If it is conflictual, then there is the much more serious possibility of tensions that could suck in the rest of Asia.

ALTERNATIVE SCENARIOS: A COOPERATIVE MODEL

The key to a cooperative model of relations between India and China may well lie in the expansion of trade and economic relations between the two countries. Economic ties between the two countries have constantly surpassed expectations since the two nations improved relations in the 1990s. It could reach a situation where India and China have a serious trading relationship that would constrain the military-strategic agendas of the two countries that are at present seen as conflicting. As the Indian economic journalist Kingshuk Nag has pointed out, with the growth of trade between the two countries, we have seen the birth of a business lobby in India that would like to see differences lessened and true economic interdependence emerge between the two countries.[12] India's demographics may also play a role in this transition since, as a country with 50 percent of the population under 25, the memory of the 1962 war and the humiliation of India is not present in the minds of the younger generation.

From a Chinese perspective, the development of Tibet requires the use of ports in the Indian Ocean region to facilitate the transit of goods to and from the western regions of China. For reasons discussed previously, Pakistan's Gwadar port may still take some time to be fully operational for Chinese businesses. With the instability in Balochistan, China is unlikely in the short to medium term to sink the kind of resources that would be required to make Gwadar an economically viable proposition and safe trade route for China. On the other hand, the Indian port of Kolkata is large enough to provide a ready-made access for Chinese and foreign goods. If China's long-term plan is to stabilize and fully integrate Tibet into the Chinese nation, then its rapid economic development could perhaps best be achieved with better and faster growing ties with India.

Chinese businesses have shown interest in increasing economic ties and expressed willingness to invest in Indian telecommunications and infrastructure enterprises. Indian caution about Chinese motives and the fear of adverse security implications have led India to resist the entry of Chinese firms into strategically crucial sectors of the Indian market, like telecommunications.[13] Chinese firms have been allowed, however, to invest in highway construction, including in the politically sensitive state of Jammu and Kashmir.[14] One of the ways out of this dilemma may be for Chinese firms to adopt the model the Japanese pursued in the 1980s and start to produce goods in India, thus alleviating Indian fears about their motives. Thus, the Chinese company Huawei has decided to invest $500 million in India and employ 6,000 personnel in order to overcome these concerns of the Indian government and security establishment.[15]

From an Indian perspective, Chinese corporations now have the skill sets, financial resources, and incentives to invest in the development of the most crucial area of the Indian economy—the infrastructure. India's ramshackle infrastructure continues to hold the country back in its attempts to develop and also discourages foreign investment. Indian estimates are that the country will have to open up $1 trillion in investment opportunities, including the opportunity to build a modern 21st-century infrastructure—something that firms all over the world are eyeing, provided India improves its investment climate and removes its bureaucratic roadblocks to the successful entry of foreign firms in the market.[16] Getting Chinese firms involved in such investments would then be a win-win situation for Indian industry.

A third part of this process would be the eventual move toward a free trade arrangement between the two countries. If achieved, it would lead to the emergence of the largest trading bloc in the world that would effectively dwarf corresponding arrangements in North America and Europe. Indian firms are wary of moving in this direction since they fear that it would encourage the dumping of cheap Chinese goods in India. In addition, they see an artificially undervalued exchange rate as favoring their Chinese competitors. The $60 billion trade is also slanted in China's favor, particularly because India mainly exports raw materials to China and gets manufactured goods in return.

A free trade arrangement could prove mutually beneficial in that it would provide Chinese investments in Indian manufacturing and allow India to move up the value chain in its production of goods.[17] This in the medium to long term would reduce the trade deficit with China. Further, China would benefit from the access to entrepreneurship of India's dynamic service sector. Rising wages and costs of production in China, the free trade agreement proponents argue, could also make Chinese firms relocate to India.[18]

If such arrangements were brought about between the two countries, it could be argued that the high level of economic interdependence would lead to a China that understood India's energy and raw material requirements and was, indeed, willing to invest in their development. Chinese firms would be willing to participate in oil and natural gas exploration, something that India has been seeking to encourage in terms of joint bidding by the two countries for foreign oil producing ventures, and to invest in the production of wind energy, since China is the largest manufacturer of wind energy equipment in the world.

From a military-strategic perspective, the growth of strong and binding ties with India would also lessen the Chinese fear of an American-led strategic encirclement of their country. All this would depend, however, on a significant shift in attitudes about the bilateral relationship in both New Delhi and Beijing. In New Delhi, it would require a recognition of Chinese security concerns in Tibet and, more importantly, a move to bring about a successful resolution of the 60 odd year border dispute between the two countries. On the Chinese part, it would require that Beijing first put the relationship with India at a higher level and work to address India's primary security concerns.

India could live with a Pakistan–China relationship that saw only the transfer of conventional weaponry to Islamabad, but it would need assurances from Beijing that there would be no further transfers of nuclear and missile technology. This is not a major concession for Beijing since it has ensured a Pakistani nuclear deterrent and investing in its enhancement would do little to actually make Pakistan more secure. It would, for example, do little to resolve the internal discord that Pakistan faces, and that, in the long run, is the greatest threat to that nation's security. In fact, attempting to enhance the nuclear capabilities of a country that some fear is headed toward radicalization would only lead to a further deterioration of the security environment in a region where China understands there is a need for long-term stability.

The other crucial change of attitude will have to come in the case of the border dispute and the Tibet issue. For China, the fear of a strengthened Tibetan secessionist movement that could potentially succeed in breaking that part of the country away from China has led to Beijing's hard-line policy in its negotiations with India, particularly on the disputed Indian northeastern province of Tawang. As Aaron Friedberg[19] points out, there remains the fear among the Chinese leadership that China could be torn apart by secessionist forces and, therefore, all efforts must be taken to prevent such a breakup. Given the location of Tibetan holy sites in the Tawang area, there has been the worry that it could be used as a symbolic means to embarrass China and stir up anti-Chinese sentiments in Tibet. Linked to this dispute is, of course, the fact that the Dalai Lama continues to live in India, is seen internationally as an influential moral leader and as the symbol of a free Tibet, and is now seeking to bring about a succession that would allow the spiritual head of the Tibetan people to be a free agent and not be under the influence of Chinese policy.

It could be argued quite cynically that a great deal of the legitimacy of the Tibet independence movement would be lost with the death of the Dalai Lama, but from the perspective of India–China relations neither side may have the luxury of allowing time and age to take their natural course. For Beijing, further strife in Tibet could easily lead to the need to take punitive measures since its authoritarian system does not really allow for the means to effectively channel dissent. Also, given how derogatory Beijing has been in its description of the Dalai Lama, it is difficult to imagine a turnaround by the political leadership of the Communist Party to work toward an effective accommodation of Tibetan interests. If this is the case, then the likelihood of a flare-up along the India–China border becomes a real possibility. This then brings up the less optimistic scenario of a conflictual model of India–China relations.

ALTERNATIVE SCENARIO: LEVELS OF CONFLICT

A conflict scenario between the two countries could be along a spectrum of alternatives ranging from militarization of the border and an arms race to a naval confrontation and the outbreak of a second India–China war. The most likely scenario that is raised in policy circles is of an expanding Chinese navy, replete with bases in the Indian Ocean region, seeking to encircle India and end up in a naval war as New Delhi seeks to break out of the ring put around it. For a variety of reasons, such a naval scenario is less likely to occur in the short to medium term, although in the long term it would be difficult to make predictions.

In the short to medium term, China is worried about the cutoff of access to the Indian Ocean and its oil supplies because of instability in the maritime states that surround it, the threat posed by piracy in the Strait of Malacca, and also by the rise of an Indian Navy that might seek to choke China's oil supplies from the Middle East and West Africa by restricting the passage of Chinese merchant shipping. China is taking both nonmilitary and military measures to try and protect its maritime interests. Militarily, China has sought to build up its naval fleet and is in the process of building one (and possibly more) aircraft carrier. Nonmilitarily, China has sought to use its infrastructure development efforts to provide alternatives to being boxed in through naval blockades.

The building of roadways and railways from China to Central Asia and Pakistan is one way to lessen the dependence on the maritime flow of traffic. China's plans for rail expansion include building a high-speed rail that goes from Beijing to London in 48 hours. While this may be the glitzy side of the development of infrastructure, the more practical side involves creating a functioning road and rail network that would integrate the countries of Asia into a large commercial network and neutralize the ability of the U.S. Navy to apply pressure on China. The other aspect of this process would involve building oil and gas pipelines from Central Asia and, possibly, Iran to China, thereby providing an alternative and possibly more secure way of transporting vital energy resources to the Chinese heartland.

From a Chinese perspective, a nonmilitary solution would help alleviate the fears of its neighbors about Chinese maritime expansion, lead to a phenomenal economic boom for its partner Asian states (Pakistan, for example, would profit enormously from the Chinese use of Gwadar port to full capacity and from the transit fees it would get for pipelines going from Iran to China over Pakistani territory), and would work to lessen American economic and, therefore, in the long run, military influence in the region.

A nonmilitary solution also allows China to not antagonize the United States and India and continue to be a free rider on the naval security and order provided by the U.S. Navy in the Indian and Pacific Oceans. As Robert Kaplan argues, a Chinese military base in Gwadar or in the Sri Lankan port of Hanambota would cause serious concern to both India and the United States, so it would be better to only have access to these ports rather than control them or have a military presence in them.[20]

For India, meeting a Chinese naval threat would be much more manageable since proximity to naval choke points, the existence of Indian island chains, and New Delhi's own naval buildup give it a significant power projection and sea denial capability in the Indian Ocean region. India's submarine fleet is to be augmented with the addition of Akula class nuclear submarines as well as an indigenously produced nuclear submarine, both of which would increase the capability of the Indian Navy to interdict Chinese shipping. India's Andaman and Nicobar Island chain, close to the Strait of Malacca, provide a natural air base from which Indian Sukhoi-30s, armed with antishipping missiles, could do considerable damage to a Chinese fleet coming into the Indian Ocean. Without comparable air cover, the Chinese fleet would be vulnerable to an Indian attack.

Other Chinese vulnerabilities would come from the fact that the bulk of China's oil comes from the Middle East and West Africa. Interdicting oil supplies would be far easier for the Indian Navy than protecting it would be for the Chinese Navy. In fact, in a future conflict between the two countries, this strategy could work to damage the Chinese war effort and bring it to a quicker resolution. But, despite Indian planning and preparations for a naval clash, it is more likely that the tensions between the two countries would erupt along the border that has still to be resolved after more than 60 years of talks, recriminations, and a border war in 1962.

For both countries, the stakes along the border have less to do with moving the line of actual control in either a northerly or southerly direction but more to do with the political ramifications of a settlement or of the continuation of certain problems associated with the lack of resolution.

From an Indian perspective, settling the border with China without getting significant concessions and the return of territory in the western sector would weaken India's case against Pakistan on the Kashmir issue. Most postcolonial states live with borders that were imposed on them and have to create their own national identities and brands of nationalism within to meet the reality of being newly independent. When the existence of the state is challenged, however, by ethno-religious groups, then the response of the ruling elite is to react by maintaining the rigidity of state boundaries since the fear is that making territorial compromises, or letting one section of the population determine its own future in an independent entity, would only serve to lead to the total disintegration of the state. Both India and China, despite their size, their military capability, and the strong centralized natures of their state apparatuses, remain deeply concerned that their countries are susceptible to failure and disintegration into smaller units.

It is this state fragility that makes Tibet and the border such a difficult issue for the two countries to resolve. For China, concessions on the border that allow the issue of Tibetan independence to remain alive would only sow the seeds for long-term instability—something that the Chinese Communist Party would be most averse to. It is for this reason that the Chinese government has started to take a harder line on the border issue with India. The presence of the Dalai Lama in India and his attempts to find a successor in his lifetime are security concerns for China as it seeks to fully and permanently integrate Tibet into China. The Chinese government would, therefore, like to see any territories where there could be a symbolic revival of the Tibetan cause to be within Chinese boundaries and under their control. That is why Tawang, over which Tibet had claims but is now in India, has emerged as a contentious issue between the two countries. China cannot allow Tawang to be a part of India as long as the complete and successful integration of Tibet does not take place.

Coupled with this issue is the fact that the Chinese Communist Party has painted itself into a corner in its dealings with the Dalai Lama. The virulent attacks on the Dalai Lama by Chinese officials make it difficult to allow both sides to sit down and work out a solution that would help resolve the issue. Further, with the Dalai Lama seeking a successor in his lifetime, it essentially means that the exiled Tibetan diaspora is seeking a spiritual leader who lives outside China and, therefore, is not under Chinese control. The Chinese government's strategy has been one of playing a waiting game—one where the Dalai Lama will die and the movement for Tibetan rights will fizzle out.[21] But until that happens, the Dalai Lama remains a symbolic leader who threatens Chinese sovereignty. There is, however, the danger that with the death of the Dalai Lama, who has been a moderating influence by calling for a nonviolent resolution to the issue, Tibetans may decide to protest violently.

From an Indian perspective, the border therefore remains a problem that is caught up in issues of state survival, national pride, and in dealing with a neighbor that has a mirror image in its security dilemma of internal fragility and the need to maintain territorial integrity. At present, neither side can give way without losing stakes in a broader game. At the ground level, the situation is further complicated by the fact that the line of actual control is six miles wide, thus leaving it rife for claims by both sides of territorial incursions. Moreover, the charge of incursions has led in the past to a barrage of nationalistic outbursts by the media of both countries. This led the then Indian prime minister to personally intervene to tone down the rhetoric that had begun to affect the relationship between the two countries.

Further, the Chinese government has sought to keep the Tawang issue alive by not requiring visas for visitors to China from that part of India, claiming that they were Chinese citizens and, therefore, did not require a visa. China also revisited the Indian claim to Jammu and Kashmir when it denied a visa to the Indian military officer who was the commander of forces in the area. And, most importantly, there remains the concern in New Delhi about Chinese incursions along the border that would effectively nibble away at it and give the tactical advantage to Beijing in a future conflict.

Confronting China along the border would be a difficult proposition for India since Beijing has built its infrastructure in Tibet to facilitate road and rail mobility. India, burdened with its own developmental challenges and its traditional neglect of the northeastern border areas, has lagged behind in building the necessary infrastructure to rapidly deploy troops in the region to sustain a defensive effort against China. In recent years, India has moved some Sukhoi squadrons to the northeast to act as a counterthreat to China, but this still leaves the Chinese with an impressive advantage in the conventional arena along the Sino-Indian border.

India's strategy on the border issue, therefore, lies in not overtly antagonizing the Chinese by providing support to the cause of the Dalai Lama. Nor has it sought to militarize the border in a way that would force Beijing to recalculate its force presence in the region. At the same time, India has maintained its position on the border and, more recently, in the joint communiqué that followed the 2010 Wen visit to India, actually adopted a tougher diplomatic posture by not making the usual statements on China's claims to Taiwan and Tibet. China in turn stayed away from mentioning its own concerns in the communiqué.[22]

This then brings up the issue of what India can do to counter the Chinese challenge, and the problem here is that it is 20 years behind the Chinese behemoth in its economic development, having started its market reforms in the early 1990s as a response to the country's financial crisis. The fact that its market reforms started at a later date has left India trailing behind China in terms of its industrial strength, its infrastructure, and its international strategy to acquire natural resources and markets. Thus, while China has, as Philippa Malgrem points out, overbid to secure resources and assets in other countries, India has cautiously moved into this area and played second fiddle to China. Consequently, it has lost out to Chinese firms in countries like Angola and Russia in the quest to secure oil exploration rights. Second, unlike China, India has not forged a foreign policy that in the further reaches of the world is shaped by economic determinism. China is able to pursue a policy of "economics matter" in its dealing with the countries of Latin America and Africa because its own national security interests, and its capacity to project power, do not extend beyond the Asian continent.

India has, therefore, a long way to go to be able to compete with China at the global level, although it is making strides by investing in Africa and through its political alliance with Brazil and South Africa. At the same time, it does have the advantage of being a large market for goods and services and so can leverage this to gain access on a reciprocal basis around the world.[23] It is this market that can give India the diplomatic support from around the world as it seeks to pursue its broader diplomatic objectives as well as its more specific ones that are focused on China.

The Chinese challenge is viewed among policy analysts in New Delhi primarily in military-strategic and Cold War terms, such as deterring the Chinese along the border and preventing Chinese encroachment in the Indian Ocean region. There is also the fear that China will not allow India to attain its rightful position as a global power by squeezing out its access to energy resources and shutting off markets. For India to meet the Chinese challenge, however, the enhancement of its military-strategic capabilities is a necessary step but not a sufficient one. A more effective way will be to rapidly develop India's own infrastructure and economy, thus providing a truly large alternative market in Asia to foreign investors and, more importantly, giving India the economic impetus to be a global economic player. An India on such a trajectory will be able to gain greater influence as Indian firms will compete globally in larger numbers with their Chinese counterparts. An India with shabby urban areas, an aging manufacturing capacity, and obsolescent infrastructure cannot hope to be taken seriously as a challenger to China. India also has an edge over China in the use of soft power that it has not yet fully exploited.

Unlike China, India has the ability to build up its secondary and tertiary educational systems to provide access to international students from Asia and Africa. It has, however, done very little in this area. Efforts to internationalize Indian education by allowing foreign students to get degrees at Indian campuses have led to less than 10,000 international students being enrolled at any given point in time in the country.[24] Yet, given the increasingly high costs of global education, this is an area where India could develop a serious international niche and use this community of students to feed its own economic efforts. As a first step, India could allow foreign universities into the country to increase and modernize the nation's educational capabilities. Government indecision and resistance from within India's academic community have made the progress on this front glacial.

Additionally, Ian Hall has argued that India, because of its growing power potential, can play the role of a spoiler in international forums, but this role while serving India's narrow interests does little to expand the country's global standing.[25] In the 1940s and 1950s, India was able to do far more, despite being an impoverished economy, because its diplomatic efforts sought to create a pan-Asian identity, to raise critical issues like nuclear disarmament and apartheid in international forums, and to create a critical space for underdeveloped nations in the world arena with the nonaligned movement. A new, globalized India needs to come up with its own big idea about the structure of global order if it wants to be able to compete with China in the international system.

CONCLUSION

For India, the challenge from China cannot be met at the military-strategic level. Such a challenge would require a massive investment in its conventional and nuclear capabilities, which the Indian government, with its commitment to national development, would not be able to fulfill. China can also easily increase the pressure on India by augmenting the conventional and nuclear capabilities of Pakistan, something it has done in the past, to keep India bogged down in South Asia.

The reliance on a military-strategic deterrent also shows a lack of understanding of the nature of the Chinese challenge as an emerging global power. Beijing has successfully leveraged its economic capability and its diplomacy to forge sound bilateral and regional ties across the world. China's multipronged approach has led to a situation where it is now the largest trading partner of strong and traditional U.S. allies, like Australia and South Korea, and the development of such strong economic ties has helped alleviate China's fears of being encircled and contained by a geographical ring of American allies. The policy of economic interdependence and quiet diplomacy has also won China friends around the world, making its own political position on sensitive issues like Tibet and Taiwan more internationally acceptable.

Given this Chinese strategy, India has to work on a long-term strategy that includes greater economic interdependence and the use of its soft power. In such a scenario, it has to keep growing its domestic economy, creating a favorable climate for investment (that would include reducing the rampant corruption in the country) and modernizing its cities, manufacturing industries, and infrastructure. Investors are willing to take the risk in China not only because of its investor-friendly policies, but because that country has invested in modernizing its industrial and infrastructural capabilities. India, in contrast, saw an over 40 percent drop in foreign investment in 2011 because of the high level of corruption in the country.[26]

While working to build up its own domestic economic and societal strength, India will have to continue being sensitive to China's concerns about the Tibetan issue by preventing elements within the exiled Tibetan community or the hawkish elements within its own policy making, military, and academic worlds from provoking a clash with China. Beijing has shown that it can rachet down the tensions between the two countries, and it is in India's interests to keep the border issue from spilling over into the other more productive areas of the relationship. This brings up the final point that in the long run economics may fundamentally transform the relationship between the two countries. With more than

$100 billion in trade, which is expected by 2015, the two countries may well find themselves in a situation where the joys of making money overcome the military-strategic concerns on both sides.

NOTES

1. Yasheng Huang, "The Myth of Economic Complementarity in Sino-Indian Relations," *The Journal of International Affairs,* 64, no. 2 (2011): p. 112.

2. Interview with Kingshuk Nag, editor, *The Times of India,* Hyderabad, March 11, 2010.

3. The term Chindia was coined by the Indian minister for the environment Jairam Ramesh. For a series of articles on the subject, see Jairam Ramesh, *Making Sense of Chindia: Reflections on China and India* (New Delhi: India Research Press, 2005), pp. 3–9.

4. Huang, "The Myth of Economic Complementarity in Sino-Indian Relations," p. 118.

5. Chung Min Lee, "China's Rise, Asia's Dilemma," *The National Interest,* issue 81, Fall 2005, p. 89.

6. Phillipa Malgrem, "The China Temptation: Are Western Investors Being Foolhardy," *The International Political Economy,* 19, no. 2 (2005): pp. 44–47.

7. Brahma Chellany, "Troubled Times for Chinese–Indian Relations: Trade Isn't Enough to Build Goodwill between the Two Asian Giants," *The Washington Times,* January 3, 2011.

8. Claude Arpi, "China's Water War with India," *The Pioneer,* June 26, 2011.

9. Griff Witte, "Pakistan Courts China as U.S. Sour," *The Washington Post,* June 23, 2011.

10. Minxin Pei, "Dangerous Misperceptions: Chinese Views of India's Rise," http://casi.ssc.upenn.edu/iit/pei.

11. Ibid.

12. Interview with Kingshuk Nag, resident editor, *The Times of India,* Hyderabad, March 20, 2009.

13. Bruce Einhorn, "Chinese Companies Try to Solve Their India Problem," *Businessweek Bloomberg,* May 9, 2010, http://www.businessweek.com/blogs/eyeonasia/archives/2010/05/chinesecompaniestrytosolvetheirindiaproblem.html.

14. "Kamal Nath Seeks Chinese Investment in J&K, North East Highways," *The Times of India,* September 16, 2010.

15. Vijay Sakhuja, "Huawei Points Way into India," *Asia Times,* January 27, 2010.

16. "India Offers $1 Trillion Investment Opportunities: Gopalan," Press Trust of India, June 29, 2011.

17. "China–India FTA Would Be a Win-Win Deal," *The Business Times,* Singapore, December 16, 2010.

18. Ibid.

19. Aaron L. Friedberg, "Hegemony with Chinese Characteristics," *The National Interest* (July/August 2011): p. 25.

20. Robert Kaplan, *Monsoon: The Indian Ocean and the Future of American Power* (New York: Random House, 2011), p. 290.

21. For a discussion of the role of the Dalai Lama, Chinese concerns, and the inability to resolve the Tibet issue, see Evan Osnos, "The Next Incarnation," *New Yorker,* vol. 86, issue, 30, October 4, 2010, pp. 62–75.

22. Sandeep Dikshit, "Let's Be Sensitive to Each Other's Concerns," *The Hindu,* December 17, 2010.

23. For a discussion of India's economic role in Africa, see Harry G. Broadman, *Africa's Silk Road: China and India's Economic Frontier* (Washington, DC: International Bank for Reconstruction and Development, 2007), pp. 79–87 and 203–8.

24. Amit Gupta, "India's Soft Power," *Indian Foreign Affairs Journal,* 1, no. 1 (2006): p. 51.

25. Ian Hall, "The Other Exception?: India as a Rising Power," *The Australian Journal of International Affairs* 64, no. 5 (2010): p. 604.

26. Jim Yardley and Vikas Bajaj, "India's Economy Slows, with Global Implications," *The New York Times,* May 30, 2012.

CHAPTER 5

India and the United States

The India–U.S. relationship has seen a major shift in the last decade due to both forces of globalization and changes in the post–Cold War international system. With globalization, and the advent of internal market reforms, India has emerged as a major international player, and the United States has sought to enter both the civilian and military markets in India. The post–Cold War international system has seen the rise of China as a near peer competitor to the United States, and in an effort to engage in offshore balancing in Asia, the United States has sought to enlist India as a potential ally. The question is will this relationship emerge as a major influence on the power politics of the Indo-Pacific region or will India and the United States be unable to move beyond their mutual suspicions and the relationship will remain one of lost potential?

BACKGROUND

In the past, U.S.–Indian relations have been marked by divergent world-views that prevented both countries from developing the type of relations that the United States had with other major democracies, despite several instances of overlapping security interests. Initial suspicions about post-independence India stemmed from its unwillingness to commit to the Western alliance in the emerging Cold War, as well as from India's adoption of a quasi-socialist economy. While the relationship briefly blossomed during and immediately after the Korean War, with India as a member of the United Nations (UN) armistice commission, it soon ran aground with the twin crises of 1956—Hungary and Suez.

India condemned the Israel–French–British invasion of Suez but was far more reluctant to condemn the Soviet Union's brutal crushing of the Hungarian revolt. Relations between the two countries again briefly flourished after the Sino-Indian war of 1962 when the United States transferred conventional weapons to India, discussed covering India under its nuclear umbrella, and for a while was inclined to set up intelligence posts in the country to monitor China. At the economic level, India became a major recipient of U.S. assistance.

The United States provided significant amounts of food aid to India in the 1960s, first to tide the country over during the Bihar famine and, later, to start an agricultural Green Revolution in the country. Subsequent attempts to get India and Pakistan to negotiate a settlement on the disputed state of Kashmir, however, made the Indian government distance itself from the United States. At the same time, growing Soviet problems with China led to a strengthening of the India–Soviet Union relationship—particularly in the sphere of military cooperation. The two countries signed a peace and friendship treaty in August 1971 that allowed New Delhi greater diplomatic and military freedom to counter Pakistan.

Difficult relations with the United States continued in 1971 during the Bangladesh war. Indian officials believe that the Nixon administration sent an aircraft carrier, the USS *Enterprise,* into the Bay of Bengal to put pressure on India to halt the military campaign against Pakistan.[1] The relationship remained cool in the 1970s both due to American disinterest—the Vietnam War and events in the Middle East holding a place of priority in U.S. foreign policy—and because India, in 1974, decided to test a nuclear device. U.S. nonproliferation measures were automatically implemented against India, and the 1974 test led to a strengthening of both U.S. nonproliferation policies (with the Glenn-Symington Amendments to the Foreign Assistance Act and the 1978 Nuclear Nonproliferation Act) and those of other Western suppliers (through the creation of the London Club in 1975 and the decision by Western nuclear suppliers to ask for fullscope safeguards over any future technology transfers to other countries). At the same time, the United States had a decreasing interest in Pakistan because it was no longer relevant as a frontline state in the Cold War.

The situation of disinterest changed after the Soviet Union's invasion of Afghanistan in 1979. The United States, seeking to contain Soviet expansion toward the Indian Ocean and the Persian Gulf, decided to supply arms to Pakistan and to use Pakistani territory as a conduit for supplying weapons to and for training the Afghan *Mujahideen.* This was done even while it became apparent that Pakistan had decided to follow India's example and initiated a nuclear weapons program. Although the personal relationship between President Reagan and Indian prime minister Indira Gandhi was cordial, and her son and successor, Rajiv Gandhi, was able to garner considerable goodwill in the United States, the rationale of the Cold War kept the two countries apart. It was also during the Rajiv Gandhi period (1984–1989) that the first discussions about transferring defense-related technology began. India expressed an interest in purchasing American avionics and power plants for its Light Combat Aircraft program.[2]

It was only after the end of the Cold War and the coming to power of the Narasimha Rao government in India in 1991 that relations began to improve. The new Indian government, recognizing that the economy was in a crisis, sought to carry out a series of structural and market reforms that relaxed previous obstacles to foreign investment in the country and allowed the economy to be rejuvenated. Indian and American groups began to meet to discuss defense cooperation, especially the transfers of technologies to assist in the development of India's conventional weapons production programs. At the same time, the first Bush administration declared in 1990 that Pakistan was not complying with nonproliferation measures and cut off military and economic assistance to Islamabad (the president could not certify under the Pressler Amendment of 1985 that Pakistan did not have a nuclear device).

The Clinton administration sought to improve relations further, but the May 1998 nuclear tests by India and Pakistan led to another series of sanctions being imposed on both countries. While subsequent congressional amendments were to pull back most of the economic sanctions, key ones remained, particularly in the area of military technology transfers. India's Light Combat Aircraft program was delayed because of its inability to obtain General Electric F-404 power plants to power the prototypes. While sanctions led to a cooling down of the relationship, the United States was proactive in maintaining peace between the two nuclear neighbors.

After the nuclear tests of 1998, Deputy Secretary of State Strobe Talbott conducted 14 rounds of meetings with India's then foreign minister Jaswant Singh in an effort to reduce the dangers emanating from both countries' going overtly nuclear. The discussions led to a shift in U.S. policy on nuclear issues in the region. The earlier position of the Clinton administration was to "cap, reduce, and rollback" the nuclear programs of both countries. This position changed, at least in the short term, to one of urging India and Pakistan to keep their nuclear forces nondeployed and at the lowest possible levels.[3]

The Clinton administration also made a significant differentiation between India, which it treated as a nuclear democracy, and other proliferating states, which it first labeled rogue states and later states of concern. By treating India and Pakistan differently, it was able to continue developing relations with both countries—although far more warmly with India than with Pakistan—while seeking to limit the damage caused by regional proliferation. At the same time, the Clinton administration successfully practiced international crisis diplomacy in the region.

In 1999, during the Kargil crisis (which followed a Pakistani advance into a remote, high-altitude part of Kashmir on the Indian side of the line of control), the United States was instrumental in getting Pakistan to withdraw its troops from the Kargil and Drass sectors of Indian Kashmir and in staving off a potential full-scale nuclear conflict between the two countries. Former White House staffer Bruce Riedel has written that President Clinton applied pressure on the Nawaz Sharif government in Pakistan to back down, and that the Pakistan military was thought to be readying its nuclear warheads.[4] The United States, however, did proceed to develop bilateral linkages with India on issues of mutual interest—one such forum being the Joint Commission of Counterterrorism.

The relationship took a turn for the better with the advent of the George W. Bush administration, which viewed India as playing an important role in future U.S. foreign policy toward Asia. As Secretary of State Colin Powell put it in his confirmation hearing:

> We must deal wisely with the world's largest democracy. Soon to be the most populous country in the world, India has the potential to help keep the peace in the vast Indian Ocean area and its periphery. We need to work harder and more consistently to assist India in this endeavor, while not neglecting our friends in Pakistan.[5]

Some have argued that this appraisal of India's position came from the administration's stance that China was no longer just a major trading partner but had become a strategic competitor that needed to be contained in Asia. This proposed strategy gained further credence after the April 2001 collision and forced landing of a Navy PC-3 surveillance aircraft by the Chinese Air Force.

By mid-2001, it seemed that India and the United States were building a new relationship that was based on military ties and an increasingly similar worldview. Thus, the Indian government was one of the first to endorse the Bush administration's National Missile Defense proposal, especially welcoming the fact that missile defense would go hand-in-hand with deep cuts in U.S. nuclear arsenals. There was also some degree of agreement between the two countries on the limitations of the International Criminal Court, particularly on the issue of peacekeepers. In addition, the two governments decided to not criticize each other in public—moving away from a policy that the Indians had followed in the Cold War days. Indian concerns about the U.S. stand on the Kyoto treaty were conveyed privately to the Bush administration. The administration, similarly, muted its criticism of India's test of a 700-kilometer medium range *Agni-1* missile in early 2002.[6]

The attacks of September 11, 2001, however, saw the United States, much to India's consternation, renew its security relationship with Pakistan.[7] India offered unconditional support to the United States, including basing rights for carrying out an air campaign over Afghanistan, but Pakistan's proximity to Afghanistan made it necessary for the United States to renew its alliance with Islamabad. India's concerns about terrorism were highlighted by the attack on the Indian parliament on December 13, 2001, which was viewed in New Delhi as an attack carried out reportedly by the banned Lashkar-e-Taiba group at the behest of Pakistan's Inter Services Intelligence (ISI).[8] India mobilized its armed forces and placed them along the border with Pakistan but decided not to pursue a military action, following a U.S. undertaking to put pressure on President Musharraf to halt cross-border infiltration. After one year of exceptionally hostile relations between India and Pakistan (with then Indian foreign minister Yashwant Sinha stating that India had a much better case to go for preemption against Pakistan than the United States had against Iraq),[9] the Indian prime minister, in April 2003, offered to talk to the Pakistani leadership in a third and final attempt to secure peace between the two countries (the first attempt was the Lahore summit of 1999, and the second, the Agra summit of 2001). The Indian government set aside its precondition that Pakistan halt all cross-border infiltration and Pakistan, in turn, ratcheted up its demands for negotiations on the core issue of Kashmir.

Serious discussions between the Indian and Pakistani governments took place, especially during the first Manmohan Singh administration, to try and resolve the Kashmir issue and to bring about a lasting peace with Pakistan. The reason such a process was possible was the feeling in both countries that there had to be movement and eventual resolution on this long-term conflict, otherwise the two would be sacrificing developmental objectives and condemning their people to lower living standards. Steve Coll documents that both countries had made considerable progress on demilitarization of the Siachen glacier but more importantly had come up with a set of proposals for resolving the Kashmir issue, which included a reduction of forces in the state, easier travel between the Indian and Pakistani sections of the state, and a movement toward greater autonomy.[10]

What led to the freezing of the peace talks was that Musharraf's position within Pakistan weakened as a result of the lawyers' agitation, and this made the Indian government balk at the thought of cutting a deal with a leader whose internal position had weakened, thereby putting into question the validity of any deal reached with him. Additionally, as Coll points out, neither India nor Pakistan had prepared their populations for a deal with the other side, and as India moved into election bargaining in 2008 (a rare situation where the country suffered from nearly 18 months of paralysis as the different political parties sought to score electoral points), it made reaching a deal with Islamabad difficult. But the final nail in the coffin was the 2008 Mumbai terror attacks.[11] Indian public opinion, politicians, and the media put the blame squarely on the Pakistani ISI, which in the past had trained jihadis to wage war in Indian Kashmir and carry out acts of terror in India. While the link to ISI could not be proved, Pakistan was forced to acknowledge that the attacks were carried out by its citizens and that the Pakistan-based jihadi group, Lashkar-e-Taiba, was involved (Bob Woodward does suggest, however, that the United States initially believed it was former ISI operatives, but this view changed to the notion that serving ISI officers were involved in planning the attack).[12]

Since the 2008 terror attack, the United States has sought to get the two countries to reengage in the peace process. American law enforcement authorities have given additional intelligence to the Indian government on the jihadi attack and put pressure on the Pakistani government to take action against such Pakistan-based groups. The U.S. role, therefore, remains one of facilitating negotiations between the two sides, which has left the two countries somewhat dissatisfied. India would like the United States to put more pressure on Islamabad to halt cross-border infiltration and more importantly work to bring Pakistan-based terrorist organizations to justice. Islamabad would like the United States to act as an intermediary between the two countries— carrying out the same role it fulfills for Israel and Palestine. The dissatisfaction with U.S. efforts is compounded because the United States and India have somewhat contradictory worldviews. These contradictions, till recently, have made collaborative efforts in the attempts to maintain international security more difficult than they should be.

U.S. WORLDVIEW AND INDIA

As the remaining superpower, since the demise of the Soviet Union, the United States is in a unique position in contemporary international relations. Not only does it have military and technological superiority over its closest rivals, but it is also positioned to dictate political and diplomatic outcomes in a way that it never could before. This was brought home during the buildup to the 2003 Gulf War when the United States withdrew its resolution in the UNSC and, with limited international support, successfully carried out regime change in Iraq. More recently, the commando raid that led to the killing of Osama bin Laden showed that the United States has managed to successfully integrate its intelligence capability with its war fighting capability to carry out precision strikes. And the NATO mission to remove Colonel Qaddafi from power saw the United States very successfully lead the coalition effort from behind.

The U.S. strategic superiority is unlikely to fade away in the near future for three reasons. First, American military superiority continues to grow not only in terms of technological prowess but increasingly in terms of training and tactics. As Barry Posen has argued, America's military supremacy rests on its control of the commons—the deep seas, airspace over 15,000 feet, and outer space.[13] While no nation has sovereignty over these environments, a country must have control over them to prosecute modern warfare successfully.

America has control over all three commons and is likely to retain this advantage for some time because of its commitment to military research and development (R&D), which provides it with a growing technological edge over potential challengers (as Posen points out, current U.S. R&D expenditure almost matches the combined defense budgets of Germany and France).[14] This capability is enhanced by two additional factors: a worldwide network of bases that extend the U.S. military reach, and the division of the world into a series of commands that can work together effectively to prosecute U.S. military strategy.[15]

This military capability can prevail over any standing military in the world, and it permitted the second Bush administration to believe that it would militarily prevail in Iraq, establish democracy there, and set the template to bring about changes in the Middle East. While the United States has control over the commons, one environment in which its military preponderance can be challenged is the land environment. There, regular and irregular forces that have sufficient manpower are motivated and, with knowledge of the terrain, have fought American forces. As we have seen in Iraq and Afghanistan, such forces, despite their technological backwardness, have been able to exact a considerable toll on the technologically superior and better-trained U.S. forces.

In short, technology does not successfully substitute for personnel on the ground. Having said that, the costs are high for a regime that opposes U.S. interests. While the United States has had problems with regime installation in Iraq, it easily succeeded in toppling Saddam Hussein's Baathist government. Any country opposing U.S. security interests, therefore, runs the risk of having its regime overthrown, unless it has a high level of domestic legitimacy. In 2011, this was once again brought home when the United States, while leading from behind, successfully helped overthrow the regime of Colonel Qaddafi in Libya.

Second, the U.S. economy remains attractive enough for foreign and domestic investors to continue to keep their investments there. In the short to medium term, China, Europe, or Japan will not be able to completely take over as an economic alternative to the United States. This has particularly been the case after the global economic collapse of 2008 where there has been an influx of foreign investment into U.S. Treasury bills. With the chaos in Europe likely to continue in the near term, the United States remains a safe haven for external investors, and this has in fact afforded the United States the ability to borrow cheaply. Thus, while the United States has problems with a ballooning deficit, and growing internal pressures to shrink the size of government and the scope of governmental expenditure, it remains the economy that is central to global economic health.

The third factor that works in favor of the United States is its soft power, particularly its attractiveness to global intellectual labor. Much has been written about the flow of migrants from the developing world into the West, but this has tended to focus on those working in the lower economic spheres in Western societies—the Mexicans in the United States, the Turks in Germany, and the North Africans in Italy. Less discussed is the flow of highly skilled or intellectual labor across boundaries, and the United States was the clear winner in this process. Highly skilled labor flows in Europe tended to be between European Union (EU) members or in the sporting arena—the global flow of soccer players into Europe.[16] But the United States was able to attract the best intellectual minds from around the world to work in its universities and high-technology industries for several reasons.

Europe, particularly the United Kingdom, had cut off financial aid to foreign students, making higher education in these countries unattractive to prospective intellectual labor imports from the rest of the world. The United States, in contrast, retained a vibrant university system that actively recruited the best minds from around the world.[17] Racism and cultural intolerance also raised their ugly faces in the 1990s, thus reducing the attractiveness of Western Europe to highly skilled professionals; the rise of le Pen in France, Haider in Austria, Bossi in Italy, and neo-Nazis in Germany contributed to making the EU the second choice for high-level professionals. Further, the inability of these states to become truly multicultural and accepting made it unlikely that they would be the best targets for anyone seeking to emigrate. A case in point was the flow of Hong Kong Chinese to Canada and the United States rather than to England. Finally, till recently, competing European and Asian firms and universities have not been able to match the higher wages and research facilities in the United States (this situation is beginning to change, as both European countries and Asian nations like Singapore are now attracting global intellectual labor). These three inducements have made the United States not just the military leader of the world but also its economic and cultural leader.

CONSTRAINTS ON AMERICA'S SECURITY AGENDA

At the same time, however, the limits of American military power and global leadership are also apparent. While the United States has the military capability to intervene and prevail in any part of the world, its more difficult task is to stay in a country for an extended period of time to carry out nation-building and the restoration of civil society. The challenges faced in Iraq and Afghanistan in terms of policing the country, restoring civil order, and helping shape democratic institutions point to the need to have forces willing to stay in a foreign country for extended periods of time to create the ideal civil situation. The United States sought to do this by including its traditional coalition partners in the war efforts.

The coalition of forces that the United States assembled in both Iraq and Afghanistan were both financially hamstrung to take over the responsibilities of the U.S. forces and also constrained by the unwillingness of their national publics to accept high levels of casualties. This led to nations withdrawing from the coalition. Further, in future wars, the traditional allies of the United States may not be the best suited for carrying out peacekeeping and peace enforcement operations in a non-Western setting. Thus, if the United States is to counter charges of being an imperial power in the non-Western world, it will require non-Western states by its side for its military efforts. In his exasperation with Paris and Berlin over the Gulf War, Secretary of Defense Donald Rumsfeld labeled France and Germany "old Europe," but, in another way, he was closer to the truth. Using European countries to establish peace only further fuels the allegations that a new kind of imperialism is being imposed on the world by the Western nations.

The other central challenge for the United States is the need to help create secular democracies around the world. While the events of September 11, 2001, demonstrated the need for a proactive military policy to target terrorism, it also brought home the realization that the international system had to move in the direction of secular democratic states. The Arab Spring of 2011 once again proved the importance of the United States' quest for global democratization as virtually every authoritarian regime in the region faced a challenge from dissident forces seeking democracy and individual freedom. The United States, both for strategic and symbolic reasons, had to tread lightly in the effort to democratize the Arab world. Strategically, several of the nations that were facing democratic dissent were American allies, and the concern in Washington was whether supporting internal protest in these nations would not only weaken traditional allies but also let loose forces within these countries that used democratic protest as an avenue to establish anti-Western, nonsecular regimes. Symbolically, U.S. interference, it was feared, would be used as an excuse to inflame Arab public opinion. In such a context, nations like India, which both have a democratic ethos and lack the stigma of the Western nations in the non-Western world, may have an important role to play in helping to bring in democratic practices to these countries. The Indian Election Commission, for instance, was asked by the Egyptian authorities to provide information on how India supervised the electoral process during national elections.

A third important concern for the United States is strategic stability in Asia and the containment of China. Strategic stability in Asia is affected by the proliferation of weapons of mass destruction (WMD), the spread of terrorism, and the rise of China as a potential hegemonic power in the region. Of these three issues, the Indian role may be the most influential in future attempts to constrain China. The Bush administration, unlike its predecessor, was to brand China a strategic competitor, and there was some discussion on how to contain it. China's military modernization efforts, its territorial dispute with Taiwan, its claims over the Paracel and Spratly Islands (which are rich in energy reserves), and its policy on the transfers of WMD and related delivery systems pose long-term concerns for the United States.

The Obama administration, entering government at the time of the worst recession in the post–World War II era, sought to enlist Chinese support in creating international order, but by December 2011, the administration had decided to reestablish the American presence in Asia in what most commentators saw as a bid to counter China. Countering China in Asia comes with its own set of problems. The United States would have to either build up a coalition of nations that would be willing to work in an attempt to contain China or, alternatively, heavily invest in establishing a strong military presence in Asia. In an era of budgetary concerns, the latter may be difficult to bring about.

Further, the huge volume of trade with China has placed the United States in a situation where it now depends on the cheap supply of goods from China to encourage consumption in the American domestic economy. Breaking away from a trading relationship that is in excess of $300 billion will be difficult for the United States to do without significant economic repercussions. Yet, if the United States at some point is to attempt to put greater diplomatic and military pressure on China, it may actually have to achieve a lesser trade dependence on that country.

The three challenges of nation-building, democratization, and containing China will require money, manpower, and a new set of alliance partners than those used traditionally by the United States. India could be a useful partner in these endeavors, but it would require recognizing the contradictions between the American and Indian worldviews and seeking to resolve them.

THE INDIAN WORLDVIEW: THE REFORMIST STATE

Indian foreign policy is best understood by recognizing that the country has assumed a somewhat unique position in international affairs because its leadership has sought to make the country into a reformist state. Typically, the international system is viewed as being divided between status quo and revolutionary states. Status quo states are those that seek to maintain the structure of the international system and the order that ensues from it.

Revolutionary states seek to dismantle the structure and the order that goes with it, partially or completely. Revolutionary states have been described as rogue states, states of concern, and, in the early 2000s, as the Axis of Evil. While one can question which states are placed in this category, especially since the newer members lack the global capacity to challenge the hegemonic power of the status quo states (unlike the way the former Soviet Union and, to a lesser degree, Mao's China did during the Cold War), the fact remains that such a category of states continues to exist.

India, on the other hand, is a reformist state—one that by and large accepts the structure and order of the international system but wishes to make incremental changes to it in order to improve its own power potential and status within the international system. India's first prime minister, Jawaharlal Nehru, envisaged such a position for India when he suggested that, while India was a poor country, it was a great country, and that it had a pivotal role to play in world affairs. This role was to try and achieve the needs of world peace and freedom that were not only part of the postcolonial revolution occurring in the post–World War II world but also critical to India's internal development and national security objectives.

As a reformist state, India has sought to participate in maintaining the status quo in the international system while shaping it so that New Delhi gets a greater say in world affairs. Thus, India has been a consistent supporter of the United Nations and has participated in more than 50 peacekeeping operations. But India's objective remains to become a permanent member of the UNSC. India has refused to sign the Nuclear Nonproliferation Treaty (NPT), but at the same time the Indian government has not assisted in the proliferation of nuclear weaponry or its associated delivery systems; in the late 1980s, for example, India refused to sell nuclear weapons to Libya.[18] Similarly, India has joined the Antarctic Club and is a pioneer member of the Law of the Seas treaty, thus signaling its commitment to international law, yet ensuring that it will influence decision making in both bodies.

The second part of the Indian foreign policy, which is also an evolutionary response to the shift in power within the international system in the 1990s, is to seek a multipolar world (as defined by Indian policymakers, it is a quest to strengthen multilateral institutions).

During the Cold War, India, through the nonaligned movement, sought to prevent the international system from becoming a tight bipolar system that put the countries of the world into two armed camps. Now India, like other major actors in the international system, would prefer to have a world order where the United States was counterbalanced by a group of powers. Former foreign minister Yashwant Sinha alluded to this, as well as to India's international ambitions, when he said:

We must also work to spread democracy at the national and also international level. Sometimes the multilateral vocation of the United States is forgotten. Almost all the significant multilateral institutions were created as a result of U.S. initiative. The United Nations, the World Bank, the International Monetary Fund [IMF] and the GATT [General Agreement on Tariffs and Trade] reincarnated now as the World Trade Organization. They needed initial guidance. Now several decades after their creation will require changes in their governance. We need to readjust the structures of decisionmaking in international bodies to reflect contemporary reality. We cannot hope to foster a democratic culture in the world until the principal international institutions are themselves democratized and made more representative.[19]

Yet, by the mid-2000s, India's room for maneuver in the international system had been significantly reduced. The India–Russia relationship, which could have served as a basis for future cooperation and for securing a multilateral international order, was restricted by the internal weaknesses of Russia and its diminished international stature. Further, after the collapse of the Soviet Union, Russia, as the successor state, sought to distance itself from its traditional ally, India, and pursue a pro-Western policy. During the premiership of Yevgeny Primakov, Russian interest in India was revived, as the Russian premier proposed a strategic partnership between India, China, and Russia.[20] In 2000, India and Russia signed the Declaration on Strategic Partnership but made it clear that it was aimed exclusively at countering terrorism and extremism. Since then, little has happened to suggest that India, China, and Russia will form a strong alliance that could potentially counter the United States. Russia's ambassador to India Alexander Kadakin argued, "Strategic partners means that we support each other in our joint vision of the world. We are against a so-called unipolar world; we stand for a multipolar world. We are for political cooperation, we are against terrorism together."[21]

India, however, has downplayed the idea of a strategic partnership. At the same time, it has continued to buy significant amounts of weaponry from Russia, including systems that will potentially enhance its nuclear force structure. These sales should not be viewed, however, as a strengthening of the Russia–India strategic partnership but, instead, as a commercial venture on the part of the Russians. For the Indians, similarly, the purchase of weaponry from Russia comes as much from the inability to conclude domestic weapons programs successfully, as from the willingness of Russia to once again throw open its arms cupboard and provide India with weapons systems that it could neither afford nor get the permission to purchase from Western suppliers. At the same time, India–Russia trade relations no longer have the importance that they did during the Cold War. Indian exports to Russia are less than 2 percent of the country's total exports, while its imports from Russia are less than 1 percent of total imports.

But perhaps the most important reason for India to downplay a Russia–India strategic partnership is that Russia can now offer little politically or economically to India. Politically, Russia is no longer the force the former Soviet Union was and consequently cannot serve as a counter to either China or the United States. Economically, Indian businesses remain pessimistic about the prospects in the Russian market.

Russian foreign minister Sergei Lavrov complained in an interview that India had yet to recognize that Russia was a market economy, and that Indian banks and other financial structures needed to accept the guarantees of private Russian banks.[22]

The decline of Russia's fortunes has led the Indian political leadership to recognize the limits of this old relationship, and, while Russia continues to serve as India's principal armorer, it is not a relationship that can be used politically to enhance India's ascension to a great power status. Thus, while being uncomfortable with America's unipolar status, India has shifted the orientation of its foreign policy to work with the United States to achieve its own greater power aspirations.

The third contradictory factor has been that India continues to seek a South Asia that is free from the influences of external powers and where it is the paramount country in the region. Such a goal would remain at odds with those of the United States, which has viewed a relationship with Pakistan as a key part of the war in Afghanistan. India has viewed with concern the perceived American attempt to equate the two countries (particularly in their nuclear policies) and believes that the United States in the past has not put enough pressure on Pakistan to halt its support to jihadi groups operating in Indian Kashmir.

These concerns about the U.S.–Pakistan relationship have been reduced both because of the buildup of the India–U.S. relationship since the times of the George W. Bush administration and because of the concurrent decline in the U.S.–Pakistan relationship due to these countries' conflicting strategic interests in Afghanistan.

From an Indian perspective, the other important aspect of U.S. foreign policy that has implications for India is that only two long-term strategic partnerships with the United States actually exist— one with Israel and the other with the United Kingdom. With these countries, the United States is the closest when it comes to consulting on operations, commitments of defense, the sharing of technology, and the willingness to apply pressure on other states to facilitate these countries' diplomatic strategies and to enhance their national security.

It would be difficult for India to create a similar strategic relationship with the United States because it neither has the historical and cultural ties that have forged these strategic relationships, nor does it want, as a reformist state, to pursue the types of policies that would cement such a relationship. India would be unwilling to be the type of military partner that the United Kingdom has been in U.S. global military efforts. The Indian unwillingness to commit to the first and second Gulf War coalitions is a case in point. Further, India does not have the type of historical and cultural-emotional ties that have forged a strong U.S.–Israel relationship. While Indian-Americans have played a role in cementing these ties,[23] it would be an exaggeration to suggest that they have the type of political and economic influence that the American Jewish community has.

Lastly, for a congruence of American and Indian worldviews, there has to be recognition of India's quest to become a global power. In the past, American policies, both intentionally and unintentionally, served to restrict such progress. The first major constraint was the U.S. lack of recognition of India's nuclear status. Despite the 1998 tests and the subsequent lengthy meetings between then deputy secretary of state Strobe Talbott and then foreign minister Jaswant Singh, official U.S. policy remained one of not recognizing India as a nuclear weapons state. Instead, the official policy was to get India to become a signatory to the NPT and to terminate its nuclear weapons program. As U.S. Assistant Secretary for

Nonproliferation John Wolf stated at the Third Session of the Preparatory Committee for the 2005 Review Conference of the Treaty on the Non-Proliferation of Nuclear Weapons (New York, May 4, 2004):

> These steps should not, however, be taken to suggest that we have "accepted" the status of either country as a nuclear weapon state under the NPT. We have not. Moreover, we will not reward either country for their decisions to acquire nuclear weapons or for the 1998 tests that made the world and the region a more dangerous place [emphasis added].
>
> We have steadfastly avoided taking any actions that would be contrary to our long-established nuclear export control policy. India and Pakistan remain ineligible under U.S. law and policy for any significant assistance to their nuclear programs. We continue to call on India and Pakistan not to conduct nuclear tests, to end the production of fissile material for nuclear weapons, to take steps to reduce regional tensions and to prevent the use of nuclear weapons [emphasis added].[24]

Such recognition was crucial, however, because it would lead to a change in the policies of all the de jure nuclear powers that were denying India its rightful nuclear status. Further, the lack of a legal nuclear status prevented the transfer of vital technologies that India required for its own modernization and economic development. These included a range of dual use and space technologies from the United States since these were crucial to the country's future economic and technological growth. For several reasons, the United States had been reluctant to transfer such technologies.[25]

Nonproliferation concerns drove such reservations since American officials were worried about the transfer of sensitive technologies to third parties. While the United States did agree to ease some of the restrictions on the sale of dual-use, space, and nuclear technologies to India,[26] the U.S. Department of Commerce made it clear that such transfers were for civilian purposes and took place within the limits set by multilateral nonproliferation regimes.[27] This has led to suggestions that the reported progress in the National Security Studies Program (NSSP) was cosmetic at best.[28] U.S. officials, however, contended that significant changes had taken place, removing the need for 25 percent of all license applications for U.S. exports to India.[29]

It was clear, however, that at some stage technology transfers in the military field would have to be considered. And as long as such multilateral limits existed, it would mean the imposition of sanctions when India took measures in the military field that are inimical to broader U.S. interests. Coupled with the problems associated with technology transfers were the divergent views on the Indian nuclear program. Despite 14 meetings between Talbott and Singh (after India's 1998 nuclear tests), the United States remained committed in the long term to having India roll back its nuclear program and sign the NPT. Resolving the nuclear issue was vitally important to India, given that it had the status of a third-tier nuclear state. What changed U.S. policy was the determination of the

George W. Bush administration, driven by concerns about China and recognizing the constraints that past policy had imposed, to reshape the foreign policy toward India.

THE BUSH ADMINISTRATION AND INDIA

The George W. Bush administration recognized the importance of India as an international actor and decided from 2005 onward to bring India to greater prominence on the global stage. The United States' strategic calculations, as Ashley Tellis points out, were driven by political, economic, and military-strategic factors. These included:

- Preventing Asia from being dominated by any single power that has the capacity to crowd out others and that would use aggressive assertion of national self-interest to threaten American presence, alliances, and ties with the regional states.
- Eliminating the threats posed by state sponsors of terrorism who may seek to use violence.
- Arresting the further spread of WMD and related technologies to other countries and sub-national entities.
- Promoting the spread of democracy not only as an end in itself but also as a strategic means of preventing illiberal polities from exporting their internal struggles over power abroad.
- Advancing the diffusion of economic development with the intent of spreading peace by means of prosperity through the expansion of a liberal international economic order.
- Protecting the global commons, especially the sea lanes of communications, through which flow not only goods and services critical to the global economy but also undesirable commerce, such as drug trading, human smuggling, and WMD technologies.
- Preserving energy security.
- Safeguarding the global environment by promoting the creation and use of innovative technology to achieve sustainable development.[30]

What the Bush administration sought to achieve, therefore, was a comprehensive transformation of the U.S.–India strategic relationship based on the assumption that India—as a major democratic nation with shared values—would seek to help maintain an America-created regional order in Asia. In this attempt to accentuate India's status, Washington was taking into account Indian security concerns as well as traditional Indian grievances vis-à-vis the United States. The tacit focus of this approach was to hedge against the growth of China in Asia, but it also included a much broader role for India within the Asian region. Additionally, the Bush administration was moving away from some of the postures taken by successive U.S. administrations during the Cold War—particularly on the issue of nuclear proliferation.

Unlike previous administrations that had been bound to nonproliferation laws and a single approach to proliferation, the Bush administration took the view that each individual case of proliferation had to be treated separately while staying within the broad ambit of U.S. and international law. More importantly, as George Perkovich points out, the nuclear nonproliferation regime was viewed as constraining the power of benign actors like the United States and India.[31] It, therefore, made sense to seek an exemption for India from the existing nonproliferation regime.

What transformed the U.S.–India relationship was the push to develop a strategic interaction between the two countries, the cornerstone of which was to be the civilian nuclear deal. In July 2005, President Bush and Prime Minister Manmohan Singh signed an agreement that fundamentally changed the nuclear relationship between the two countries. George Perkovich argues that on the American side the deal was orchestrated by a small group of people (Condoleeza Rice, Philip Zelikow, and Nicholas Burns) with the following objectives in mind:

1. To dissuade or prevent China from competing harmfully with it, the United States must mobilize states along China's periphery to balance Chinese power.

2. India is a rising power with great intrinsic merits, including its attachment to democracy, and is a natural partner with the United States in the global system. The United States should cultivate a partnership with India and enhance India's international power. A more powerful and collegial India will balance China's power in Asia.

3. To win over India, the United States should change national and international laws and rules that bar technology cooperation with India due to India's nuclear weapons and ballistic missile programs. Changing these rules is necessary to cement the partnership, and such changes also will help India bolster its strategic capabilities, including nuclear weapons and ballistic missiles, which will further balance China's strategic power.

4. India will have to increase its use of nuclear energy in order to fuel economic growth and reduce its rate of greenhouse gas emissions.

5. India never has been a threat to the United States or the liberal international system. India's possession of nuclear weapons breaks no international treaty. India has been a responsible steward of nuclear technology, material, and know-how. India is not a proliferation threat that a smart counterproliferation strategy must combat; rather it is a partner to cultivate in isolating terrorists and rogue states that are proliferation threats. India's exclusion as an accepted nuclear weapons power is a historical anomaly that should be corrected.

6. The established global nonproliferation regime is predicated on rules that do not sufficiently discriminate between bad actors and good actors. Universal equal compliance with rules will never happen because bad guys will always exist and cheat. The objective should be not to constrain or burden good actors, including the United States and India, but rather to concentrate power on removing or nullifying bad actors. If negotiation and enforcement processes are hung up on equal treatment and mutual obligations, they are a waste of time and political capital.[32]

The most fundamental change of the second Bush administration, however, was the rewriting of the relationship with India in the nuclear realm. Recognizing that one of the sticking points in the relationship between the two countries was U.S. sanctions on India's nuclear program, the Indian and American negotiators began to untie the Gordian knot by proposing that India be brought in from the cold. The sticking point in the relationship had been the fact that India had not signed the Nuclear Non-Proliferation Treaty and had gone on to test nuclear weapons for a second time in 1998. The Clinton administration had first sanctioned India on the nuclear tests but had then gone on to reduce tensions as the United States and India had initiated a dialogue to reconcile India's security concerns with the United States' nonproliferation objectives.[33]

By 2002, the Indian government had entered into a dialogue with the Bush administration and indicated that it was willing to make significant concessions for the resumption of fuel supplies to its civilian nuclear reactors. Specifically, India indicated the willingness to put its civilian nuclear reactors under international safeguards.[34] What changed U.S. policy, however, was, as Ashley Tellis points out, the Bush administration's comprehensive review of India's nuclear capability. The Bush administration, writes Tellis, recognized that India was unwilling to give up its nuclear weapons as long as regional rivals possessed them. Further, Indian nuclear weapons were not a threat to the United States or its larger geopolitical interests. In some cases, they could actually promote U.S. policies. Lastly, existing technological resources in India's public and private sectors posed a greater proliferation threat if leaked to other countries.[35]

In July 2005, the two countries agreed to a deal whereby India agreed to place an export control regime in uniformity with U.S. and international export control laws on nuclear technology. It also agreed to separate its military and civilian nuclear facilities and to put the civilian ones under international safeguards. It agreed to make progress on the Fissile Material Cutoff Treaty, to refrain from transferring enrichment and reprocessing technologies to states that do not have them, and to harmonize its own laws with the Missile Technology Control Regime and the Nuclear Suppliers Group.[36] In return, the United States agreed to ease technology restrictions on India, take Indian research organizations like the Indian Space Research Organization off the sanctions list, and ensure full cooperation in the civilian nuclear field with India.[37] Moreover, the United States moved the International Atomic Energy Agency to sign an additional protocol with it, thus permitting international technology and fuel supplies to India.

The crux of the nuclear treaty was that it allowed India to move from a de facto nuclear status to a de jure nuclear status since it opened the doors for the transfer of technology and nuclear fuel to India, both of which had been restricted, if not cut off, in the wake of the first and then second set of nuclear tests. Yet, from a developmental perspective, both nuclear energy and technology transfers were vital for the future development of India. India's chronic power shortages and the booming growth in the population, as well as the increasing prosperity of the country, meant that energy generation was a priority for the country. India's energy consumption is expected to double from 375.8 million tons of oil equivalent to 812 million tons of oil equivalent by 2030, driven by growing urbanization, automation, and a bourgeoning population.[38] Given the lack of proven oil reserves, and environmental concerns over extracting natural gas by hydraulic fracturing, nuclear power became one of the few proven options for India to work with as it planned for the future economic development of the country. In such circumstances, removing the restrictions that had constrained the growth of India's nuclear power industry became critical. Technology transfers, particularly in the field of space and computing, were also important to the growth of India's technological and scientific capacity but were also constrained by the sanctions and restrictions placed on the country since the first nuclear test of 1974. The nuclear agreement with the United States, therefore, was crucial to unlocking international restrictions on the future developmental efforts of the country. Further, at the foreign policy and security level, the agreement essentially tied India to a policy of nuclear restraint that it had been following since the 1974 test.

Since 1974, the country while going nuclear did not seek to transfer nuclear technology to other states, even though both Iran and Libya had made such requests to India. It also refused to participate in the Iraqi ballistic missiles program. Nor did India seek to develop a large nuclear force, and, in fact, till the tests of 1998, the Indian nuclear program had proceeded at a glacial pace. Ashley Tellis wrote an article in Orbis, suggesting that India could gain the confidence of the international community toward its nuclear intentions if it went slow, kept its numbers low, and did not manufacture intercontinental ballistic missiles—the path that the Indian government had decided to pursue.[39] From an American perspective, the real concern lay in India's public and private sectors, either for profit or inadvertently, leaking sensitive technologies to other nations. Reports of retired Indian nuclear scientists freelancing in Iran were part of such concerns. What emerged, therefore, was an agreement that fundamentally transformed the U.S.–India relationship and set the stage for far greater cooperation between the two nations. In real terms, any examination of the India–U.S. relationship has to be broken down into five parts: the government-to-government relationship; the military-to-military relationship; the Bangalore and Silicon Valley relationship; the connection between Indian students and American universities; and finally, the ties between the Indian-American diaspora and India.

GOVERNMENT TO GOVERNMENT

As the world's largest democracy and the world's most powerful democracy, the relationship between the two countries should be exceptionally strong. Both share common values, and while the Indian government is content with the structure of the democratic international order, it would just like to enhance its position within this structure. Yet, after nearly two years of the Obama administration being in office, there was a feeling in Washington that the relationship had run adrift. As Nicholas Burns, Richard Armitage, and Richard Fontaine described it, "Past projects remain incomplete, few new ideas have been embraced by both sides, and the forward momentum that characterized recent cooperation has subsided. The Obama administration has taken significant steps to break through this inertia, including with its Strategic Dialogue this spring and President Obama's planned state visit to India in November 2010. Yet there remains a sense among observers in both countries that this critical relationship is falling short of its promise."[40]

The reasons for this sense of drift came from the seeming lack of attention paid by the Obama administration to India in the first two years of his presidency. The American president's focus was on Iraq and Afghanistan, and when it came to his first state visit to Asia, the president initially chose Indonesia and Australia as the countries to visit rather than the big three—China, Japan, and India. Additionally, India, despite the talk of a strategic partnership, was actually charting an independent path in its foreign policy that was at times at variance with that of U.S. interests. In December 2009, in Copenhagen, India, China, Brazil, and South Africa played the role of spoilers in the climate change negotiations, forcing a dilution of the most serious proposals to suit their interests.[41] Obama's campaign speeches about penalizing companies that took jobs abroad was seen as an attack on the outsourcing of jobs to India's vibrant information technology industry. And Pakistan, as always, remained as an irritant in the India–U.S. relationship since New Delhi believed that Washington could do more to rein in the jihadi activities of its ally. The Obama administration, like others before it, pointed out that it did not have the type of influence that New Delhi believed it did in the Pakistani capital (a fact probably borne out by the Raymond Davis affair and the killing of bin Laden, both of which showed the deep distrust between the two countries and the fact that the United States did not have the sort of leverage that would permit it to strong-arm Pakistan on crucial issues).

Ashley Tellis also points out that given the Obama administration's problem-solving approach to international politics, India, with its relative stability and its vibrant economic growth, had not, "received the attention that is understandably showered on the Obama administration's worst headaches—but that is only a tribute to India's inherent stability in what is otherwise a regional sea of troubles."[42] Yet, the first state dinner hosted by President Obama was for Prime Minister Manmohan Singh in November 2009 and a year later the American president made his first trip to India.

Writing on what the U.S. president should do to get the Indo-U.S. relationship out of a stall, Armitage, Burns, and Fontaine suggested that, "In order to chart a more ambitious U.S.–India strategic partnership, we believe that the United States should commit, publicly and explicitly, to work with India in support of its permanent membership in an enlarged U.N. Security Council; seek a broad expansion of bilateral trade and investment, beginning with a Bilateral Investment Treaty; greatly expand the security relationship and boost defense trade; support Indian membership in key export control organizations, a step toward integrating India into global nonproliferation efforts; and liberalize U.S. export controls, including the removal of Indian Space Research Organization (ISRO) subsidiaries from the U.S. Entity List."[43]

Several of these issues, however, are more of ideals on a long-term wish list and unlikely to change in the near future. While in India, President Obama took the step of stating that India should be a permanent member of the UNSC, but Indian commentators were less than enthused by his pronouncement. Analysts pointed out that in the past the United States had supported Japan and even Brazil to become permanent members of the UNSC, but these attempts had gone nowhere. In the case of Brazil, for instance, when the government in Brasilia pursued an independent foreign policy, the United States dropped the issue from its agenda.[44] There was also the concern that being a permanent member did not necessarily mean being a permanent member with veto, since the five existing permanent members were against expanding the number of nations having veto power.

On the issue of India joining global nonproliferation regimes like Nuclear Supplier Group, the problem lies in India not being party to the NPT or to any of the treaties—Pelindaba and Bangkok for example—that create Nuclear Weapons Free Zones (NWFZ). So, the United States would have to lobby for a waiver of this condition—something that the other members of the group might not agree to.[45] Similarly, in the case of the Missile Technology Control Regime, membership is based on consensus, and India is unlikely to get that if it is unwilling to sign the NPT. The Australia Group (AG)—which seeks to control the proliferation of chemical and biological weapons—requires a third party to forward an expression of interest in membership to the AG chair. India meets the requirements for the AG, so this is the most likely one that the United States could sponsor its membership to. But sources argue that even this one could take a long time since India has yet to convincingly demonstrate that it has effective monitoring and control measures against the diversion of sensitive chemicals.[46]

Another sticking point in the government-to-government relationship is the nuclear liability issue, which has prevented the successful implementation of the nuclear agreement by allowing for U.S. nuclear technology sales to India. The Indian parliament has passed a liability law that allows lawsuits against not only the operators of nuclear power plants but also the suppliers for defective parts or services.[47] This law would harm U.S. suppliers, say American sources, who unlike French and Russian suppliers would not have the state and its resources to back them up.[48] Another aspect of the Obama visit was the suggestion that restrictions on cooperation in high-technology sectors would be removed, but actual progress in this area has taken place very slowly.

But the most serious differences come from the fact that India continues to pursue an independent foreign policy that at times runs contrary to American interests. India's relationship with Iran was particularly irksome to both the Bush and Obama administrations, which saw Tehran as a major strategic challenge in the Indian Ocean region. American pressure was able to stop many Indian businesses, most notably India's largest industrial group, Reliance, from doing business with Iran and the Indian government shelved the plans for an Iran–Pakistan–India natural gas pipeline. Indian leaders, however, do see energy as the driver to maintaining relations with Iran.[49] Myanmar is seen as another nation where India should be doing more, with Washington charging that New Delhi does little to criticize and reform the Myanmar government.

The other major area of difference is over the proposed way to deal with China. Indian commentators have argued that the United States would like India to join a circle of democracy and challenge China. The Indian government has remained reluctant to openly antagonize Beijing and, therefore, has been a less than enthusiastic partner in this proposed coalition.

MILITARY TO MILITARY

As described earlier, military-to-military relations have improved in the past decade, with joint naval and air exercises between the two countries, increased arms sales, and the belief that India may be ready to flex its muscles on the international stage. While there have been a series of military exercises between the two countries, they are a long way from interoperability or joint operations. The first is due to the vagaries of the Indian weapons acquisition process (and the Indian experience with various weapons supplying states), while the latter is due to the continued caution in the Indian political elite about using military power extraregionally and aligning itself too closely with the United States.

Till the new millennium, the Indian arms acquisition process was determined by the availability of hard currency resources and the willingness of suppliers to provide weapons. For a developing nation with chronic hard currency shortages, devoting scare resources to militarization while urgent developmental priorities went unattended to was always going to be an unacceptable path to take. In the 1960s, for example, India moved away from its post-1962 military buildup, which was a response to the defeat in the China war, and instead concentrated its resources on feeding its people in the wake of the Bihar famine of the late 1960s. Similarly, in the 1990s, the economic and financial crisis of 1991 led to a scaling down of ambitious plans to modernize and expand the capabilities of the different branches of the Indian armed services. In such circumstances, the willingness of a supplier like the former Soviet Union, which was willing to accept payment in rupees and make soft loans, to provide weapons made it possible for India to maintain its military force structure.

The other factor that shaped India's acquisition process was the arms embargoes it faced from supplier nations. In the 1960s, the United States terminated the supply of arms and spare parts to both India and Pakistan, although it hurt the latter country far more because its arsenal was overwhelmingly of American origin at that point of time. Similarly, following the nuclear tests of 1998, India once again saw the cutoff of critical U.S. technologies including those on the Light Combat Aircraft project. Maintaining autonomy in the realm of arms imports, therefore, has been crucial to India's acquisition efforts.

In the 21st century, the availability of hard currency resources is no longer a problem as the country's economic growth has provided it with the necessary resources to make large-scale purchases in the international market. In fact, the Indian government, by some estimates, is likely to buy $80 billion worth of weaponry by 2015. Autonomy remains a concern because India's scientific and defense production base still does not provide the capability to manufacture high-quality weaponry or to provide an alternative in case of the cutoff of military sales by another nation. More recently, a third factor has been added to these two traditional Indian concerns. The Indian government sees arms acquisition as a way to gain influence and access in foreign capitals and, as a consequence, this has led to a strategy of spreading the wealth around. This trend was first demonstrated in the purchase of aircraft for the Indian civil aviation industry where the government decided to buy planes from both Boeing and Airbus in an effort to keep both the United States and Europe happy. What do these factors mean in terms of the U.S.–India military relationship?

It has been argued that arms sales would be the way to cement the relationship between the two countries and, indeed, President Obama sent a letter to the Indian prime minister, Dr. Manmohan Singh, arguing precisely this point. President Obama wrote:

> Let me reassure you that the US is a willing, capable and reliable defence partner to India. High-tech defence sales are increasingly a cornerstone of our strategic partnership. I want to underscore the strategic importance the United States attaches to the selection of a US proposal in India's MMRCA competition. The US is offering India two of the most advanced multi-mission combat aircraft in the world—the Boeing FA/18IN and the Lockheed Martin F16IN. These aircraft have a demonstrated qualitative military advantage over any current fourth generation plus aircraft. . . . I view the MMRCA acquisition as a key step along this path. I respectfully ask that your Government will give its full consideration to the commercial, technical and strategic merit to the US proposal.[50]

Yet, the president's urging fell on deaf ears, as the Indian government shortlisted two European planes in the fighter competition—the EADS Eurofighter and the Dassault Rafale—and eventually gave the contract to Dassault. The decision was seen as a setback to the India–U.S. military relationship for, as Ashley Tellis put it, India bought a plane but not an aircraft.[51] The MMRCA decision, however, was based very much on the perception in New Delhi of the limits of the India–U.S. military relationship. Indian analysts saw several limitations in the purchase of American aircraft. There was the concern that the United States would cut off the supply of spare parts and there were also worries about the, "excessive restrictions placed on users and the end-user monitoring on the aircraft, which undermine sovereignty and make the Indian establishment uncomfortable."[52] It was also believed that American companies would not honor their end of the bargain in terms of technology transfers to India—one of the crucial parts of selecting an aircraft for the Indian Air Force. But the geopolitical and economic calculus played a major role in the decision as well. India had already purchased C-130J transport aircraft and P-8 naval aircraft from the United States and is expected to ink a deal to buy 10 C-17 Globemaster aircraft as well. The view in New Delhi was that the United States, while not receiving the MMRCA contract, was getting an equivalent value in other arms sales—since it is likely that U.S. companies like Boeing will win the contract to supply transport and attack helicopters to the Indian military. On the other hand, by buying European, India was ensuring that it had some influence in European capitals as well.

What we are likely to see in the case of arms sales, therefore, is that India continues to acquire systems from both Europe and the United States and maintains its long-standing ties with Russia, as seen by the fact that it entered into an agreement to codevelop and produce a fifth-generation fighter aircraft (FGFA) with the Russians. Until the level of trust in New Delhi about U.S. dependability rises, India will continue to buy secondary systems from the United States, thereby building the relationship gradually but not compromising its sovereignty.

Questions about the United States as a dependable ally, paradoxically, also come from the troubled U.S.–Pakistan relationship, since Indian analysts point to that as a case where the United States has terminated arms supplies when short-term objectives have been met. This question of dependability, coupled with the Indian government's inherent caution about using force unilaterally (or as part of an American operation) in an extraregional context, makes the growth of the military-to-military relationship between the two countries a gradual and long-term process. The economic ties between the two countries, particularly the link between Bangalore and Silicon Valley, are more promising for the future growth of the relationship.

BANGALORE AND SILICON VALLEY

Bangalore and Silicon Valley symbolize the growing technological cooperation between the businesses of the United States and India and have led to the creation of a "flat world"—a term popularized by Thomas Friedman who was quoting the Indian software entrepreneur, Nandan Nilekani. India's software industry now has more than $50 billion in global sales, and its progress has not been slowed by foreign competition, pressures in the United States to halt outsourcing, and the general slowdown in the global economy since 2008. In essence, software and IT were the obvious choice for the India–U.S. business ventures because the decentralized, high-tech, high-education nature of the industry made it difficult for the Indian state, with its heavy-handed application of industrial regulations, to control. Thus, while areas like the retail industry and financial services have seen U.S. companies run into the Indian wall of bureaucratic red tape and protectionism, the software industry, being a new frontier, was able to flourish and generate a new partnership between the two countries. Cisco perhaps best symbolizes the synergistic nature of this relationship. As mentioned earlier, Cisco officials point out that they now have two global headquarters with San Jose as Cisco West and Bangalore as Cisco East and within a seven hour flight radius of either headquarter, 70 percent of the world was covered.[53]

The problem for industry in both countries is that India's software industry, and the consequent outsourcing of business, was seen as sending American jobs to other countries—an emotional issue at the best of times, but made more sensitive by the economic downturn that began in 2007–2008. Thus, sections of the American public see India as the country where their jobs went, while Indians on the other hand feel that they are being unfairly scapegoated for the globalization of the IT industry. Additionally, the cut in the number of H-1 visas being issued to countries is also viewed as being hostile to Indian interests.

At the same time, India's labor laws and protectionist policies still make it difficult for most American firms to invest in the country as witnessed by the problems Walmart has faced in trying to establish a presence in India. So, what is more likely in the short to medium term is the increase in business in the software sector and, despite the opposition in the United States, an increasing number of service-related and value-added operations being carried out in India.

INDIAN STUDENTS AND AMERICAN UNIVERSITIES

In many ways, this may be the strongest tie between the two countries for over the last decade the number of Indian students in the United States has increased and almost doubled from roughly 66,000 to more than 104,000 out of a 2010 total of 690,921 international students in the country.[54] While large numbers of students stay on to work in American academia and industry—with remarkable success—an increasing number are now going home to open their own startups or to work for Indian academic and research organizations.[55] Those who return are taking with them an American education, American values, and American business practices, all of which in the long run will only help to grow the bonds between the two countries. Those who stay are among the most innovative and creative leaders of America's high-technology revolution.[56] This connection will continue to flourish for several reasons: Indian-Americans remitting funds to look after their families in India and to invest in India; the rediscovery of India by first-generation Indian-Americans; and the fact that a rising India enhances and improves the profile of the Indian-American community. According to 2008 data, Indian-Americans were sending $10.8 billion to India annually, thus making this diaspora group the largest remitters of funds to India. It has been suggested that such remittances would stop once the generation that had migrated to the United States died off, but the flow of new Indians into the United States continues.

Coupled with this trend is the discovery of India by the first generation of Indian-Americans. These young people are going to India to seek their roots but more importantly are interested in the emergence of India as a major world actor. For this diaspora group, the emergence of India also has important career and professional benefits, since they are the most likely interlocutors for corporations, businesses, and universities that are seeking to establish a presence in India. Consequently, the Indian-American community will remain one with strong ties to the home nation.

India–U.S. relations, therefore, are likely to follow the trajectory of relationships that other democracies have with the United States. Shared values will bring the countries together, economic and educational ties will grow in a globalized world, and the bonds of diasporas will link the nations for some time to come. On the other hand, like all democracies, India will have substantive policy differences with the United States not only because of regional differences but also because there is a great difference in the levels of wealth and development between the two countries. What we are likely to see, therefore, is a U.S.–India relationship where significant political differences remain and India continues to chart its own unique course in international affairs. At the same time, given the drivers of economic, technological, and cultural interconnectedness in a globalized world, the two countries will continue to be brought together.

ACKNOWLEDGMENT

Portions of this chapter are adapted from Amit Gupta, "The U.S. India Relationship: Strategic Partnership or Complementary Interest?" Strategic Studies Institute, U.S. Army War College, 2005. Available at http://strategicstudiesinstitute.army.mil/pubs/download.cfm?q=596.

NOTES

1. Dennis Kux, *Estranged Democracies: India and the United States* (Washington, DC: National Defense University Press, 1993), p. 307.

2. Raju G. C. Thomas, "U.S. Transfers of 'Dual-Use' Technologies to India," *Asian Survey* XXX, no. 9 (1990): pp. 840–43.

3. Strobe Talbott, "Dealing with the Bomb in South Asia," *Foreign Affairs,* vol. 78, issue 2, March 1999, p. 120. For greater details, see Talbott, *Engaging India: Diplomacy, Democracy, and the Bomb* (Washington, DC: Brookings Institution Press, 2004).

4. See Bruce Riedel, "American Diplomacy and the 1999 Kargil Summit at Blair House," *Policy Paper Series 2002,* Center for the Advanced Study of India.

5. *Washington File,* January 17, 2001.

6. Dennis Kux, "India's Fine Balance," *Foreign Affairs,* vol. 81, issue 3, May/June 2002, p. 97.

7. Ibid.

8. Ranjit Bhushan, "Shock Therapy," *Outlook India,* December 24, 2001.

9. B. Muralidhar Reddy, "Pak. Rejects Sinha's 'Talk of Preemption,'" *The Hindu,* April 4, 2003.

10. Steve Coll, "The Back Channel: Reporter at Large," *The New Yorker,* vol. 85, issue 3, March 2, 2009, p. 38.

11. Ibid.

12. Bob Woodward, *Obama's Wars* (New York: Simon and Schuster, 2010), p. 46.

13. Barry R. Posen, "Command of the Commons: The Military Foundations of U.S. Hegemony," *International Security,* vol. 28, issue 1, Summer 2003, pp. 7–15.

14. Ibid., p. 10.

15. Ibid., pp. 16–19.

16. See Pierre Lanfranchi and Matthew Taylor, *Moving with the Ball: Migration of Professional Footballers* (New York: Berg Press, 2001), pp. 69–110 and 167–90.

17. On the outflow of global intellectual labor, see Ben Wildavsky, *The Great Brain Race: How Global Universities Are Reshaping the World* (Princeton, NJ: Princeton University Press, 2010).

18. For a discussion of the restrictive nature of Indian arms transfer policies, see Amit Gupta, "I Want My M-i-G: How India's Force Structure and Military Doctrine Are Determined," *Asian Survey,* XXXV, no. 5 (1995): pp. 441–58.

19. Speech to The Brookings Institution, Washington, DC, September 9, 2002.

20. For a discussion of the pros and cons of such a relationship, see Galina Yaskina, "Russia–China–India: Prospects for Trilateral Cooperation," *Far Eastern Affairs,* 31, no. 1 (2003): pp. 16–27.

21. Amit Baruah, "India, Russia May Invite China to Join Fighter Aircraft Project," *The Hindu,* June 27, 2004.

22. Amit Baruah, "Multilateralism the Best Solution," *The Hindu,* October 11, 2004.

23. See Robert Hathaway, "Unfinished Passage: India, Indian Americans, and the U.S. Congress," *The Washington Quarterly,* 24, no. 2 (2001): pp. 21–22.

24. Available at http://www.state.gov/t/np/rls/rm/32293.htm.

25. For a discussion of U.S. concerns, see Anupam Srivastava, "Positive-Sum Game Accruals in US–India Relations," *Bharat Rakshak Monitor* 51 (2002), http://www.bharatrakshak.com/MONITOR/ISSUE5-1/anupam.html.

26. Sridhar Krishnaswami, "U.S. to Ease Curbs on Space, N-Facilities," *The Hindu,* September 20, 2004.

27. K. Alan Kronstadt, "India–U.S. Relations," *CRS Issue Brief for Congress,* July 29, 2004, p. 15.

28. R. Ramachandran, "India, U.S. & Trade in Technology," *The Hindu,* September 27, 2004.

29. Matthew S. Borman, "NSSP: U.S., India Interests in Action," *The Hindu,* October 2, 2004.

30. Ashley Tellis, "What Should We Expect from India as a Strategic Partner," in Henry D. Sokolski (ed.), *Gauging U.S.–Indian Strategic Cooperation* (Carlisle, PA: Strategic Studies Institute, Army War College), pp. 241–42.

31. George Perkovich, "Global Implications of the US–India deal," *Daedalus,* Winter 2010, p. 22.

32. George Perkovich, "Faulty Promises: The U.S.–India Nuclear," *Policy Outlook Carnegie Nonproliferation South Asia,* Carnegie Endowment for International Peace, Washington, DC, September 2005, pp. 1–2.

33. C. Raja Mohan, *Impossible Allies: Nuclear India, United States, and the global order* (New Delhi: India Research Press, 2006), p. 17.

34. Ibid., p. 23.

35. Ashley J. Tellis, *India as a Global Player: An Action Agenda for the United States* (Washington, DC: Carnegie Endowment for International Peace, July 2005), p. 7.

36. Teresita C. Schaffer, *India and the United States in the 21st Century: Reinventing Partnership* (Washington, DC: Center for Strategic and International Studies, 2009), p. 96.

37. Ibid., p. 95.

38. Tanvi Madan, "India," *The Brookings Foreign Policy Energy Security Studies,* Washington, DC, 2006, p. 7.

39. Ashley J. Tellis, "The Strategic Consequences of a Nuclear India," *Orbis* 46, no. 1 (Winter 2002): pp. 41–43.

40. Richard L. Armitage, R. Nicholas Burns, and Richard Fontaine, *Natural Allies: A Blueprint for the Future of U.S.–India Relations* (Washington, DC: Center for New American Security, 2010), p. 3.

41. Barbara Crossette, "The Elephant in the Room," *Foreign Policy,* January/February 2010, p. 30.

42. Ashley Tellis, "Obama in India. Building a Global Partnership: Challenges, Risks, and Opportunities," *Policy Outlook,* Carnegie Endowment for International Peace, October 28, 2010, p. 3.

43. Armitage, Burns, and Fontaine, *Natural Allies,* p. 4.

44. John Cherian, "American Agenda," *Frontline,* vol. 27, issue 24, November 20–December 3, 2010.

45. R. Ramachandran, "Just a Promise," *Frontline,* vol. 27, issue 24, November 20–December 3, 2010.

46. Ibid.

47. "Nuclear Liability High Priority for Obama's Visit to India," *Nucleonics Week,* November 4, 2010.

48. "A Damp Squib: India and America," *The Economist,* October 30, 2010.

49. Cherian, "American Agenda."

50. Ashok K. Mehta, "US Stumped by Europe," *Daily Pioneer,* May 11, 2011.

51. Narayan Lakshman, "Top India Analyst Criticises MMRCA Decision," *The Hindu,* April 28, 2011.

52. Rohit Vishwanath, "It's Smart Diplomacy," *The Times of India,* May 10, 2011.

53. Briefing to author in Bangalore, March 15, 2009.

54. Source Institute for International Education, Washington, DC, Open Doors 2010, http://www.iie.org/en/Research-and-Publications/Open-Doors.

55. Archana Rai, "Thriving Economy Lures NRIs Back to India," *The Economic Times,* April 29, 2011.

56. AnnaLee Saxenian chronicles the impact of Chinese and Indian immigrant entrepreneurs in the 1990s in Silicon Valley; see Saxenian, "Silicon Valley's New Immigrant Entrepreneurs," Working Paper 15, The Center for Comparative Immigration Studies, University of California San Diego, May 2000.

CHAPTER 6

The Indian-American Diaspora and Its Impact on Politics and Foreign Policy

In a complex, globalized environment, the role of transnational actors like diaspora groups becomes important in shaping relations between home (where the diaspora originates from) and host nations (where the diaspora now resides). Diaspora groups mobilize political forces within the host nation to help secure the stated objectives of the home nation. They also, on occasion, work as influential actors who seek to reshape the political and economic agendas within the home country—especially if these agendas lead to discriminatory practices against particular ethnic or minority groups. As Parag Khanna explains:

> Diasporas influence domestic politics and foreign policy in some of the most important states such as the US, Great Britain and China. They are also crucial agents of economic development: the volume of remittances flowing each year dwarfs all official foreign aid from governments.
>
> And they are, of course, the key mechanism of cultural transmission in the world. Studying diasporas reminds us that there are other ways to think about how identity, power and space come together beyond just states.[1]

The Indian diaspora is now estimated to be more than 25 million people and its presence is global even though its economic and political influence varies greatly from country to country. Though a slim majority in Fiji and Trinidad, the Indian diaspora in these countries faces political and cultural discrimination. In Malaysia, the Indian diaspora is discriminated against in terms of education and employment by the Bhumiputra policies of that country. In Australia and New Zealand, the diaspora has flourished with a New Zealand Indian (of Fijian descent), Arvind Netam, actually becoming the governor-general of the country.

In the United Kingdom, Indians have faced discrimination in the 1960s and 1970s but have since been integrated into the society. A similar situation exists in Canada, although neither Indian diaspora group has emerged as a superstar in economic and educational terms. It is in the United States, however, that the Indian diaspora has been the most successful, affluent, and influential. Indians are high wage–earning professionals or successful businessmen—usually in the high-value information technology sector. The next generation has sought to enter those areas of American society where it can make a contribution to the future of the country. This is perhaps visibly marked by the sudden mushrooming of Indian-Americans on American television, leading to the actor Kunal Nayyar saying that as far as American television is concerned, Indians are the new blacks.[2] Indian-Americans are a community that are punching above their weight within America and, like other diaspora communities in the world, have the potential to be significant transnational actors.

This chapter examines the attempts of the Indian-American diaspora to influence politics and particularly the relationship between the United States and India. In doing so, it makes the argument that the diaspora, while rich, motivated, and potentially influential, is divided by ethnic, religious, and generational lines. These divisions are leading to varying impacts on American foreign policy, India–U.S. relations, and even on the Indian political system itself. Given that the diaspora keeps renewing itself through continuing migration, however, it is likely to be a factor in the U.S.–India relationship economically, politically, and culturally.

BACKGROUND

The Indian-American diaspora now numbers close to 2.8 million people[3] and is both prosperous and educated, with median household income of $90,717[4] and with 80 percent of the men and 50 percent of the women possessing college degrees. For a relatively new diaspora—only migrating to the United States in large numbers from the 1960s—the Indian diaspora has built up a fairly impressive reputation for itself as a political force in the country.

Indian activist groups have set up an organization along the lines of the American Israel Public Affairs Committee (AIPAC)—the U.S. India Political Action Committee (USINPAC)—to help promote Indian and Indian-American interests in the United States. USINPAC was one of the groups credited with helping ensure that the U.S.–India nuclear deal cleared Congress, and this has led to the hype that the Indian-American diaspora is a highly influential lobby that can proactively shape Indian-American interests and U.S. foreign policy. There are also a variety of groupings along regional, caste, and religious lines that have emerged as specific interest groups in the American context.

It is important to note that the Indian-American diaspora is split along generational, ideological, and ethno-religious lines, leading to the diaspora engaging in discrete political issues and in a few instances coming together to lobby for legislation that is vital to U.S.–Indian relations. More importantly, in an era when we are witnessing the emergence of digital diasporas, there is an increasing impact of diaspora groups on the politics of home nations, leading these groups to be less of the instruments for enabling home or host country objectives and, instead, moving their own agendas.

In the United States, Indian-Americans are viewed as the educated, technologically savvy, and wealthy minority that not only has a growing political influence but is a group that may attain a bargaining power comparable to that of the American Jewish community. Indian activist groups are actively working to promote Indian and Indian-American interests in the United States. In fact, this is the role that the USINPAC is seeking to achieve. One of its objectives is to, "provide a national platform for local leaders and organizations and give them the ability to leverage their activities and coordinate their efforts with like-minded people in our community and country."

Similarly, in India, the Indian-American community is now viewed as helping further Indian foreign policy and security goals as well as contributing toward its economic development. The Government of India's High Level Committee Report on the Indian Diaspora states:

> A section of financially powerful and politically well connected Indo-Americans has emerged during the last decade. They have effectively mobilized on issues ranging from the nuclear tests in 1998 to Kargil, played a crucial role in generating a favourable climate of opinion in Congress and defeating anti-India legislation there, and lobbied effectively on other issues of concern to the Indian community. They have also demonstrated willingness to contribute financially to Indian causes, such as relief for the Orissa cyclone and the Latur and Gujarat earthquakes, higher technical education and innumerable charitable causes.

The report continues:

> For the first time, India has a constituency in the US with real influence and status. The Indian community in the United States constitutes an invaluable asset in strengthening India's relationship with the world's only superpower.[5]

While the Indian-American diaspora's progress and political mobilization have been commendable, the claims about the community's political power are somewhat overstated. The Indian diaspora's role as a facilitator of foreign policy will require a greater commitment from the Indian government in developing stronger ties with the Indian-American community as well as providing greater incentives to it. Further, the best lobbying efforts cannot work if there is a fundamental divergence of political views between the United States and India—as was the case when the Indian parliament unanimously condemned the 2003 American-led war in Iraq.

THE RISE OF DIASPORA POLITICS

The revival of interest in diasporas came with the end of the Cold War. Analysts who had hitherto focused on state actors now started to examine, in an era of globalization, the role of substate and suprastate actors like diaspora groups.[6] Newly democratic nations, like Poland and the Czech Republic, also sought to avail of the political, economic, and technological benefits that their diaspora communities could provide. In doing so, these countries were hoping that their diasporas would provide the same type of support that the Jewish, Irish, and Chinese diasporas had provided to their home countries. While there was a worldwide interest in utilizing the latent potential of diasporas, the question that arises is: Why do diaspora groups decide to facilitate activities of the home country?

As Yossi Shain has argued, "Politics in the home country [for a diaspora group] is important for their political identity in America, and they are more likely to support those regimes whose policies coincide with American liberalism and/or US foreign objectives and actively oppose those which do not. They tend to embrace their homeland in a way that is not threatening to their identity within the parameters of American pluralism, but they must defend themselves against the charge of divided loyalties."[7] An India with foreign policy views that diverge significantly from those of the United States, or one that sheds its liberal-democratic and secular credentials to adopt more religious and nationalistic ones, is likely to receive less support among the diaspora.

Further, from the perspective of the Indian government, the diaspora's attention can also focus on issues that are embarrassing or threatening to the government in New Delhi. The move to place caste as a form of racial oppression on the United Nations agenda and the International Conference of Dalit groups are examples of the diaspora working against the prevailing power structure in India.[8] At the same time, the Indian diaspora in the United States will have to survive a series of challenges, not the least of which is generational change, and create a public policy agenda that works to provide leadership and guidance on policy issues in the United States.

THE INDIAN-AMERICAN COMMUNITY:
FROM INVISIBLE TO THE NEW BLACK?

Till recently, Indian-Americans were an almost invisible community. It had not assimilated as much as succeeded and disappeared into American society.

It was a community with a low political profile and its cultural impact on the United States was low. Americans ate at Indian restaurants, occasionally visited a Hindu temple out of curiosity, and, despite the prosperity of the Indian community, saw the average Indian as an Apu-like character who ran a convenience store and prefixed every sentence with a "Blimey, Mr. Homer Simpson."

An additional part of the problem was that the Indians in America had (and continue to have) a weak sense of national identity, choosing instead to identify with their different regional, linguistic, and religious groupings. Thus, there are Indian Muslim, Indian Christian, and Indian Hindu community organizations, with umbrella organizations called the Indian-American Christian Association and the Federation of Indian Muslim Associations. Similarly, different ethnic and linguistic groups have set up their own national associations: the Federation of Kerala Associations in North America, Federation of Gujarati Associations in North America, Telugu Association of North America, and the Bengali Association of North America are some examples. In some cities, there are Tamil Brahmin, Sri Lankan Tamil, and Tamil organizations.

Caste-based organizations have also been set up; for example, there exists a Brahmin Society of New York that comprises of Gujarati Brahmins.[9] The pull of religious and ethno-linguistic ties leads to a diffusion of mobilization efforts as groups tend to focus their resources on parochial as opposed to national or diasporic interests. Thus, Gujarati Americans became very active, after a meeting with former president Bill Clinton who advised them on how to work to raise funds for earthquake and disaster victims in Gujarat.

Coupled with this phenomenon is the problem of a cultural freeze. This is a situation where immigrants retain the traditions, culture, and values of their home country even though these may have been significantly modified in their country of origin. The second major wave of Indian immigrants came in the 1960s and once in the United States froze part of their culture and attitudes. As Samuel Huntington has pointed out, this is not an uncommon occurrence. Writing about early settlers in America, Huntington states, "The initial settlers bring their own culture and institutions with them. These are perpetuated in the new territory, while changes take place in the homeland."[10] Cultural freezes may not be conducive to the modern national identity that India projects. The excessive emphasis on caste and religion among the diaspora works against modern India's portrayal of itself as a secular state as well as against ongoing trends in Indian society. As Catarina Kinvall and Ted Svensson have persuasively argued, it is the fear of cultural contamination from the decadent West as well as more specific cases of racial intolerance that have led the Indian diaspora to create overseas branches and chapters of organizations like the Rashtriya Svayamsevak Sangh (RSS) and the Vishwa Hindu Parishad (VHP). Not only do these groups have agendas in the host nation but they also push their agenda in the home nation—in this case one of Hindu supremacy—as a vital part of their international agenda.[11] An Indian diaspora that lives and works with attitudes that do not fit into modern India can only be viewed as hindering the relationship with the host state and encouraging tensions in the home state. One of the strongest support groups for the creation of a Sikh state of Khalistan, for example, came in the 1980s from the Canadian Sikh community and residual separatist elements remain within that society.

CAUSES FOR POLITICAL MOBILIZATION

In the 1990s, however, there was a growing political mobilization by the Indian-American community as well as a move by the Indian government to try and woo its expatriate groups. As Robert Hathaway argues, the Indian community had by the 1990s grown in size and started to make its influence felt among congressional members and their staffs. By 2004, the India caucus in Congress had the largest membership (186) of any such political group. Congressmen, who in the past had supported cutting foreign aid to India, now strenuously opposed such moves.

When India carried out a series of nuclear tests in 1998, American nonproliferation laws were automatically enforced and India was subject to both economic and military sanctions. Yet, within a year legislators had given the Clinton administration the authority to waive all the sanctions (this being done in a legislature where, as Hathaway states, knowledge about South Asia was still quite limited).[12] The lobbying efforts of the Indian-American community were obviously significant in bringing about this shift in congressional attitude, although other factors did play a role in revoking of the sanctions.[13]

THE INDIAN GOVERNMENT'S ATTITUDE

Coupled with rise of Indian-American activism has been a shift in the policies of the Indian government toward its greater diasporic community. In the past, India had typically adopted a hands-off approach toward its diaspora communities. Jawaharlal Nehru said that these communities should not call themselves Indian and, instead, identify with, and assimilate into, their host countries. It was only in the early 1990s, when India dropped its socialist pattern of economic development and initiated market reforms, that there was a drive to encourage nonresident Indian (NRI) investments in the country (even though for two decades prior to this decision Indians in the Persian Gulf countries had been repatriating large amounts of money to their families in India and bringing about local and state-level development through these financial inputs). Since then, both the Indian central government and Indian state governments started developing ties with the Indian diaspora and particularly with the Indian-American community.

This culminated in the development of Person of Indian Origin and Overseas Citizen of India cards.

In 2012, at the annual Pravasi Bharatiya Divas, an annual meeting held by the Indian government to meet the Indian diaspora, the Indian prime minister, Dr. Manmohan Singh, announced that diasporic Indians would be allowed to vote in the Indian elections, with non-resident Indians actually being allowed to register at local consulates and then participate in the state assembly elections of 2012—a remarkably quick move for the Indian bureaucracy.[14] What this step does is to make the Indian diaspora stakeholders in the future of their home country and not just providers of investments and remittances.

Reasons for Political Activism

Yossi Shain argues that a diaspora group starts to participate in American political life once it gains a sense of confidence about its role in that society and "involvement in US foreign policy is in fact often one of the clearest indications that an ethnic community has 'arrived' in American society, and that it has demonstrated its willingness not only to reinforce and uphold American values such as democracy and pluralism inside America, but promote these values abroad."[15] The Indian-American community has arrived in that its political participation has shifted from symbolic to tactical and strategic goals. The objectives of Indian-Americans were usually symbolic, for they aimed at such gestures as getting a local politician to attend cultural events or to sign a photograph. As one Indian-American activist commented, "Indians tend to sell themselves cheaply and American politicians know it. Sometimes giving a contribution just to get a photo with your Senator is considered a great accomplishment."[16] In part, such a lack of political awareness also came from the community's transplantation into a political milieu that they were unfamiliar with. Indian immigrants were unfamiliar, for example, with a political system that required lobbying efforts to achieve goals.

For several reasons, however, the community became more politically active. It reached critical mass with a concentrated population in certain major metropolitan areas; the community's population also doubled from 1990 to 2000, touching approximately 1.7 million. Further, the community was prosperous and could therefore, potentially, organize fairly effectively. Second, it is digitally connected both within the United States and to the home nation. One of the consequences of the Indian information technology boom has been a growing web presence of both official and unofficial organizations in India that can be tapped into by the diasporic community. At the same time, India's print media has also recognized the importance of establishing a web presence and is now readily available to those interested in following the news in their own region. As Deepika Bahri points out, "Since these new technologies of representation became available, the relative isolation of expatriate South Asians in their discrete locations in Northern countries (Canada and the United States) has been effectively offset by the presence of a large, virtual, instant community that may be geographically scattered but is electronically—and sometimes epistemologically and ideologically—connected and contiguous."[17]

Thus, the Gujarati American community was able to respond rapidly and effectively to the 2001 Bhuj earthquake (to the extent of getting former president Clinton to help raise contributions for the earthquake relief effort). Similarly, the 2002 sectarian riots in Gujarat gained international attention because they were the first riots in India that the digital age was able to transmit globally (the 1984 anti-Sikh riots in India, which followed the assassination of Indira Gandhi, saw a far greater loss of life but did not receive as much international attention). Secular Indian groups, both in India and abroad, were able to mobilize and use the web to highlight the tragedy and the incompetence of the Indian and Gujarat governments in dealing with the upsurge of violence.[18] What hurt the Bharatiya Janata Party (BJP), which was the ruling party at that point of time, even more was the mobilization by secular as well as some religious groups in the United States to deny Narendra Modi, the chief minister of Gujarat and a rising star in the BJP, a visa to the United States.[19] The denial of the visa was particularly damaging since Modi is viewed as a future prime ministerial candidate by the BJP, and not allowing him to go to the United States took away some of his credibility both nationally and internationally.

Third, in the past decade, a new generation of Indian-Americans have attained political maturity. They have organized, are politically aware, understand the process in Washington, and have a range of interests that they seek to promote. Thus, Desis Rising Up and Moving (DRUM) fights for the rights of working class South Asians along the east coast and has sought to organize taxi drivers in New York and northern Virginia. The Indian-American Leadership Initiative Public Action Committee (IALIPAC) seeks to train young Indians in political activism and works to support the campaigns of Indian-Americans who are running for legislative office. While in Washington, DC, groups like Desi Power Hour have provided the network for Indian-Americans to promote their careers.[20]

More importantly, two Indian-Americans have become governors of two of the most conservative states in the American South—Bobby Jindal in Louisiana and Nikki Haley in South Carolina. The cases of both are interesting since they have sought to de-emphasize their Indian identities, with Jindal converting to Catholicism and Haley, although of Sikh descent, becoming an evangelical Christian—a fact that upset both older and younger Indian-Americans who had been born in this country and did not see why they had to apologize for their religion and identity.[21] Jindal, in fact, was reluctant to give his support to the passage of the U.S.–India nuclear deal and only came on board in the latter stages of the campaign.

The main reason for increasing political proactiveness is, however, twofold. One is that the first generation of Indian-Americans, who migrated to the United States, was too busy establishing itself to have the time and the money to invest in a political career. The second generation comes from wealthy families and is confident of its Americanness in an increasingly multicultural America. Further, the community has been willing to mobilize financially for candidates of Indian origin. Thus, USINPAC was able to raise $300,000 for candidates of Indian origin and with pro-India views, and as many as six Indian-Americans competed for races to the House of Representatives (although Bobby Jindal's win in 2007 was probably another big catalyst to the growing confidence of Indian-Americans).[22]

Fourth, a portion of the Indian diaspora now comprises the children and siblings of the Indian elite. Increasingly, Indian businessmen, bureaucrats, military personnel, and, to a lesser extent, politicians have their children studying or living in the United States. This elite group has the ability to reach the most relevant sectors of Indian decision making with their complaints and concerns (as they did when the Indian parliament passed a resolution in April 2003 condemning the Iraq war). It is also an elite group that for practical reasons—particularly business reasons—maintains a strong connection with the home country.

Lastly, diaspora groups may be passive in terms of their identity, as Scandinavian groups in the United States have become, or they may be proactive. What changes this attitude and makes a diaspora conscious of its identity is a critical event that signals discrimination or conflict either within the host country or in the homeland. In the Indian case, three major events have worked to raise political consciousness and mobilize the diaspora. The first event was the growing tensions between India and Pakistan that were exacerbated with India's 1998 decision to test nuclear weapons. The second was the terrorist attacks of September 11, 2001, in the United States. The third was the U.S.–India nuclear deal of 2008, and more recently, the continued terrorist attacks that are launched from Pakistani soil and aimed at Indian cities have also helped mobilize Indian advocacy groups.

The tests were followed by an automatic imposition of economic and military sanctions by the U.S. government. Consequently, Indian groups worked actively to have these sanctions rolled back. Since then, the same groups have been active in attempting to increase U.S.–India cooperation, in helping forge a strategic relationship with Jewish groups in the United States (under the assumption that there was a mutual interest in curbing radical Islam and, more particularly, terrorism), and in working to counter Pakistani lobbying efforts in the United States.

Of these, the link with Jewish groups is the most interesting since it is an attempt to piggyback on the lobbying skills of these groups to achieve certain political ends—most notably the sale of defense technologies like Israel's Phalcon airborne warning system and the Arrow antiballistic missile (both of which have American components and, therefore, require the permission of the State Department).[23] Indian groups have worked alongside pro-Israeli groups to have the U.S. government remove its objections to the sale.

There was also some discussion about a U.S.–India–Israel strategic relationship that is aimed at countering terrorism. In September 2002, a 21-member delegation comprised of members of B'nai B'rith International, the American Jewish Committee, the Jewish Institute of National Security Affairs, and the American Israeli Public Affairs Committee met with then Indian prime minister Atal Behari Vajpayee in New York. A representative from the delegation said, "We also spoke about the blossoming of relations between India and Israel. We dwelt on the common thread of terrorism that the democracies of India, Israel, and the US face. We spoke about the intensifying cooperation in the US between the Indian-American community and the American Jewish community."[24] The delegation also discussed how the two immigrant communities could work together on mutually important issues. The Indian prime minister reportedly expressed a desire for enhanced cooperation between American Jewish organizations and the Indian-American community.[25]

In May 2003, the then Indian national security advisor, Brajesh Mishra, spoke to the American Jewish Committee about the need for concerted action by the United States, India, and Israel on security issues. He also praised the growing cooperation between Indian and Jewish groups in the United States:

> The end of the Cold War also ushered in a major transformation in India's relations with USA. Our Prime Minister has referred to the two countries as "natural allies." The US National Security Strategy report, released last September by President Bush, asserts that the two countries have common strategic interests. India, the United States and Israel have some fundamental similarities. We are all democracies, sharing a common vision of pluralism, tolerance and equal opportunity. Stronger India–US relations and India–Israel relations have a natural logic. I am pleased to see so many distinguished members of the United States Congress here today. They are friends of Israel. They are also friends of India. The Caucus on India and Indian-Americans in the House of Representatives has nearly 160 members. It is perhaps the largest single country-Caucus in the House, testifying to the growing bonds of friendship between the world's oldest and largest democracies. The increasing contact between the AJC and Indian-American community organizations is another positive reflection of the shared values of our peoples.

He continued, "Our principal theme here today is a collective remembrance of the horrors of terrorism and a celebration of the alliance of free societies involved in combating this scourge. The US, India and Israel have all been prime targets of terrorism. They have to jointly face the same ugly face of modern day terrorism."[26]

This commonality of interests, therefore, has both national and international implications. Domestically, it allows the Indian-American community to harness the skills of a larger and more skillful lobbying group to help attain mutual goals. Internationally, it may allow India to procure weapons that have been denied by the United States to China—one of India's regional competitors. From the Israeli perspective, it strengthens both military-strategic and diplomatic ties with India. This not only provides Israel with an important regional ally in the fight against radical Islamic groups, but also weans away Indian diplomatic support to the Arab states. Such lobbying efforts will also continue on the issue of terrorism. As terrorist activity continues in India, and Pakistan sponsors these insurgents, a strong case is made among Indian-American circles for lobbying the American government to put pressure on Pakistan to end its support for such organizations.

The question remains, however, whether this a long-term phenomenon or a short-term tactical alliance based on common threat perceptions. In India, several political parties, particularly the Congress, cautioned the then BJP government against developing strong ties with Israel at the risk of alienating the Islamic countries in general and the Arab world in particular. The current government, consisting of a Congress-led alliance, however, continued the strong ties, and pro-Israel groups actually came out in support of the U.S.–India nuclear agreement.[27]

There also remain residual feelings in India about the need for politically distancing the country from the United States. The belief is that in the long term such an alliance could make India extremely dependent on the United States and circumscribe its freedom to maneuver in the international system. As the former Indian foreign minister Natwar Singh put it, "The broad foreign policy framework left behind by Nehru has stood us in good stead. There is no other foreign policy India can follow without becoming a satellite. The people of India will not allow this country to be a camp follower of any country, howsoever powerful."[28] This was seen in the nuclear debate in India where one of the fears was that India would become too beholden to the United States and lose its autonomy in foreign policy. Further, there are those within the Indian political system who remain uncomfortable with the idea of a unipolar international system. This discomfort was partially reflected in the Indian parliament's unanimous condemnation of the Iraq war.

The other event that catalyzed Indian-American political action was the terrorist attacks of September 11, 2001. In the aftermath of 9/11, Indians in America were attacked (particularly Sikhs).[29] According to one estimate, 15,000 lost their jobs because of new federal regulations specifying that only U.S. citizens could man airport security checkpoints. Thus, the invisible and prosperous Indian minority suddenly found that being wealthy and law-abiding did not prevent an individual from being pulled out of line at an airport or being ejected from a plane because the pilot did not feel comfortable having a dark-skinned Indian onboard.[30] The combination of these factors has created a belief both in the United States and in India that the Indian-American diaspora, along with its various lobbying and political action groups, will play a role for India similar to that of the Jewish community and AIPAC in its support for Israel. However, there are several reasons that point to the fact that this may have been an overoptimistic assessment.

First, as Krishna Kumar, then of the Indian-American Policy Institute, argued in 2002, the Indian diaspora in the United States is miniscule, and even if it doubled in the next decade to approximately 3.5 million, it will still be numerically insignificant in a country of nearly 300 million people. Secondly, the Jewish community has been in the United States for a much longer period of time and, therefore, has a larger donor base for both political contributions and philanthropy. The Indian community reportedly contributed about $7 million to the 2000 presidential elections. When one takes into account the fact that nearly $1 billion was spent in the campaign, the total contribution of Indian-American groups is very small and does not carry the type of influence that it is believed to have. As seen with the success of Indian-American candidates, however, this trend is changing and the community is becoming increasingly willing to fund and participate in political affairs.

Further, Indian-Americans remain, like most Asian Americans, fairly apolitical. As one political activist pointed out, during the 2002 elections, only 10,000 of about 45,000 Indian-Americans living in Massachusetts were registered to vote.[31] Moving Indians away from such political apathy will obviously take time. Nor is the community geographically concentrated, as a part of the Jewish community is in New York or the Cuban community is in Miami, to have significant political influence in crucial electoral states.

The clout and mobilization capabilities of the community are also exaggerated, as can be seen by the attempt to remove Representative Cynthia McKinney of Georgia from Congress. After Representative McKinney called for the Balkanization of India, Indian-American activist groups sought to unseat her. The attempt was successful but also underlined the limits of Indian-American mobilization capability. According to Dr. Narsi Narasimhan of the Indian Professionals Network of Atlanta, one of the groups spearheading the effort, Indian-Americans probably donated about $20,000 in the bid to dislodge the incumbent. It was only when out of state Jewish American contributions started to pour in, however, that the financial tide turned significantly against Representative McKinney. Very few Indian-Americans outside Atlanta made financial contributions and even within

Atlanta only about 100 people contributed. (In fact, Ms. McKinney once again won the democratic primary in 2004 and was subsequently elected to the House of Representatives—only to lose the 2006 Democratic primary to Hank Johnson.)[32] On the other hand, the national furor that was created after Virginia Senate Republican candidate George Allen called an Indian-American staffer a "Macaca" and lost the elections shows that the community can generate political protest if sufficiently motivated.[33]

Thirdly, as Samuel Huntington argued, for institutions to survive, they must be able to weather a generational change. The question then arises, will the next generation of Indian-Americans have the same type of affinity with the home country that their parents have? The answer is at best a mixed one and can be discerned by how young Indian-Americans define their identity. The terms they use include Indian-Americans, South Asian Americans, Hindu Americans, and Indian Muslim Americans, to name a few. This suggests that rather than being unified, the next generation may well break into disparate groups based on caste, ethnic, and religious identities.

Coupled with the general shift in identity is the shift in the attitude on the India–Pakistan issue. Several young Indian-American policy activists interviewed by this author stated that, as far as they were concerned, the rivalry between the South Asian neighbors was a dead issue. They were Americans with positive feelings for India but did not want, quite understandably, to be dragged into the nationalistic and religious rivalries of the subcontinent. One factor that would work in favor of maintaining such a diasporic identity, however, is the fact that there continues to be heavy first generation migration into the country that brings a large pool of educated labor into the country with political concerns about the home country.

Finally, one needs to examine what the long-term economic stakes the Indian community has in the home country. One may argue that the stakes of the Indian diaspora of other countries are much higher than those of its constituents in the United States. More than 6 million Indians working in the Persian Gulf countries and this group, for several reasons, has higher stakes in maintaining stronger ties with India and in identifying themselves as Indians.[34] Most of the Indian labor force in the Gulf cannot bring its families to those countries because of the financial restrictions placed by host governments (only white-collar employees have high enough incomes to qualify for bringing in their families).

Moreover, the inability to get citizenship in these countries has meant that the Indian diaspora has been forced to develop stronger economic, political, and even educational ties with India. Thus, the Gulf Indians have set up 38 schools that follow the Indian higher secondary curriculum—this permits their children to be automatically considered for admission to Indian universities.[35] Those who cannot bring their families remit significant amounts to their households in India and, in fact, it is these remittances that have provided significant hard currency earnings to the Indian government since the mid-1970s (the Gulf Indians provide more than half the NRI investments in India). The Gulf Indians have also made generous financial contributions whenever India has faced natural calamities or war. They made significant financial donations during the India–Pakistan conflict over Kargil in 1999 and following the Gujarat earthquake of 2001. Further, the Gulf Indians have invested heavily in special Indian government bond issues like the India Millennium Deposit bonds.[36] In contrast, the Indian-American community has been able to move entire households to the United States and, more importantly, to secure citizenship. This naturally leads to a diffusion of ties with the home country.

Yet, the wealth of the Indian diaspora, particularly its North American branch, is noticeable in the form of remittances to India. The flow of foreign direct investment into the country—something that the Indian government pointed out was an indicator of the foreign investor community's long-term stakes in the host economy[37]—has played a major role in shaping development in certain states of India and in supporting Indian families.

By 2011, remittances to India had grown to $58 billion, with the Indian diaspora overtaking the Chinese one in terms of hard currency repatriations.[38] Of this the bulk has come from North America and the Gulf region, with the North American countries in 2009 providing 38 percent of remittances, while 27 percent of total remittances came from the Gulf.[39] By 2011, however, the Gulf had overtaken North America, but this can possibly be attributed to the political and financial uncertainties in the Gulf coupled with the desire of international investors to seek refuge in U.S. dollars.[40]

Nor can the Indian-American diaspora be viewed as a major supplier of technology. Most of the technologies that India needs would require Congressional approval and there is little that the Indian-American community could do to facilitate such transfers. The reluctance of the American strategic community to transfer the Arrow antiballistic missile and the continued U.S. insistence that India, ideally, sign the Nuclear Nonproliferation Treaty are examples of the continued resistance in American governmental circles to open the technological cupboard to India and to treat it as an equal partner.

Perhaps the best way to understand the political mobilization efforts of the Indian-American community is to recognize that from being a group in themselves they have become a group for themselves. A great deal of the political mobilization that is taking place is to enhance the economic standing of the community, to secure legal protection for it, and to develop the networking ties that would promote the careers of the next generation of Indian-Americans. But part of this approach has included a shift toward dealing with issues that impact on the India–U.S. relationship, with concerns ranging from terrorism and freedom of religion to the nuclear deal.

Indian Government Approach

Coupled with these factors has been the lackadaisical approach of successive Indian governments on how to cultivate and nurture links with the Indian diaspora. While, as mentioned earlier, the Indian government would actively seek remittances from the Indian diaspora, little was done to provide constitutional and legal rights to these groupings. Dual citizenship, which would not only have provided legal guarantees to the diaspora that they were welcome in India but also have created strong emotional ties to the home country, was rejected as an option by successive Indian governments. Yet for Indians living in ethnically and racially tense nations like apartheid era South Africa and Fiji, this would have provided a lifeline that they could depend on in case conditions in their host country became intolerable.

The Indian government's main objections stemmed from the inability to check the backgrounds of those who applied for dual citizenship and the more practical fact that people from Bangladesh and Pakistan could claim dual nationality and create internal security problems in India. The issue was magnified with the arrest in the United States of the Pakistani American David Headley over his links to the November 28, 2008, Mumbai terror attacks. For an Indian government that was already suspicious of people of Indian descent, this provided the excuse to be even more restrictive in the granting of visas to foreigners to come to India.

When the Indian government offered dual nationality, it was done with definite commercial and economic interests in mind. Indians from only a select group of Western nations and Singapore were permitted to apply for dual citizenship. Members of the Indian diaspora from Trinidad and Fiji, where communities exist in sensitive ethnic divides, were denied the right to claim citizenship—while they perhaps required such a tie the most. It may, therefore, be the non-American part of the Indian diaspora that will be the one to strongly identify with India and work toward further cooperation with it.

Finally, diaspora groups, as Shain argues, tend to support the home country as long as it fits into the interests of the host nation. When these interests diverge, the diaspora group tends to side with its country of domicile rather than its country of origin.[41] The development of significantly better ties between India and the United States have come about not primarily because of the lobbying efforts of Indian-Americans but, instead, due to a changed political perception in both countries. In the United States, in the latter part of the Clinton administration, interest arose in trying to develop a better relationship with India. India's market reforms, coupled with the recognition in Washington that India was an emerging power, led to a push for a better relationship with the United States. In New Delhi, there was a recognition that India had to adjust to the existence of a unipolar international system.

Thus, it would be premature for the Indian government to expect that the diaspora will work to help further Indian goals in foreign, economic, and security policy over an extended period of time. What the Indian government needs to do, and the High Level Committee Report on the Indian Diaspora addresses this, is to create the type of cultural, emotional, and economic links that will withstand the transition from a predominantly Indian-born diaspora to an American-born one. The Chinese government has done this with its establishment of Confucian centers around the world, which are seen as not only reaching out to the diaspora but also helping integrate the Taiwanese part of it into the mainstream Chinese model.

In practical terms, the Indian government will have to create cultural and educational centers in the United States so that young Indians can learn about India and the current trends within Indian society. Further, a serious move to establish India chairs in universities around the United States will have to be attempted. Both the central and state governments of India have slowly started to try to establish university chairs around the world. Coupled with such efforts, there has to be a set of study-abroad programs that can take young members of the diaspora from all over the world to India. Indian universities and think tanks should be encouraged to create summer courses for American colleges that would permit young Indian-Americans to come to India, study about it, and get to travel around the country. It is remarkable that existing Indian government programs are covering virtually every country in the world but do not make a concerted effort to attract the Indian diaspora.

There is also the need to attract retired Indians to come and contribute to the country's developmental efforts. This could be done in several ways. One could be to get diaspora donations to set up a technologically advanced university and staff it with retired or visiting faculty—this has already been done in Bangladesh with the creation of a North South University. Another strategy may be to establish an Indian International Voluntary Service that permits members of the diaspora to come and contribute to national developmental efforts—an Indian-style peace corps.

As far as technological development is concerned, the focus should be not on acquiring dual-use technologies but instead focusing on the technologies of peace. India continues to have severe energy problems, and it would be useful to engage the Indian-American scientific community in developing alternative energy programs. Similarly, scientific programs that provide improved transportation capabilities as well as cheaper methods to carry out construction projects should be pursued. As part of this process, the Indian government would be well served to develop a database of Indian-Americans and the skills that they can potentially contribute. The other crucial area is making India genuinely investment-friendly for the diaspora investor. Indian bureaucratic red tape and corruption have forced NRIs to put their money in stocks and in savings accounts. If the

Indian government wants to tap into the overseas community's entrepreneurial skills, it will have to create a favorable climate for investing in India. Then only will there be a genuine, long-term connection between India and its diaspora.

ACKNOWLEDGMENT

Portions of this chapter are adapted from Amit Gupta, "The Indian Diaspora's Political Efforts in the United States." Observer Research Foundation, ORF Occasional Paper, September 2004. Available at http://www.orfonline.org/cms/export/orfonline/modules/occasionalpaper/attachments/op040918116339808 4234.pdf.

NOTES

1. Vikram Khanna, "Merging Identity, Power and Space; Indian–American Author Parag Khanna Discusses the Importance of Diasporas in the Multipolar World of the 21st Century," *The Business Times,* Singapore, July 5, 2011.

2. Indian-Americans are on shows like *Covert Affairs, The Office, The Big Bang Theory,* and *Rules of Engagement.* Nayyar's comments are available at http://www.deadline.com/2010/07/tca-big-bang-co-stars-kunal-nayyar-simon-helberg-on-indians-jews-in-showbiz/.

3. Richard Springer, "Indian Americans Number 2.8 Million," *India West,* vol. XXXVI, issue 28, June 3, 2011, p. 1.

4. Joel Kotkin and Shashi Parulekar, "India Conquers the World; After a Long Eclipse, an Ancient Country Finally Returns as a Force in Global Business and Culture," *Newsweek,* August 8, 2011.

5. *High Level Committee Report on the Indian Diaspora* (New Delhi: Government of India, January 8, 2002), pp. xx–xxi.

6. See, for example, Joel Kotkin's book, *Tribes* (New York: Random House, 1993), that examines the emergence of global diasporas like the Chinese, Indians, and Jews.

7. Yossi Shain, *Marketing the American Creed Abroad: Diaspora in the U.S. and Their Homelands* (Cambridge and New York: Cambridge University Press, 1999), pp. 8–9.

8. Gail Omvedt, "Dalits Mobilizing," *The Hindu,* May 27, 2003.

9. Madhulika S. Khandelwal, *Becoming American, Being Indian* (Ithaca, NY: Cornell University Press, 2002), p. 165.

10. Samuel P. Huntington, *Who Are We? The Challenges to America's National Security* (New York: Simon and Schuster, 2004), pp. 41–42.

11. Catarina Kinvall and Ted Svensson, "Hindu Nationalism, Diaspora Politics, and Nation-Building in India," *Australian Journal of International Affairs,* 64, no. 3 (2010): p. 286.

12. Robert Hathaway, "Unfinished Passage: India, Indian Americans, and the U.S. Congress," *The Washington Quarterly,* 24, no. 2 (2001): pp. 21–22.

13. Hathaway argues elsewhere that congressional pressures to continue the sale of food grains to Pakistan also led to a shift in congressional attitude. See Robert M. Hathaway, "Confrontation and Retreat: The U.S. Congress and the South Asian Nuclear Tests," *Arms Control Today,* January/February 2000.

14. Ishani Duttagupta, "Pravasi Bharatiya Divas 2012: Key Takeaways for Overseas Indians," *The Economic Times,* January 14, 2012.

15. Yossi Shain, *Marketing the American Creed Abroad*, p. 8.

16. Interview with Anna Pediyakal, India Abroad Center for Political Awareness, July 23, 2002.

17. Deepika Bahri, "The Digital Diaspora: South Asians in the New Pax Electronica," in Makarand Paranjape (ed.), *IN Diaspora* (New Delhi: Indialog Publications, 2001), p. 223.

18. See, for instance, the report, "The International Initiative for Justice in Gujarat," December 19, 2002, http://www.onlinevolunteers.org/gujarat/reports/iijg/.

19. Suresh Nambath, "When Modi Was Denied the Visa," *The Hindu*, March 22, 2011.

20. Krissah Thompson, "Indian Americans Take Next Step in Political Ascent; Record Number Seek Office Moving from the Sidelines to Candidacy," *The Washington Post*, July 6, 2010.

21. Samuel G. Freedman, "Pride and Concern Follow Success of Indian-Americans," *The New York Times*, July 10, 2010.

22. Thomson, "Indian Americans Take Next Step in Political Ascent."

23. Peter Slevin and Bradley Graham, "Indian Arms Plan Worries State Dept.," *The Washington Post*, July 23, 2002.

24. Ganesh S. Lakshman, "American Jews Moot India–US–Israel Coalition against terror," *The Hindustan Times*, September 14, 2002.

25. Ibid.

26. Address by Shri Brajesh Mishra, National Security Advisor of India at the American Jewish Committee Annual Dinner, May 08, 2003, http://meadev.nic.in/speeches/bmnsaad. html.

27. Allison Marz Freedman, "USINPAC and the U.S.–India Nuclear Deal: Lasting Influence or One Shot Victory?" *CUREJ—College Undergraduate Research Electronic Journal*, August 2009, p. 47.

28. "Bad Domestic Policy Can Never Produce Good Diplomacy," *Frontline*, vol. 19, issue 16, August 3–16, 2002.

29. For details, see "American Backlash: Terrorists Bring War Home in More Ways than One," http://www.iapolicy.org.

30. For discrimination against the Indian–U.S. community after September 11, 2001, see, Vijay Prashad, *Uncle Swami: South Asians in America Today* (New York: The New Press, 2012), pp. 3–8.

31. Ela Dutt, "What the Results Mean for Indian American Interests," *News India Times*, November 22, 2002.

32. "A Conversation with Dr. Narsi Narasimhan—Getting Involved in the Political Process," *Desijournal*, htttp://www.desijournal.com/article.asp?articleId+79.

33. For a discussion, see Chris Good, "Will Macaca Hurt George Allen in 2012?" http://www.theatlantic.com/politics/archive/2011/02/will-macaca-haunt-george-allen-in-2012/71513/.

34. *The High Level Committee Report on the Indian Diaspora* (New Delhi: Government of India, January 8, 2002), pp. 20–22.

35. Ibid., p. 22.

36. Ibid., p. 22.

37. Economic Survey, 2002–2003, Ministry of Finance and Company Affairs, Government of India, http://indiabudget.nic.in/es2002–03/chapt2003/chap612.pdf.

38. Sankeet Mohapatra, Dilip Ratha, and Ani Silwal, "Outlook of Remittance Flows 2012–2014," The World Bank, *Migration and Development Brief 17*, December 1, 2011, p. 3.

39. "Remittances from Overseas Indians: Modes of Transfer; Transaction Cost and Time Taken," *RBI Monthly Bulletin,* April 2010, p. 787.

40. "Indian Banks Shrug Off Arab Spring as Expats Keep Cash Flowing," *Arabic Knowledge@Wharton,* http://knowledge.wharton.upenn.edu/arabic/article.cfm?articleid=2724.

41. Yossi Shain, *Marketing the American Creed Abroad,* pp. 8–9.

CHAPTER 7

Russia

The fourth major part of India's foreign and security policy lies in its relationship with Russia. Since the advent of the 21st century, the relationship between the two countries has changed from what it was with the erstwhile Soviet Union at the height of the Cold War. At that point of time, the two countries were bound by strong political, military-strategic, and economic ties, with India very much the junior partner in the relationship. In the new millennium, with the change in India's economic capabilities, the relationship has become a more equal one, with India being actively courted by Moscow to remain a major customer for Russian weapons and civilian technology. For India, the connection is not just one of military technology but also one of shaping political alliances in a unipolar world. Yet this relationship too has, in the post–Cold War era, developed its own set of problems as Russia feels threatened by the rise of India's economic power and the independence it gives to New Delhi in its arms acquisition and economic programs.

BACKGROUND

Although the Soviet Union gave diplomatic recognition to India after it gained independence in 1947, Stalin was suspicious of Jawaharlal Nehru, who he viewed as an agent of Western imperialism. Stalin, therefore, refused to meet Vijayalaxmi Pandit, India's first ambassador to Moscow and Nehru's sister. While India's role in the Korean War saw the Communist bloc lessen its suspicions about India, it was only after the death of Stalin and the rise of Khrushchev that the Soviet Union moved to build its relationship with India. Economic assistance in the

1950s was followed by military assistance in the 1960s, starting with the Soviet willingness to first sell and then permit India to manufacture the MiG-21 fighter in the country. The two countries established a rupee–ruble trade agreement that allowed India, which at that point of time faced a severe shortage of hard currency, to buy goods and oil from the Soviet Union.

Indo-Soviet relations reached their peak in 1971 when the countries signed a peace and friendship treaty that gave India the freedom to prosecute its war against Pakistan that led to the eventual independence of Bangladesh. By the late 1970s, India gave its support to Moscow when the Soviet Union invaded Afghanistan. The Indian decision was seen to violate its nonaligned position in international affairs, but New Delhi by then was too vested in its relationship with the Soviet Union to try and maintain equidistance between the great powers or to even move its economy toward a free market regime. What had developed by then, both in the case of the Indian elite and the Indian public opinion, were strong pro-Soviet sentiments because the country was seen as one that had stood by India in its moments of need. In fact, it was argued that there were four great permanent strategic relationships in the world: the U.S.–U.K. relationship, the U.S.–Israel relationship, the China–Pakistan relationship, and the India–Soviet Union relationship.

What changed the situation for India was the collapse of the Soviet Union in 1991. The death of the Soviet empire destroyed India's existing worldview and called into question the policy of nonalignment. At same time, the successor state of Russia, under the leadership of Boris Yeltsin, was more concerned in projecting itself as a Western nation and in building up its relations with Europe.[1] The expectation in Moscow was that the United States and Russia would form a strategic partnership to carry out great power management of world affairs. The relationship with India went into the doldrums, and for India this was particularly difficult since its supply of Soviet-era weaponry required spare parts that were no longer easily available in the chaos that followed the demise of the Soviet Union.

As Anuradha Chenoy argues, Russia's economic troubles in the 1990s and the collapse of the domestic market led to a revival of ties with India, particularly in the defense sphere:

> It was with Yeltsin's visit, followed by meetings in 1994 and 1997, that India and Russia once again felt that a strategic partnership could be worked out. The reality of globalisation and the revival of a trend towards a multipolar world pushed the two countries into a strategic and economic alliance. In Russia, the neo-liberal economic policies, which advocated a complete destruction of Soviet-type institutions and market-led growth, led to a complete collapse of the financial and economic system. Levels of foreign aid and investment were far below expectations and were completely tied to the import of Western goods. The trade balance between Russia and the West was skewed against Russian goods. The secure COMECON (Council for Mutual Economic Assistance) trading bloc was over.

In these circumstances Russia once again had to seek its old allies, in India, West Asia and South East Asia. Russia then made a second shift in its strategic thinking. While ideological proximity and alliance with the West was to be given emphasis (not necessarily priority), Russian foreign policy aims were to be realised in the CIS (Commonwealth of Independent States) near abroad and with old allies in West Asia and Asia. The appointment of Yevgeny Primakov as Foreign Minister in 1996 concretised this shift.[2]

Primakov's call for a Russia–India–China strategic alliance was met with little enthusiasm in Beijing and New Delhi as the alliance was perceived as being anti-American in its orientation.[3] The important change in this period was Moscow's recognition that international arms sales served the economic, political, and military-strategic interests of Russia, and India, as one of the major importers of former Soviet weaponry, was looked on as a valued customer. By 1996, the two countries had inked a deal for the Indian purchase of 40 Su-30MKI fighters and an agreement to license-produce an additional 140 aircraft in India.

What brought India–Russia relations to an even keel, however, was the visit of Russian president Vladimir Putin to India in October 2000. Putin signed a strategic partnership declaration with India but, more importantly, agreed to sell a range of weapons systems to India that included the *Admiral Gorshkov* aircraft carrier, Su-30 aircraft, and T-90 tanks.[4] The deal was mutually beneficial since it infused much needed hard currency into the Russian economy and helped bolster the Russian arms industry (the *Gorshkov* sale helped revive the fortunes of the shipyard at which it was to be retrofitted, while the Su-30 MKI became the cornerstone of the new India–Russia defense cooperation model). On the Indian side, the country was able to start to modernize its armed forces after the delay caused by the financial crisis of the early 1990s. At that time the supply of U.S. weaponry was not possible because of supplier restrictions.

But the visit also showed that the India–Russia relationship had moved beyond the political and emotional links of the Cold War period and was now based on pragmatic economic calculations—although there was discussion about the need to coordinate policies in a multipolar world. The focus was on trade, both civil and military, and was to be conducted in hard currency. In a post-socialist market economy, both countries had higher expectations about the quality of products and the terms of the contracts. Indian companies were no longer able to pass on lesser quality products into the Russian economy,[5] while India became, as in the case of weapons sales, far more demanding that the Russians stick to the prices, terms, and delivery schedules that they had agreed to (the latter issue became a major problem in the case of the delivery of the aircraft carrier *Gorshkov* to India).

While these concerns were to create tensions in the relationship, a set of mutual concerns and complementary views on world affairs meant that the two countries could have a working strategic partnership. These included terrorism, arms sales, contesting unipolarity both bilaterally and through the BRIC coalition, and the development of a strong energy relationship between the two countries.

As Kuchins points out, Russia's last two wars were against Muslims in Afghanistan and then the battle in Chechnya.[6] Terrorism on Russia's southern flank, therefore, remains a central concern to the country. The fact that the bulk of these terror groups have connections to the Afghanistan–Pakistan region make India–Russia cooperation in this area an imperative. The two countries have set up working groups to address this problem regionally. A key part to that regional settlement would be a post-U.S. solution in Afghanistan that did not permit extremist elements from controlling the government in Kabul (although India would also like a government that was not blatantly pro-Pakistani and continued to take into consideration Indian interests). As part of this process, India would like to be a full-fledged member of the Shanghai Cooperation Organization (SCO)—a group consisting of the Central Asian Republics, Russia, and China—since this would not only help India shape the security framework in the region but also let it develop plans to extract energy supplies from the region.

Arms sales remain the key component of the India–Russia relationship, although they have in recent years witnessed tensions between the two countries. For India, despite the growth in its economic fortunes and the fact that it would like to diversify its supplier base, weaponry of Russian origin remain the mainstay of its arsenal. There are several reasons for this. First, the Russians have been willing to part with systems and technology that till recently the West was unwilling to give to India (and in the nuclear field continue to do so). Thus, Russia agreed to the leasing of two Akula class nuclear submarines to India just as in the 1990s it had leased a Charlie class nuclear boat to India. Faced with increasing competition in the Indian market for what till the past decade was a near monopoly for Russian weapons, it is likely that Russia will continue to provide such systems to India. This is a particularly valuable asset for India since its own arms industry has been unable to meet the technological or numerical requirements of what the Indian armed forces need in their future modernization efforts. Moreover, India was able to customize Russian weapons systems, by including subcomponents that were indigenously manufactured as well as acquired from Western and Israeli sources, to not only suit India's requirements but also to become a more formidable weapons system. That was particularly the case with the Su-30MKI fighter, where India was able to incorporate French and Israeli subsystems into the aircraft. Second, as India continues to develop its own domestic arms production capabilities, the link with Russia, in terms of the joint development of weapons programs, has given India's defense science base a way to move up the technological ladder as well as provide weapons systems that are required by the Indian armed forces. The latter has always been an issue since the Indian armed services have questioned the quality and effectiveness of indigenously produced weapons systems. Thus, the Brahmos missile—a collaborative effort between India and Russia—gave the country a missile that could be land-, air-, and sea-launched and that could achieve supersonic speeds. More recently, the two countries reached an agreement to jointly develop a fifth-generation fighter aircraft (FGFA), thus providing India with an air power capability that it would be unable to acquire from the West (critics do, however, have reservations about whether the fighter will actually be a true fifth-generation plane comparable to the F-22 Raptor). India has agreed to provide about $5.5 billion as its share for the joint development of the airplane. Again, since one of India's long-term goals is to build up its defense science capabilities, such joint programs do provide it with the basis to further develop in the field of aeronautics. In fact, the Indian government was so confident about the benefits that would come from the FGFA collaboration that it reportedly turned down the offer to purchase the F-35 Lightning from the United States.[7] Although the degree to which India will actually participate in the development of the plane has been questioned.[8]

More recently, the relationship has run into some turbulence because of the delays in providing new weaponry to India, the fact that Russian weapons are not matching their stated standards, and hefty cost overruns, with the Russians playing hardball with their Indian counterparts. Thus, India recently refused to accept updated Kilo submarines because the Klub missile system that was added to it did not work properly.[9] Similarly, the Russians have told the Indian Navy that they require an additional $1.2 billion to complete the refurbishment of the carrier *Gorshkov* (now renamed *Vikramaditya*).[10] This puts India over a barrel since it has bought the supporting air wing based on the configuration of the carrier. India's naval chief publicly complained that the Russians had used Indian money to modernize their shipyard facilities and, in doing so, were now able to attract new business and push the Indian carrier project onto the back burner.[11] Also, the India–Russia medium-range transport aircraft project has run into funding problems.

What the Russians have also been doing is essentially tying the availability of certain weapons systems to the purchase of others. Thus, one of the reasons for buying the *Gorshkov* was that the Russians would subsequently sweeten the pot by offering India strategic systems like the Akula-class submarines and Tu-22 Backfire bombers (the Backfire deal was subsequently scrapped).[12] Further, when deals fall through in one area, there have been repercussions in the purchase of other weapons. When India declined to purchase Russian nuclear reactors after coming close to inking the deal, Moscow retaliated by asking for price increases on a series of weapons programs that included the *Gorshkov* and the Su-30MKI fighters.[13]

One should stress, however, that this is not the end of the India–Russia military relationship in the way that the Egypt–Soviet Union relationship ended in the early 1970s. The Indian defense minister was quick to distance his government from the remarks of the Indian Navy chief about the delays and price increase associated with the *Gorshkov* project. Further, the Indian government continues to be interested in oil exploration in Sakhalin, has entered into an agreement with Russia to develop an FGFA, and retains plans for the joint development of a transport aircraft. What we are likely to see, therefore, is a continued link with Russia, but at the same time, India will move toward other suppliers to reduce the critical dependence on Moscow in some fields.[14]

In the area of armaments, Russia, because of its cash-strapped arms industry, will continue to share technology and scientific collaboration with India since New Delhi will be willing to fund Russian research and development efforts. While Beijing is also willing to provide such research and development subsidies, lingering suspicions about China's intentions will likely prevent the building of a similar military technology relationship with that country.

Russia, more than any other Western nation, is willing to share technology with India and actually seek collaborations with Indian defense science and the broader Indian scientific community. The MMRCA fighter competition was instructive in this regard because, despite the size of the deal and the desire of various Western aeronautical companies to get a long-term share of the Indian market, there was no real attempt to try and entice India by making it a collaborative partner in newly emerging weapons programs. The argument made in Western circles was that India would not be able to absorb some of the technology transfers it required nor would it be able to effectively contribute to more advanced weapons programs. There was also the question whether India had reached the level of trust that the United States had with other long-term Western allies to merit the sale of advanced systems or for that matter to even have a seat at the table for acquiring cutting-edge technology.

Until India develops a significant domestic defense science and industrial capability, it will remain dependent on external suppliers for both weapons systems and technology transfers. This will make the India–Russia arms relationship flourish in the near to medium term since both countries benefit from it. India, in the near future, is unlikely to significantly alter its foreign policy in a way that would make it one of the key allies of the West, thereby facilitating the type of technology transfers that would displace Russia.

BRICS?

The term Brazil, Russia, India, China (BRICs) was coined by Jim O'Neill of Goldman Sachs in 2001 to describe emerging nations in the globalized economy that were likely to emerge as central players in the world economy and global policymaking and affect trade, capital markets, energy policy, and investment decisions (South Africa has since been added to this grouping, making it BRICS).[15] Since then, the economies of all four nations have grown and there has been increased collaboration between them on economic and political issues, leading to the belief that they can be a coordinated force in international affairs. On the other hand, the fact remains that the differences between them and the greater opportunities afforded by working with the West have led to what, the *Economist* has argued, can sometimes be written off as a catchy term to attract investors.[16] The question addressed here is, can the BRICS forum be an arena for enhanced cooperation between India and Russia? Put simply, the answer is no since Indian foreign policy has evolved considerably since the death of the Soviet Union and India's own global standing has grown substantially in the 20 years since the demise of the Soviet Union.

During the Cold War, India was economically and militarily too weak to not depend on the Soviet Union for political and military support. Moreover, the Soviet Union had the capability to provide such support to India both through the transfer of weapons and technology and also by using its own political clout in international forums like the United Nations. In the 20 years following the demise of the Soviet Union, the impressive growth of the Indian economy as well as the country's military capabilities has made Russian support somewhat redundant. In the Soviet era, India was forced to largely buy Soviet equipment because of financial constraints. Such constraints no longer exist as India has become one of the largest arms markets in the world, with suppliers scrambling to get a share of what is believed to be an $80 billion market. Nor is Russia capable of providing the political support that the erstwhile Soviet Union was able to. As the defeated superpower, Moscow has lacked the ability to impose its political views in international forums, and the India–Russia relationship consequently does not have the type of compelling need that the old India–Soviet Union relationship did. The lack of a significant volume of trade between the two countries, in spite of the continuing Indian dependence on Russian weaponry, is perhaps symptomatic of how this relationship has changed in the new millennium.

Trade between the two countries reached close to $9 billion by the end of 2011, and the countries have stated that they want to increase bilateral trade to about $15 billion (double the amount at the end of 2010) by 2015.[17] In the same period of time, India–China trade is targeted to reach $100 billion, and if past indicators are any guide that amount is likely to be surpassed by New Delhi and Beijing. The fact is that in a post–Cold War world, Russia has become a secondary economic partner of India.

One must also raise the issue of whether the Russian elite and policymakers can work with countries that they view as essentially developing or would rather prefer to be linked to the developed world. The age-old Russian dilemma of identity—European or Asian—in the globalized world has become a choice between considering oneself part of the developed world club or being viewed as an emerging economy. The Russian elite preference would be to be viewed as European and developed and thus distance itself from the BRICS agenda.

In terms of Indian foreign policy, New Delhi has been playing a fairly nuanced diplomatic game by seeking particular types of diplomatic alliances for specific negotiation frameworks. Thus in some contexts it has sought to use the

G3 framework—India, Brazil, and South Africa—to promote its interests while at the Copenhagen Climate Change Summit in 2009 it worked with an alliance of like-minded nations, the so-called BASIC group—Brazil, South Africa, India, and China—to focus the outcome of the conference in a direction that was more suited to India's long-term developmental efforts and environmental plans. A more fruitful venue for the two nations to cooperate would be in the Shanghai Cooperation Organization (SCO), which focuses on security in Central Asia.

The SCO was created in 2001 with China, Russia, Kazakhstan, Kyrgyzstan, Uzbekistan, and Tajikistan as its members, with the goals of combating the three threats of religious extremism, ethnic separatism, and international terrorism.[18] Since then, it has moved toward becoming an organization with a growing institutional character, regular meetings at different governmental levels including head of state, and increasingly a push toward greater economic cooperation. Underlining this movement, some Western analysts argue, has been the objective of creating a Central Asian sphere of influence that shuts out the United States.[19]

As the organization has grown, and economic cooperation has come to the forefront, there has been concern in Russia that China is gaining an ascendancy within the organization and relegating Moscow to the junior partner status in the relationship. In economic terms, this makes perfect sense since China views the SCO as potentially providing it with the basis for regional leadership as well as serving as an institution that promotes economic development. In the past decade, Beijing's trade with the SCO countries has risen from $12 billion to more than $90 billion, and China would like to expand it even further.[20] China would like to bring about "the realization of infrastructure interoperability, as well as speed up the diversification of financing channels."[21] Making infrastructure interoperable would permit the movement of goods and services and tie in the SCO region to the Chinese economy. To make this economic integration more palatable, China has also launched an extensive soft power campaign that has led to the establishment of Confucius Institutes to teach Chinese in all the Central Asian states except Turkmenistan, and has also helped develop an SCO University that brings together some 50-plus universities across China and Eurasia.[22]

For China, the stakes are high in bringing the SCO nations into its economic and political orbit. Economically, energy supplies from the region will help quench China's growing demands for energy for its rapidly growing economy. In geo-strategic terms, oil and natural gas pipelines from Central Asia lessen the dependence on the sea lanes that are prone to being blocked by nations hostile to China. Politically, working with the SCO nations helps lower the danger of support for jihadi terrorism and anti-China insurgencies in China's sensitive western regions. After the 2011 terror attacks in the Uighur region, China was quick to point out that the terror attacks had originated from Pakistan, and this led the Pakistani leadership to go post-haste to Beijing to smooth things over.

Russia, therefore, sees the rise of China in the region as a challenge to its own position and its predominance over the Central Asian states. With this in mind, it is encouraging India to join the SCO, even though it is unclear what the criteria will be for admitting new members to the organization. The Indian government itself has argued that until the statutory obligations required of new members are made clear, India could not join the new organization.

An India in the SCO helps balance China, but geographic constraints, Pakistani suspicions, and the extent of Chinese economic largesse limit what India can do in the organization. Given China's geographic proximity, it would be difficult for India to counter the advantages China provides in terms of the movement of trade and services. Pakistani suspicions also limit the role India can play in that Islamabad would be likely to work with Beijing to marginalize the influence of New Delhi in the region. This would particularly be the case on any Afghan settlement where Pakistan would not brook any perceived challenges to its interests in that country.

A greater problem comes from the fact that neither Russia nor India will be able to provide a successful economic alternative to China in the near future. In the wake of the 2008 economic crisis, Russia broached the idea that the SCO nations consider trade in their own currencies, thereby bypassing the dollar. While China agreed, it went on to offer a $10 billion credit line to the SCO countries—something that was taken up by the member states, most particularly Kazakhstan.[23] China has gone on to suggest that bilateral trade between China and Kazakhstan increase to $40 billion by 2015, and the two countries have agreed to a $1 billion currency swap agreement.[24] Despite such constraints, the Russians actively seek Indian membership because, "If we admit India, the SCO will contain not two heavyweights—Russia and China—but three. It will make things much easier for us."[25]

While India has more limited resources than China, it is viewed positively by the elites in SCO countries who see themselves not just as Muslim but also as culturally Indo-European. More importantly, they recognize that living geographically sandwiched between two giants—Russia and China—maintaining economic and political links with India provides a necessary buffer from the two larger neighbors exerting greater pressure and influence.

Additionally, like Russia and India, they are concerned about jihadi activities, and these nations would like to pursue an independent foreign policy that would permit them to benefit from ties with both their larger neighbors. Most importantly, like Russia and India, these nations would like to see a settlement in Afghanistan that does not end up with a destabilization of the region by permitting another Taliban-style regime to take over in Kabul.

From a Russian and Indian perspective, the ability to influence events in Kabul remains paramount, and the best way to do this is to create a situation where the northern supply route to Afghanistan remains open and the countries of the region work to both stabilize a post-U.S. Afghanistan. The latter would require a commitment by both India and Russia to build infrastructure in the country as well as work to strengthen the institutions of the country.

In the latter case, the Indian government after considerable hesitation, due largely to the concern that any proactive measures would anger Pakistan, has agreed to train Afghan security forces and contingents of the military in India.[26] In effect, this means that India will be committing itself to the future of an independent government in Kabul. Parts of such a strategy are falling into place, as can be seen by the Indian decision to try and build a railroad from Afghanistan's mineral-rich heartland to the Iranian port of Chah Bahar.[27] Such a project would bring lucrative contracts for Indian firms and allow India to get a share of Afghanistan's mineral wealth. It would also serve a strategic purpose since it would create a second route for Afghan goods to reach the ocean and thus reduce the importance of Pakistan. Due to the fact that Afghan goods transit primarily through Pakistan, Islamabad has been able to put blocks at the border to put political pressure on Kabul whenever the need has arisen. Such a rail system, however, would be prone to attacks by the Taliban and, therefore, is viewed as a high-risk project.

For any of these ventures to succeed, what is needed is for Afghanistan's neighbors to work with each other to stabilize the country, and, as some observers point out, in effect this means ensuring that Pakistan and India are able to contain their rivalry within that nation.[28] In actual fact, the situation is more heavily weighted in favor of Pakistan because of the advantage provided by its geographic proximity, the high stakes it sees in maintaining strategic depth in Afghanistan, and the presence of a large Pashtun population on its side of the border. Afghans have, therefore, suggested that Afghanistan also send troops and security forces for training in Pakistan, although with the caveat that they should be monitored both before and after they received training in order to weed out possible spies.[29]

Any peace settlement in Afghanistan would have to take into account and satisfy Pakistan's security considerations, but it cannot be one where the Taliban or other extremist forces return to create the antebellum political situation that existed in Afghanistan before 2001. It is with this in mind that the Russian government has agreed to give military and financial assistance to the Afghan security forces and to increase contributions to the Afghan reconstruction process.[30] Thus, a consensus is emerging among Afghanistan's most influential neighbors on the need to maintain a government in Kabul that is not overtly influenced by Pakistan but is neither hostile to its eastern neighbor's interests. Russia and India may be able to make great cooperative efforts in the near future to address this immediate geo-strategic issue.

In conclusion, the India–Russia relationship has shifted from the one that existed during the Cold War, where India was the junior partner that depended on the former Soviet Union for weaponry, oil, and the Rupee-Ruble trade. Now, in a globalized post–Cold War setting, the relationship is on a more even footing as India emerges both economically and militarily as a more powerful global actor. In fact, barring the military relationship, which provides India with a range of strategic weaponry as well as more advanced technologies, the two countries now have divergent paths in the international system. For the two nations to once again develop a truly strong strategic relationship would require a reorientation of Russian thinking to work more comprehensively with India to establish regional order. An opportunity for this exists in Afghanistan, and it will be interesting to see if the Russian government is willing to invest in a foreign policy endeavor that is still surrounded by bad memories of the Soviet invasion of the 1970s.

ACKNOWLEDGMENT

Portions of this chapter are adapted from Amit Gupta, "India's Military Aviation Market: Opportunities for the United States." Strategic Studies Quarterly, Summer 2009, pp. 52–71. Available at http://www.au.af.mil/au/ssq/2009/Summer/gupta.pdf.

NOTES

1. Rajiv Sikri, *Challenge and Strategy: Rethinking India's Foreign Policy* (New Delhi: Sage, 2009), p. 155.

2. Anuradha M. Chenoy, "A Defining Moment," *Frontline,* vol. 17, issue 21, October 14–27, 2000.

3. Andrew C. Kuchins, "Russia's Relations with China and India: Strategic Partnerships, Yes; Strategic Alliances, No," *Demokratizatsiya,* 9, no. 2 (2001): p. 260.

4. John Cherian, "The Defence Deals," *Frontline,* vol. 17, issue 21, October 14–27, 2000.

5. Gulshan Sachdev, "Reviving Economic Interests," *Frontline,* vol. 17, issue 21, October 14–27, 2000.

6. Kuchins, "Russia's Relations with China and India," p. 262.

7. Rajat Pandit, "With Own 5G Jet Plan India 'Rejects' U.S. Offer," *The Times of India,* January 30, 2011.

8. Sudha Ramachandran, "India, Russia Still Brothers in Arms," *Asia Times,* October 27, 2007.

9. Rahul Bedi, "Klub-S Missile Snags Delay Delivery of Indian Sub," *Jane's Defence Weekly,* January 23, 2008.

10. "No Renegotiation on Price of Gorshkov: Navy Chief," *Hindu,* December 4, 2007.

11. Sandeep Unnithan, "Battle over Gorshkov," *India Today,* December 7, 2007.

12. Ibid.

13. Seema Mustafa, "Angry Russia Hikes Cost of Deals," *Asian Age,* November 19, 2007.

14. Gurmeet Kanwal, "Indo-Russian Partnership," *Deccan Herald,* December 25, 2007.

15. Jim O'Neill, "The World, BRICs Dream and India," *Silicon India,* May 2006, p. 10.

16. "International: The Trillion Dollar Club; The BRICs," *The Economist,* April 17, 2010, p. 64.

17. Jon Grevatt, "India and Russia Sign Initial FGFA Design Contract," *Jane's Defence Weekly,* January 5, 2011.

18. Jing-Dong Yuan, "China's Role in Establishing and Building the Shanghai Cooperation Organization (SCO)," *Journal of Contemporary China* 19, no. 67 (2010): p. 856.

19. Stephen Aris, "The Shanghai Cooperation Organisation: 'Tackling the Three Evils'. A Regional Response to Non-Traditional Security Challenges or an Anti-Western Bloc?," *Europe–Asia Studies* 61, no. 3 (2009): pp. 458–59.

20. "Shanghai Bloc's International Clout Rising—Chinese Envoy to Russia," *Xinhua* (New China News Agency), November 6, 2011.

21. Ibid.

22. Raffaello Pantucci and Alexandros Petersen, "Russia's Eastern Anxieties," *The International Herald Tribune,* October 18, 2011.

23. Russia seen backing Indian SCO membership bid to dilute Chinese influence, Report from Russian newspaper *Kommersant,* June 15, 2011, provided by BBC Worldwide Monitoring, June 15, 2011.

24. Ibid.

25. Ibid.

26. Alex Rodriguez, Mark Magnier, "Pakistan–India Tensions Ease Amid New Concerns; Islamabad, Worried about Afghanistan, Makes a Trade Overture," *Los Angeles Times,* November 7, 2011.

27. Dean Nelson, "India Plans 'World's Most Dangerous Railroad' from Afghanistan to Iran," *The Telegraph,* November 2, 2011.

28. Dean Nelson, "Afghanistan Is a Proxy War between India and Pakistan; When Afghanistan's President Hamid Karzai Visited New Delhi Earlier Last Month to Sign a Strategic Partnership Deal, He Quickly Reassured Islamabad It Remained Kabul's Most Important Partner," *The Telegraph,* November 2, 2011.

29. Text of report by Afghan independent Tolo TV, December 4, 2011, supplied by BBC World Monitoring Service, *BBC Monitoring South Asia—Political,* December 5, 2011.

30. Hadi Sadeqi, "Asian Triangle Will Emerge!," *Daily Afghanistan,* December 18, 2011.

CHAPTER 8

India and the Indo-Pacific

In 2010, Secretary of State Hillary Clinton coined the term Indo-Pacific. The significance of it lay in the fact that for the first time a U.S. official had brought the Indian and Pacific Oceans together into one economic, political, and military-strategic sphere. The implications for India from Secretary Clinton's statements were perhaps obvious. As the secretary explained, "Earlier this year, we launched the U.S.–India Strategic Dialogue. And one of the core issues we addressed is India's growing engagement and integration into East Asia, because we believe that India is a key player in this region and on the global stage. That's why President Obama is also beginning his own major trip to Asia next week with a stop in India. His trip will bring together two of our top priorities—renewed American leadership in Asia and a U.S.–India partnership that is elevated to an entirely new level. . . . And we are expanding our work with the Indian navy in the Pacific, because we understand how important the Indo-Pacific basin is to global trade and commerce."[1] How does India fit into the broader Indo-Pacific region? What are its security and economic compulsions and how do the changing patterns of power rivalry in the region create both opportunities and challenges for India?

BACKGROUND

Indian interests in the Indian Ocean region, Southeast Asia, and East Asia have been pursued, with varying degrees of emphasis, by every government since the times of Jawaharlal Nehru. As Christophe Jaffrelot points out, Indian nationalists saw links with Southeast Asia as a central part of Indian identity and the newly independent Indian government sought to foster these ties.[2] In 1947, it held the

Asian Relations Conference in Delhi with the view to creating a forum for discussing Asian affairs and reaching agreements on positions. Later, at the Bandung Conference in 1955, India, along with China, laid out the principles of peaceful coexistence, which were welcomed by most Asian states. Further eastward, India had a good relationship with Japan that emerged from its historical links during World War II, where while the Royal Indian Army defeated the Japanese in Burma, some Indian troops fought on the side of the Japanese and became part of the Indian nationalist discourse. Later, during the Tokyo war crimes trials, the Indian judge, Radha Binod Pal, was the sole dissenter for which he is remembered in Japan with a memorial outside the Yasukune shrine—in fact, when Prime Minister Abe visited India, he made it a point to go to Kolkata to meet Pal's son.[3]

On the other side of the Indian Ocean, India sought to build ties with the countries of the Middle East. India sought to project its Islamic heritage as a means to reach connectivity with some nations, while with others, most notably Nasser's Egypt, the common secular themes of anticolonialism, nationalism, and socialism were seen as creating long-lasting bonds.

In both cases, however, Indian efforts met with limited success. Pakistan's diplomacy in the Middle East and in the Persian Gulf was more relevant to the needs of those nations as Islamabad was able to use religious and military ties to build long-lasting bonds with those nations and leverage these ties against India. Islamabad was thus able to successfully shut out India from the Organization of the Islamic Conference (OIC), thereby creating a situation where the world's third largest Islamic country did not have a voice in the organization.

In the case of South East Asia, Yong and Mun point out:

> The Asian Relations Conference and the Bandung Conference were high points in the early attempts by the newly emerging Asian states to create a free and neutral pan-Asian identity and presence in the international order. In this, there was clear convergence of interests between an emerging India and the Southeast Asia nation-states in waiting. Nonalignment and freedom from foreign domination were commonly held ideals and Nehru's vision of an Asia that would be uncommitted to either of the two power blocs appealed to like-minded Asian nationalists, most notably Aung San and Sukarno. But these ideals would fade by the 1960s, when Southeast Asian states, having attained independence to become nation-states in their own right, began articulating their own foreign policies in light of their respective national interests. With that, Indian interests and those of the new states of Southeast Asia began to diverge.[4]

By the 1960s, political influences had shifted India's focus in other directions, most notably the growing link with the Soviet Union. This saw India distancing itself from the non-Communist states of South East Asia, even though there was little that the Communist states of South East Asia had to offer India. In fact, when the Association of South East Asian Nations (ASEAN) was formed, India was not invited to join the group, while Burma and Sri Lanka were. As for Japan, its geographical distance from India, its preoccupation with the security region of North East Asia, its ties to the United States in the Cold War, and its strong economic focus on other parts of Asia—due in part to India's post-independence closed economy—led to ties between the two countries being restricted to some economic connections and cultural ties.[5]

The situation did not change in the 1970s as neither ASEAN nor India had incentives to build a more comprehensive relationship. The ASEAN countries reacted with unease about India's links with the Soviet Union and the Indian proposal for a regional security convention met with a lukewarm response. The ASEAN countries had few economic interests in India.[6] India, in turn, was pursuing bilateral relationships, the most important of which was with Communist Vietnam—an act that created further discomfort for the ASEAN states. The relationship with Vietnam reached its apogee in the 1980s when India recognized the Heng Samrin regime in Cambodia, which went squarely against ASEAN policy at the time. Added to the concern of the ASEAN nations were India's own constraints, which came from geopolitics and the worldview of the Indian elite. Rajiv Sikri points out that despite not having a history of conflict with South East Asia, India could not develop economic ties with the region since both Bangladesh and Burma blocked the transit of Indian goods through their territories, thus taking away the creation of a connected economic zone between India and South East Asia. Culturally, Sikri writes, the obsession of the Indian postcolonial elite with the West meant that there was little attention paid to the countries with whom India should have had natural ties.[7]

By the 1990s, however, the situation changed whereby India refocused its attentions on South East and East Asia. The death of the Soviet Union, India's own financial crisis of 1991, the subsequent move toward market reforms and globalization, and the economic dynamism of the East Asian tigers led to the government of Prime Minister Narasimha Rao deciding to pursue a "Look East" policy.

Along with economic interests, strategic interests have also driven the Indian approach to its eastern flank. The rise of China and the growing economic connectivity between the ASEAN and East Asian states with China led to the fear of India being shut out of the region. On the other hand, Asian countries saw India as providing some balance against a China whose economic footprint, while beneficial to all, was matched with concerns about its growing military capabilities.[8]

On its western flank, in the Indo-Pacific, India has three key interests. India's demand for energy will grow rapidly due to both population and developmental necessities, with India already importing close to 72 percent of its oil. Additionally, P. R. Kumaraswamy says that the export of labor services to the Persian Gulf, where more than 6 million Indians now work, is of equal importance since it provides valuable hard currency and has led to increased development in particular regions in India.[9] The southern state of Kerala has perhaps benefitted the most from the connection with the Persian Gulf, and the importance of that region was brought home at the start of the great recession in 2008 when thousands of Indians were forced to leave the area because they had lost their jobs.

INDIAN INTERESTS

If one takes the Indo-Pacific region as stretching from the Persian Gulf to the western part of the Pacific, then Indian interests in this region have been growing both because of economic and security concerns and due to the need to counter Chinese expansion. Indian oil and natural gas supplies depend on a smooth relationship with the nations of the Persian Gulf since alternative sources are shut off to India. Natural gas from Myanmar and Bangladesh, for example, has not been available primarily for political reasons. An attempt by India's Tata industrial group to set up a gas plant in Bangladesh, for example, ran into problems on political grounds.[10] Equally important is the continued presence of the 6 million plus labor force in the region. Indian expatriate labor from the Gulf generates roughly $12 billion in hard currency earnings, and as mentioned earlier, there are domestic developmental and employment consequences of such overseas employment.

The other reasons that the Persian Gulf nations are crucial in the Indian foreign policy process are the religious and emotional ties that bind India's Muslim minority to the Arab world. With a population of 178 million, Indian Muslims cannot be counted as a minority but, instead, should be thought of as a nation within a nation. The religious and emotional ties of these citizens to Saudi Arabia—because of the holy sites of Mecca and Medina—and the connection of India's Shia population—which may be either the second or third largest Shia population in the world, depending on whose numbers you take—to Iran make it necessary for the Indian government to maintain cordial relations with these governments. It was this pressure that for decades ensured that India did not establish full-scale diplomatic relations with Israel. At the same time, this policy had little impact on Indian efforts to enhance the nation's external interests. The Islamic countries of the Arab world were to side with Pakistan in all the India–Pakistan conflicts and were unwilling, as mentioned earlier, to let India join the OIC. Due to the fact that Indian foreign policy had, since independence, attempted to use multilateral forums to pursue India's objectives, losing out on the OIC membership was seen as a blow to India's interests. It was also a setback in the attempts to curb Pakistan's influence since Islamabad, as a full member of the OIC, was able to get the organization to adopt what was seen in New Delhi as an anti-Indian position.

The Persian Gulf states are also important for two other reasons. First, in a globalized environment, they serve as potential future investors in India. Gulf state investors have sought to invest in a range of activities from the railways to information technology. Dubai Ports World, which was forced to sell the six ports it had acquired in the United States, has acquired five container terminals in the country, which account for 40 percent of India's container terminal operations.[11] More recently, Dubai Ports has spent more than a billion dollars to build a port in the south Indian city of Kochi to move increasing amounts of cargo to Europe and China.[12] In fact, since 2008, the Indian government has sought to encourage the Sovereign Wealth Funds of the Gulf Cooperation Council (GCC) countries to invest in India. Similar attempts have also been made with Saudi Arabia and Kuwait.[13] Getting other countries to make foreign direct investments in India has been difficult as India's bureaucratic red tape and the long and cumbersome decision-making process has tended to discourage investors. In such a situation, the Gulf countries become a welcome economic asset, and the new trend toward investment in India may also introduce a more balanced diplomacy on these countries' part vis-à-vis the India–Pakistan situation. Given the current security and investment situation in Pakistan, India has become a better bet in terms of investments, and this has seen all the Gulf states move in that direction.

The other reason is the emerging security architecture in the region where India, with its emerging military capabilities, is increasingly becoming an actor to be reckoned with. A key part of this turn of events is the situation in Iran. Indian interests in Iran came from a set of interrelated factors, as Abhijit Iyer-Mitra writes:

> The reasons for that friendship were energy (which India needs desperately and from diverse sources), a bargaining lever against America, a conduit to playing the great game in Central Asia and finally to encircle Pakistan. Iran obliged (possibly unwittingly) on all counts.[14]

India has had centuries-old ties with Iran, although more recently the relationship has been based on energy and on the desire to work with Iran to deal with emerging security issues in the region. Thus, India's second largest supplier of petroleum is Iran, which provides 12 percent of its oil supplies.[15] India has invested in the Pars oil field in Iran and had discussed the development of an Iran–Pakistan–India pipeline. India has also inked an agreement to build a liquefied natural gas plant in Iran and to buy 5 million tons of LNG annually from Iran.[16] As India's energy requirements grow, the availability of Iranian energy would be vital for Indian future development.

Politically, both India and Iran have been concerned about the kind of future regime that will emerge in Afghanistan. During the Taliban's rule of Afghanistan, both India and Iran supported the Northern Alliance and the relationship between the two countries was a fairly cordial one. Iran actually worked in the OIC to prevent the tabling of a resolution that would have been critical of India's actions in Kashmir.[17]

Relations between the two countries started to sour as India began to improve its relationship with the United States. As the U.S.–India relationship began to improve, Iran began to express its displeasure about the change in the relationship. What brought matters to a head was India bowing to U.S. pressure and agreeing to vote against Iran's nuclear ambitions at the International Atomic Energy Agency. In successive resolutions in 2005 and 2006 India voted against Iran, stating that Tehran as a member of the Nuclear Nonproliferation Treaty (NPT) should abide by its provisions. At the same time, New Delhi sought to try and placate Tehran by stating that as an NPT member Iran had a legitimate right to the benefits of nuclear energy. For India, going along with the U.S. position was crucial since not doing so would have jeopardized the India–U.S. nuclear pact.[18] In 2011, India was also forced into the position of paying for Iranian oil through a complicated payment deal that routed money through Turkey and the United Arab Emirates to pay for the petroleum. The need for this complicated routing arose from a call by the United States and its allies for nations to not use the Asian Clearing Union currency swap system to pay Iran. India responded by paying through a German bank, but even that arrangement broke down when the European Union placed sanctions on Iran.[19]

Additionally, there is the pressure placed on India by the Arab countries who have their own reasons for worrying about Iran—particularly due to its emerging nuclear program. Sudha Ramachandran quotes P. R. Kumaraswamy on this to suggest that while India can resist Iranian pressure, it finds it harder to do so to the Arab countries because the Arab countries play a more important role in influencing Indian foreign policy.[20]

More recently, the United States has exerted diplomatic pressure to get India to reduce its dependence on Iranian oil—something that it is seeking all countries that purchase Iranian oil to do—and the Indians responded by cutting purchases by 15 percent.[21] Recognizing the Indian dependence on Iranian oil, the United States agreed to a special waiver for India and several other countries so that they could gradually move away from buying Iranian oil. The six-month waiver would permit India and other countries to seek alternative suppliers of oil—although interestingly enough China was not included in the waiver by the American government.[22]

Iran has responded by publicly criticizing Indian actions in Kashmir, although this can be viewed as part of a broader foreign policy strategy on Tehran's part. While the Sunni Arab nations have sought to create the bogey of a rising Shia Iran, the government in Tehran has attempted to counter this by trying to create pan-Islamic solidarity by bringing about a common front on the oppression of Muslim communities around the world. Thus, the Iranians have included the plight of the Muslims in Kashmir along with their campaign for Palestinians. This foreign policy tactic generates sympathy in the Arab world since their own governments have been less than enthusiastic in recent times about championing the Palestinian cause. Instead, it has been Turkey and Iran that have been in the forefront of espousing Palestinian rights. The emphasis on Kashmir, however, has irked the Indian government whose policy has consistently involved treating Kashmir as a domestic issue and the territorial dispute over it with Pakistan as a bilateral issue.

While there are contentious issues between India and Iran, two key issues make it difficult for New Delhi to completely abandon Iran. First, there is the issue of transcontinental transit. Given the less-than-cordial relations with its neighbors, India has to seek alternative routes for trade and transit and in this context the Iranian port of Bandar Abbas becomes important. The Indian government would like to use Bandar Abbas as a hub to transport goods past the Caspian into Russia and Europe (a north–south corridor). The other and more difficult issue is Afghanistan.

With the United States having stated that it will withdraw all troops from Afghanistan by 2014, and some believe that it may happen even sooner to accommodate domestic political demands, it will be the regional players who will have to pick up the pieces of an Afghanistan that could go back into a civil war situation or into long-term instability. To prevent this from happening and to retain Indian influence in Afghanistan, which is seen as vital to the country's long-term security interests as well as a counter to Pakistan, India will require the help of Iran, the Central Asian nations, and possibly Russia to help stabilize a post-U.S. Afghanistan. As one commentator notes, "That would, however, require a powerful vision and strategic cooperation, including intelligence sharing and political coordination at an unprecedented level, for which serious preparations have to begin right away. In fact, with western forces stepping out, in a manner not very different from the Soviet withdrawal from the country in 1989, India may find it necessary to initiate the evolution of a regional mechanism, where neither Pakistan nor China is left out, so that Afghanistan—a country prone to multiple influences—has a realistic chance to rebuild."[23]

Iran would be particularly important since it could be used as the supply conduit to provide supplies to an India-friendly, non-Taliban regime in Kabul. The general consensus is that a regime in Kabul that was adequately funded and reasonably armed would possibly be able to ward off advances from the Taliban and the Haqqani network and thus allow Afghanistan to neither fall in the hands of Islamic fundamentalists, who would permit it to become, once again, an epicenter for terrorist groups, nor allow a pro-Pakistani government to come to power.

Yet, as observers point out, it is easy to overestimate the India–Iran relationship for it is actually based on limited interests and does not threaten India's relations with other countries. The India–Iran relationship is predominantly based on energy supplies and attempts to broaden the energy relationship have floundered. The Iran–Pakistan–India pipeline has been put on the back burner and is unlikely to find external investors who are willing to risk funding an unpredictable Iran, and despite the signing of the deal to supply LNG, none has flowed from Iran to India. India's former ambassador to Iran, K.C. Singh, summed up the underlying problems of doing business with Iran. First, there was the difficulty of doing business with Iran, and secondly there was the stigma of doing business with Iran.[24] In contrast, it is India's relations with the Arab states of the Gulf that are more important both economically and politically.

More than 6 million Indians live and work in the Gulf and they mainly come from a select group of states, thus localizing their impact on India's domestic economy—predominantly Andhra Pradesh and Kerala.[25] More than 1.5 million live in the United Arab Emirates and account for 33 percent of the population.[26] More importantly, India–GCC trade is expected to reach $130 billion by 2013–2014 and the GCC countries supply 45 percent of India's petroleum (with Qatar being the largest supplier of natural gas to India at approximately 5 million tons of LNG annually to India).[27] Given this economic imperative, Pant argues that India would like the status quo to continue in the Gulf.[28]

In operational terms, this would mean keeping the Straits of Hormuz and Bab-el-Mandeb open in order to ensure India's energy security, and with this in mind India has conducted naval exercises with a number of Gulf countries. It has also signed defense cooperation agreements with the major GCC countries that mirror those inked by the major powers.[29] So, what does this changed context mean for Indian policy toward the Gulf states?

If we look at the expansion of Indian commercial and economic interests in the western Indian Ocean region and the growth in Indian military capabilities, then it would seem that India is headed for playing a more influential role in the Gulf region. The expansion of the Indian Navy, with the growth of its carrier fleet and its acquisition of Russian nuclear submarines, along with its own indigenously developed nuclear submarine, suggests an increased Indian presence and role in the region. Added to this expanding naval capability is an Air Force that has aerial refuellers, airborne early warning systems, and long-range strike aircraft in the form of the Su-30 MKI. Yet, India, as observers suggest, has to be careful about how it projects power in the region. It cannot, as C. Raja Mohan points out, go the route of the Royal Navy that had maintained imperial control over the Indian Ocean. In a globalized 21st-century world, attempting to be an imperial power would only lead to resistance from the rest of the littoral states. Nor is it likely to happen given India's own political agendas and worldview. The role India can play is also constrained, for now, by the turmoil within the South Asian region. Indian actions would have to take into account the security considerations of its neighbors, most notably Pakistan. On the other hand, there are opportunities for India to work with the countries of the region precisely because of the changes in the international system. First, C. Raja Mohan writes, is the fact that India, while not a junior partner to the United States, does share both values and objectives with the United States on the security structure in the Indian Ocean. Both are against terrorism and the spread of weapons of mass destruction (WMD), for democracy, and for the free flow of energy supplies. Second, there is the growing role of the Gulf states in maintaining international security. Qatar, for example, was the first Arab country to commit its air force to aid in the NATO air campaign in Libya in 2011. Earlier, the United Arab Emirates had sent its forces to be part of the International Security Assistance Force in Afghanistan. Along with this emphasis on security has been the overall rise of Asia as an economic power, leading to what Mohammed el-Erian, the head of Pimco, describes as a tectonic shift in the international system. What this leads to is that:

> At the same time, the Gulf and Indian Ocean littoral states are beginning to see that the rise of Asia is offering a valuable alternative to their traditional dependence on the West for economic assistance and military support. This has created an entirely new context for thinking about the balance of power throughout the entire region.[30]

Within this framework, it is argued that India can play the role of a bridging power that can use its leverage with the United States and Iran to help shape a security architecture within the region.[31] Other nations, most notably China, would also be considered for such a role, and Beijing certainly has the advantage in that its economic ties in the region are extensive. But Indian observers suggest that India has certain advantages like being a democracy that might work to its advantage if New Delhi pursues a correct foreign policy toward the region, which would include "a sustained strategic dialogue with the Gulf security elites, elevating the current defense exchanges to higher level, conduct of joint military exercises, deeper links with regional navies, establishing military training programs, servicing arrangements for military equipment, and eventual equipment transfers to the region as India becomes part of the globalizing defense industry."[32]

In attempting to become part of the security architecture of the Gulf, India will have to reset its foreign and security policy in ways that might be difficult for New Delhi to accomplish. Current Indian policy, for example, is to avoid expeditionary actions, which is exactly what greater operations in the Gulf would eventually involve. There is also the problem of how India's Muslim population would perceive any actions in the Gulf. The Shia–Sunni split in India's population is roughly 20:80, and taking sides with either the Iranians or the Arabs would potentially have problems with one of the two Muslim dominations. Working with the United States might be even more problematic since the Iraq war led to anger and protests by India's Muslim population, as evidenced by the demonstrations against President George W. Bush when he visited India.

The issue of leverage with Iran and the United States has also to be questioned since New Delhi has, if one goes with the conclusions from the earlier argument, little influence on Tehran. It has been unable to bring to fruition energy deals with that country and nor has it brought about significant security cooperation with the United States on Iran. India's stance on the Iranian nuclear program would essentially be a deal breaker in terms of creating more long-term India–Iran cooperation, and it is clear that New Delhi has decided for military and political reasons to side with the international community on this issue.

Neither has leverage with the United States reached the stage where India can act as a proxy in certain scenarios to replace the United States. Indian relations with the United States are certainly better than they were a decade ago and the India–U.S. nuclear deal led to speculation that it would serve as the basis for a more solid and comprehensive relationship, but the subsequent Indian decision to purchase the Rafale—an arms purchase that the United States had put sufficient emphasis on and had hoped would go its way—shows the limits of the relationship. Moreover, while India cannot be the junior partner of the United States, it does have to show that it has a commitment to using its military strength to uphold the existing order in the Indian Ocean region. To some extent, New Delhi has shown that will with its decision, after much hesitancy, to combat piracy in the Indian Ocean region. But it will need more to establish New Delhi as an alternative to Washington in the region's strategic calculus.

The Indian reluctance to move beyond baby steps in the security sphere also brings up the dilemma of how to counter Chinese moves in the Indian Ocean region. India lacks the economic instruments that China has used to gain acceptance in the region and particularly in the Gulf region. It is China that provided Saudi Arabia with medium-range ballistic missiles, engaged in military and economic cooperation with Israel, and built up a strong energy relationship with Iran. India's inherent political caution and its economic constraints have not permitted the emergence of a similar policy from New Delhi. Unless India moves to be more proactive in the region, which may involve coming down on one side of the Arab–Iranian dispute, it is unlikely to be taken more seriously than China in the region.

Lastly, there comes the more recent risk that has emerged from the Arab Spring—that of supporting authoritarian regimes in the Gulf, however prosperous they may be. The Arab Spring has had its impact on the oil-less states of the Arab world and, so far at least, the oil-rich nations have been able to prevent internal dissent from rising—Libya of course being the notable exception. Getting into security arrangements with authoritarian regimes, however, may be a proposition that India is not likely to agree to since it would be overtly tying itself to regimes that may neither be stable in the long run or may generate domestic criticism if these regimes were marked by internal turmoil.

AUSTRALIA

The southern tip of the Indo-Pacific region would include Australia, a country with which India has only begun to interact seriously in the past decade. As my friend Jason Sharman, who is a Professor at Griffith University in Queensland, says, the India–Australia relationship used to be based on three things: cricket, Commonwealth, and curry. There were good reasons for this. As part of the Western alliance, Australia did not share a security perspective with India that was nonaligned and under nonalignment had tilted toward the Soviet Union.[33] Even after the death of the Cold War, the relationship did not grow since Australia was focused on the Asia-Pacific region and subsequently in the growth of the economic relationship with China. In part this was due to Australia's strategic outlook, for as one observer noted, while Australia was a three-ocean continent, it predominantly focused on two—the Pacific and the Antarctic—in its foreign policy orientation. It is only in the past decade that the relationship has grown, with the Australian government recognizing the role that India can play and due to the growth of economic ties between the two countries, particularly the outflow of Indian students into Australia for a higher education.

Australian foreign and security policy toward Asia must be examined in terms of Canberra's broader perceptions of international security and the perceived role of Australia in a unipolar international system. Australian security and foreign policy has been driven by certain constants that are now beginning to be modified to suit the emerging security system in Asia.

First, Australian policymakers have traditionally recognized that the country would be hard-pressed to defend itself and, therefore, have sought alliances with great powers. Until World War II, the alliance was with the United Kingdom, and after the war, the alliance was with the United States. Second, while Australia was in Asia, it was not part of Asia. In fact, there was a fear of the Asian neighbors—the so-called yellow peril—which saw, at various times, security threats from China, Japan, and Indonesia. Third, Australia was a white Anglo-Saxon country with an avowedly racist immigration policy, the White Australia Policy, that deliberately sought to exclude nonwhite people from Australia.[34] Fourth, there was a belief that Australia was an important actor in international affairs.

Australia's security has traditionally been tied to alliances with outside powers—first, the United Kingdom, and since World War II, the United States—an alliance that was formally codified with the ANZUS treaty of 1951. This led to Australia sending expeditionary forces to participate in the major wars of the last century and intervening, when necessary, to stabilize the immediate region in Southeast Asia and the Southwest Pacific (although the latter actions were both out of alliance obligations and the independently determined need to secure the immediate region). More recently, in November 2011, the Australian government signed an agreement that will allow the United States to annually rotate up to 2,500 Marines into the country and to use Australia's barren north for both training and basing aircraft. In such a situation, one has to raise the question of why Australia would be interested in building strategic ties with India and why

New Delhi would want such a relationship to emerge. The answers lie in the Indian need for energy, the maintenance of security in the Indian Ocean region, and of course the rise of China. They also come from the fact that India and Australia share similar characteristics.

As Rory Medcalf writes, Australia, like India, is a lonely power in that, "Despite all their other connections, Australia and India are fundamentally lonely powers in the global system: neither belongs to a natural bloc, and both sustain stable, democratic systems in an environment that is often less than sympathetic to their interests."[35] Thus, for both countries going outside their natural geographic zones and seeking friends and allies makes complete sense.

For India, Australia provides a reliable supply of energy as New Delhi looks globally for energy supplies and sees this quest being challenged by China. In 2009, Australia and India concluded a 20-year contract worth 25 billion Australian dollars to supply liquefied natural gas to India.[36] For India, which was shut out of Bangladeshi, Iranian, and Burmese natural gas supplies for political reasons, the Australian deal was a vital success in the country's global quest for energy. India had also hoped to secure uranium from Australia to fuel its ambitious nuclear energy plans and, initially, the John Howard government in 2007 agreed in principle to be the provider of the mineral. The Howard government's decision was probably taken in part to help the United States which by then had started to build up India as a counter to China but also to promote Australia's own interests. The argument made was that if Australia was selling to China, why could it not sell to the other large nation in Asia, India? What made the Howard government's decision all the more significant was that there had been a bipartisan consensus in Australia between the Liberal and Labor parties to not sell uranium to countries that were not signatories to the NPT. In 2009, the Labor government of Kevin Rudd reversed the Howard decision and backed away from the sale.[37] In 2011, Rudd's successor, Julia Gillard, agreed to change Australian policy to sell uranium to India (although she expected considerable opposition from within her own party).[38] Australia would be an important supplier to India both because of its political reliability and ease of doing business and framing contracts in the country. The issue of security in the Indian Ocean is one where the two nations can cooperate quite effectively since the constraints that apply to India in the Persian Gulf or for that matter in South East Asia are not present in the relationship with Canberra.

In a 2011 paper brought out by the Heritage Foundation, Sydney's Lowy Institute, and New Delhi's Observer Research Foundation, the authors identified sea-lane security, counterterrorism, nonproliferation, and disaster relief as possible areas in which Australia and India could cooperate.[39] Maritime security is important for both nations since a bulk of their trade passes through either the Indian or Pacific Oceans, and meeting challenges like piracy require cooperation. Although India has favored bilateral attempts to combat piracy, it is argued that antipiracy operations could constitute greater cooperation between the United States, India, and Australia, and perhaps lead in the future to discussions in broader international forums.[40] Counterterrorism is an area where all three nations could cooperate and Indian antiterrorism units, which were found wanting in the 2008 Mumbai attack, could receive better training from both Australia and the United States. But the main issue on which India would have an interest in seeking a strategic relationship with Australia is how to deal with the rise of China.

AUSTRALIA AND ASIA

For Australia, the broader Asian region is really North East Asia—specifically China and Japan. China (despite the 2003 U.S.–Australia free trade agreement) is now Australia's largest trading partner while Japan is now its second-largest partner (after having been the largest trading partner for some years).[41] The Australians share the same dilemmas that other Asian states face about the peace and stability in Asia. First, they are concerned about how to shape the relationship with China, and second, they are worried about an emerging rivalry between the United States and China in the Asian region adversely impacting Australia. Like other Asian countries, Australia recognizes the enormous economic value that China's rise is bringing to the region—a large portion of Australia's commodity exports now goes to China and probably the main reason that Australia did not fall into a recession after the 2008 global financial crisis was the sale of commodities to China. At the same time, like other countries in the region, it is concerned about China's possible political and military forays.

Hugh White points out that the rise of China could go along several paths. The ideal path would be one where Beijing accepted American hegemony and continued a peaceful rise to the position of a great power—albeit under American tutelage. White, however, is not optimistic about such an outcome and, therefore, projects other potentially disastrous outcomes like a Cold War between China and the United States, China successfully shutting the United States out of Asia (an alternative that would be difficult for Australia to accept), and, worst of all, armed conflict between the two countries.[42]

Given Australia's economic connection with China and its worries about Chinese expansionism in Asia, Canberra has sought to strengthen its alliances with traditional allies like the United States and Japan but also, since 2007, sought to strengthen the relationship with India and other nations in the region. For India, the Australians perceive its greater involvement in Asian regional institutions as a hedge against China. Rory Medcalf makes the case for such cooperation by arguing that:

> The two countries have a strong interest in working together to help accommodate China's rise but in such a way that Beijing does not become destabilisingly dominant.

Australia and India could thus affirm the intent to develop Asian regional bodies in which they are both members, which help to sustain deep US engagement in the region, and which could help reduce the risks of conflict.[43]

For Australia, the acceptable rise of China would possibly include the following elements that are, in fact, shared by other Asian states. First, China must show a commitment to an Asian Free Trade Zone (FTZ) that extends beyond increasing economic integration. For such an FTZ to work, the Chinese would have to help establish secure trade routes and facilitate the reduction of tensions in the various subregions of Asia. China's attitude to issues of insecurity in Asia has been one of taking a backseat to ones that are not central to its own security dilemma. Thus, Beijing was reluctantly dragged into the six-party talks to help find a solution to the North Korean nuclear issue. Making an FTZ work, however, will require China to play a more proactive role in managing regional security issues.

Second, like every other country in the Asian region, Australia would like to see a peaceful resolution of the Taiwan issue. A peaceful reunification would go a long way to assure other countries about the fact that Beijing has not only transformed economically, but also finally and firmly moved away from the politics of a Cold War, revolutionary, non–status quo state.

Third, China will have to take a serious stance on nonproliferation. When the Libyans handed over the bomb design they got from Pakistani scientist A. Q. Khan, it turned out to be of Chinese origin. The Chinese could do more to halt North Korea's onward march to a WMD force, especially since their own security environment would worsen dramatically if the North Koreans went overtly nuclear—particularly if it resulted in Japan deciding to exercise its nuclear option.

Finally, Australia would like to work hard to lessen potential tensions between the United States and China as well as between Japan and China. Being on good terms with all three states, Australia would like to use its good offices to help facilitate mutual understanding between these countries. In return, it would like China to be willing to make symbolic gestures to keep relations on an even keel. Australia would like China to be refraining from engaging in damaging exchanges with Japan, as happened over the Yasukuni shrine during the Koizumi administration, or the tensions that erupted between the two countries over the Japanese seizing of a Chinese fishing boat in disputed waters.[44] Getting China to accept Japan's return to a normal role in international relations, as Alan Dupont suggests, would be another issue.[45] Australia would also see its role as helping the United States and China create a joint vision on the future of the Asia-Pacific region. Getting China to work along these lines will require strong Australian diplomatic efforts with both the United States and Japan—countries with whom it is already talking about the emerging security system in Asia. In this context, a recent joint policy paper by Indian, American, and Australian think tanks called for a U.S.–India–Australia trilateral dialogue similar to the U.S.–India–Japan trilateral dialogue and the U.S.–Japan–Australia trilateral dialogue.[46]

INDIA AND JAPAN

The India–Japan relationship has blossomed in the past decade because of the rise of China and both countries' efforts to hedge against this growth in Beijing's power. Facilitating this shift has been the growth of U.S.–India relations, which have allowed traditional U.S. allies like South Korea, Australia, and Japan to reshape their foreign policies to take advantage of the regional maneuverability provided by engaging with India in Asia. In the Japanese context, the new relationship has emerged due to common concerns about China, the need to maintain maritime security, the opportunity provided by the economic growth of India, and the fact that India is a democratic state.

The affinity provided by sharing common democratic values is an important one for India, which in its immediate neighborhood faces states that have had a difficult time ensuring that democratic systems stay in place. This in part explains the tensions between India and its neighbors, with the latter worrying about what impact the existence of a large, cantankerous, and noisy democracy on their borders will have on their own people. No such tensions exist further from South Asia, where India's physical size, its military capability, its economic market, and its democratic ideals become advantageous to nations that seek to bring about a new security architecture in Asia. In the Japanese case, the unique history with India, where New Delhi does not put the history of World War II as a burden on Tokyo's shoulders, is an additional advantage toward framing a cooperative relationship.

Economically speaking, trade between the two countries has lagged behind that between China and India, with the bilateral trade being about $13 billion in 2008.[47] And in terms of Japan–China trade, the India–Japan trade relationship is insignificant. In terms of Official Development Assistance, however, India has become the largest recipient of official Japanese assistance. The problem is that Japan lagged behind other investors in India since its focus was on South East Asia.[48] There is now, however, a renewed commitment toward India given Tokyo's decision to invest in the Delhi–Mumbai Industrial Corridor. The corridor is to consist of 24 industrial cities built from scratch along a 920 mile route. India will commit $4.5 billion to the project and the Japanese government is expected to match this amount to kick-start the project. The Indian government believes that this initial commitment will encourage other investors to come up with the rest of the $90 odd billion required to complete the ambitious project, which would require not only the building of industry but also of infrastructure.[49] The project when it gets off the ground would dramatically reshape the economic potential of what is already one of the most booming parts of the nation, but skeptics point out that corruption, a creaking bureaucracy, battles over land acquisition could make the project a failure.[50] On the other hand, the success of the Japanese in making the New Delhi metro an efficient and cost-effective system leads analysts to be more optimistic about the prospects of this joint venture.

Perhaps the most important economic contribution Japan can make to India is in the energy field. Because of the atomic bombings of Hiroshima and Nagasaki, Japan has been in the forefront of opposing the proliferation of nuclear weapons, and this has been one of the reasons for discord in the India–Japan relationship. Since the U.S.–India nuclear deal, however, Japan has engaged India about the transfer of nuclear technology. Indo-Japanese talks were stalled after the Fukushima disaster. Since then Japan has reached nuclear technology agreements with Vietnam, Jordan, South Korea, and Russia, but according to foreign minister Kiochiro Gemba, Japan still hoped to reach agreements with Brazil, India, and Turkey.[51] Hurt by a decline in external demands for its traditional exports, Japan needs the revenues that its nuclear exports would bring. In the Indian context though, Japan can provide energy and environmental products that are of pressing need to India, which has to resolve the environmental problems of its growing population as well as meet its rapidly increasing demand for energy. Japan will set up three projects in India—a solar power generation system, a seawater desalination plant, and a gas-fired power generation plant—along the Delhi–Mumbai Industrial Corridor.[52]

But the most important change in the Japan–India relationship is emerging in the security realm because of the rise of Chinese power and the unease with which it is looked at in both Tokyo and New Delhi. In 2001, the two countries initiated a strategic dialogue that has since grown, in 2008, into an agreement for a Strategic and Global Partnership.[53] The partnership covers areas such as sea-lane safety, defense collaboration, disaster management, and counterterrorism. As one observer pointed out, the strategic relationship between the two countries would help counter the power disequilibrium in Asia that is emerging from the rise of China.[54]

INDIA AND THE INDO-PACIFIC

The Indian interests in the Indo-Pacific region emerge from energy requirements, the need for maritime security, a continuance of free trade, and working to accommodate or manage the rise of China. In one sense, all of these issues have some connection to the rise of China: Beijing's lockdown of existing energy supplies and its claims to large swaths of potentially rich energy zones like the South China Sea raise concerns in Asian capitals; for some nations in Asia maritime security is compromised by the rise of the Chinese Navy; and trade, as Japan found out when China stopped the export of rare earth minerals, can be held hostage to geopolitics.

The response in Asia has been to bring about a set of multilateral institutions that, on the one hand, bring the nations of the region together in economic networks and, on the other hand, bring together these countries in a political framework where certain rules for maintaining regional order can be made. Additionally, some degree of security cooperation has emerged between these nations as common problems like piracy, the transfer of WMD, and the potential threat to shipping lanes have required coordinated responses. In this environment, India, till recently, was, as C. Raja Mohan put it, concentrated on its national development and essentially pursued a policy of wanting the great powers to vacate the Indian Ocean.[55] With the rise of Chinese naval power and China's broader goals, this approach has changed as India now seeks to engage countries in the region to enhance its own maritime security.

Engagement with these nations, however, is complicated by the fact that the whole of Asia depends on the Chinese economy for its current and future health. Thus, major U.S. allies like South Korea, Japan, and Australia (as well as the vulnerable-to-Chinese-takeover nation of Taiwan) all have stronger trade relationships with Beijing than they do with Washington, but it is the latter who they see as their security guarantor. India falls within the same security dilemma for while it has significant security issues with China it is Beijing that is now New Delhi's largest trading partner. Thus, like all Asian nations, India is attempting to reconcile its economic ties and security concerns with China. Coupled with the economic pressure is the fact that India has yet to feel comfortable with closer security relationships—that might border on alliances—with other Asian nations.

As a consequence, the vehicle for increased security has been the development of the term strategic partnership. In essence, it offers nations the ability to engage in a security dialogue without creating the tensions brought about by a formal alliance. Thus, by engaging in a strategic partnership, nations can exchange ideas on what may be common security interests and they can carry out joint military exercises without projecting the hostility and countermeasures that a formal alliance system engenders. Thus, in the past decade, India has engaged in military exercises with many of the nations of Asia as well as the United States, and these have been useful in allowing the participating nations to work toward understanding each other's military cultures, working toward interoperability, and in planning for future possible security contingencies.

It has also allowed India to move away from the old defensive policy of countering Chinese moves in the Indian Ocean by slowly moving into China's sphere of influence—notably the South China Sea and North East Asia. The military cooperation with Vietnam and Japan should be seen in this context as an attempt to reverse the Chinese strategy of encroachment into South Asia by encroaching into what Beijing views as its own preserve.

While not creating a formal alliance structure, the new set of strategic partnerships may do what Indian strategists had thought would be a viable deterrent against China in the 1960s. At that point of time, Indian strategic thinkers were calling for the development of an Indian nuclear weapons program with the express purpose of countering China. The twist was, however, as the Indian economist Raj Krishna wrote, that India did not need to match the Chinese weapon for weapon in the attempt to achieve nuclear deterrence.[56] Instead, Krishna argued that India need only build a limited number of bombs and in doing so would complicate China's strategic calculus since Beijing would now have to deal with American, Russian, and Indian nuclear forces in the region. That, consequently, would lead to what Krishna called the "division of labor of deterrence," since India's nuclear forces would create further strategic uncertainty for China. The current move toward strategic partnerships in the region could work in a similar way since it might increase Chinese uncertainty and thereby lead to more caution on Beijing's part in exercising its military capability.

The Indo-Pacific region is also emerging as the area of international economic opportunity with China and potentially India becoming the two drivers for global demand. Under the old Asia-Pacific rubric of economic cooperation, India was excluded from the benefits of joining regional economic forums. Moreover, its restrictive trade and economic policies made Indian participation in such ventures somewhat meaningless. As the Indian economy grows and there is an inexorable move toward integrating India into the global economy, we are seeing New Delhi becoming eager to join regional economic arrangements. At the same time, the nations of the region are working to finally include India into these economic groups. The stakes are high for New Delhi since how well it enters these regional economic groups may well determine the future of India's long-term economic progress.

NOTES

1. Hillary Rodham Clinton, "America's Engagement in the Asia-Pacific," Remarks, Kahala Hotel, Honolulu, HI, October 28, 2010, http://www.state.gov/secretary/rm/2010/10/150141.htm.

2. Christophe Jaffrelot, "India's Look East Policy: An Asianist Strategy in Perspective," *India Review* 2, no. 2 (2003): p. 37.

3. http://news.bbc.co.uk/2/hi/southasia/6960017.stm.

4. Tan Tai Yong and See Chak Mun, "The Evolution of India–ASEAN Relations," *India Review* 8, no. 1 (2009): p. 22.

5. For a discussion, see Purnendra Jain, "Westward Ho! Japan Eyes India Strategically," *Japanese Studies* 28, no. 1 (2008): p. 17.

6. Tan Tai Yong and See Chak Mun, "The Evolution of India–ASEAN Relations," p. 22.

7. Rajiv Sikri, "India's 'Look East' Policy," *Asia-Pacific Review* 16, no. 1 (2009): p. 132.

8. Ibid., pp. 134–35.

9. P. R. Kumaraswamy, "Realism Replacing Rhetoric: Factors Shaping India's Middle East Policy," *The Round Table* 97, no. 397 (2008): p. 581.

10. Smrutti S. Pattanaik, "Bangladesh and the TATA Investment: Playing Politics with Economics," *IDSA COMMENT,* May 11, 2006, http://www.idsa.in/idsastrategiccomments/BangladeshandtheTATAInvestmentSSPattanaik110506.

11. "Dubai Ports World to Invest $2 Billion in India Operations," *Domain B.Com,* March 12, 2007, http://www.domain-b.com/economy/infrastructure/ports/20070312operations.html.

12. "Dubai Ports World's India Container Port to Challenge Colombo," *Business Standard,* May 13, 2010.

13. Zakir Hussain, "India Woos GCC's Sovereign Wealth Fund: Policy, Scope and Precautions," IDSA Policy Brief, June 26, 2009, http://idsa.in/policybrief/IndiaWoosGCCsSovereignWealthFundzhussain260609.

14. Abhijit Iyer-Mitra, "Debate: Is a Nuclear Iran Good for India?," *Article #3423,* Institute for Peace and Conflict Studies, New Delhi, July 11, 2011, http://www.ipcs.org/article/india/debate-is-a-nuclear-iran-good-for-india-3423.html.

15. Sudha Ramachandran, "India–Iran Relations at Nadir," *Asia Times,* December 4, 2010.

16. K. Alan Kronstadt and Kenneth Katzman, "India–Iran Relations and U.S. Interests," *CRS Report for Congress,* RS22486, August 6, 2007, p. 6.

17. Ramachandran, "India–Iran Relations at Nadir."

18. Kronstadt and Katzman, "India–Iran Relations and U.S. Interests."

19. Atul Aneja, "Oil Payment Row and India–Iran Ties," *The Hindu,* August 1, 2011.

20. Ramachandran, "India–Iran Relations at Nadir."

21. Jim Yardley, "India's Diplomatic Balancing Act; with Iranian Delegation in Delhi, Clinton Seeks to Isolate Tehran Further," *International Herald Tribune,* May 9, 2012.

22. Tracey Quek, "U.S. Exempts India from Iran Sanctions; Strategic Move Ahead of Talks Follows Cuts by India in Iranian Oil Purchases," *The Straits Times,* June 13, 2012.

23. Aneja, "Oil Payment Row and India–Iran Ties."

24. "Indo-Iranian Relationship: Former Ambassadors to Iran Share Their Views," *The Hindu,* March 15, 2011.

25. "India Has Stakes in Wider Gulf Region: Indian NSA," December 6, 2011, Defense Forum of India, http://defenceforumindia.com/foreign-relations/28308-india-has-stakes-wider-gulf-region-indian.html.

26. Samir Pradhan, "India's Economic and Political Presence in the Gulf: A Gulf Perspective," *India's Growing Role in the Gulf: Implications for the United States,* Gulf Research Center Dubai, 2009, pp.19–20.

27. Harsh Pant, "India's Relations with Iran: Much Ado about Nothing," *The Washington Quarterly,* 34, no. 1 (2011): pp. 67–68.

28. Ibid.

29. Ibid, p. 68.

30. C. Raja Mohan, "India's Strategic Challenges in the Indian Ocean and the Gulf," *India's Growing Role in the Gulf: Implications for the United States,* Gulf Research Center Dubai, 2009, p. 61.

31. Pradhan, "India's Economic and Political Presence in the Gulf," p. 16.

32. Raja Mohan, "India's Strategic Challenges in the Indian Ocean and the Gulf," p. 66.

33. For a discussion of the early India–Australia relationship and its limitations, see Sally Percival Wood, "So Where the Bloody Hell Are We? The Search for Substance in Australia–India Relations," *The Fearless Nadia Papers,* vol. 1, 2011, pp. 2–4.

34. For a discussion of the White Australia policy and the reasons for its demise, see Gwenda Tavan, "The Dismantling of the White Australia Policy: Elite Conspiracy or Will of the Australian People?" *Australian Journal of Political Science,* 39, no. 1 (March 2004): pp. 109–25.

35. Rory Medcalf, "Problems to Partnership: A Plan for Australia–India Strategic Ties," *Lowy Institute Policy Brief,* November 2009, p. 10.

36. Ibid, p. 4.

37. Katharine Murphy, "Digging in on Uranium," *The Age,* Melbourne, November 17, 2011, p. 13.

38. Greg Sheridan and Imre Salusinszky, "PM's Uranium Backflip Opens US Door to Delhi. PLAN TO END INDIAN EXPORT BAN OPENS RIFTS IN LABOR," *The Australian,* November 16, 2011.

39. Shared Goals, *Converging Interests:A Plan for U.S.–Australia–India Cooperation in the Indo–Pacific,* Washington, DC, The Heritage Foundation, 2011, p. ii.

40. Ibid, p. 5.

41. See "Australia's Top 10 Two-Way Trading Partners and Australia's Top 10 Exports, Goods & Services," http://www.dfat.gov.au/trade/focus/081201_top10_twoway_exports.html.

42. Hugh White, "The Limits to Optimism: Australia and the Rise of China," *Australian Journal of International Affairs,* 59, no. 4 (2005): p. 477.

43. Medcalf, "Problems to Partnership," p. 9.

44. Peter Ford, "China Japan Territorial Spat over a Fishing Boat Flares," *The Christian Science Monitor,* September 10, 2010.

45. Alan Dupont, "Unsheathing the Samurai Sword: Japan's Changing Security Policy," *Lowy Institute Paper 03,* 2004, p. 58.

46. "Shared Goals, Converging Interests: A Plan for U.S.–Australia–India Cooperation in the Indo–Pacific," The Heritage Foundation, Washington, DC, 2011, p. 2.

47. Figures from February 2011, http://www.mofa.go.jp/region/asia-paci/india/index.html.

48. Madhuchanda Ghosh, "India and Japan's Growing Synergy: From a Political to a Strategic Focus," *Asian Survey,* 48, no. 2 (2008): p. 294.

49. "India Plans Industrial Corridor Bigger than Japan," *The Economic Times,* October 26, 2011.

50. Ibid.

51. Anthony Rowley, "Japan MPs Okay 4 Nuke Deals," *The Business Times,* Singapore, December 10, 2011.

52. "Japan, India to Push Ahead on Three Infrastructure Projects," *BBC Monitoring Asia Pacific*—Political, December 25, 2011.

53. Rajaram Panda and Victoria Tuke, "India–Japan–US Trilateral Dialogue: A Promising Initiative," *IDSA Issue Brief,* November 22, 2011, p. 4.

54. Brahma Chellany, "Toward Asian Power Equilibrium," *The Hindu,* November 1, 2008.

55. C. Raja Mohan, "Indo-Pacific Naval Cooperation Open to India and Canberra," *The Australian,* November 2, 2011.

56. Raj Krishna, "India and the Bomb," *India Quarterly* 21, no. 2 (1965): p. 128.

CHAPTER 9

India: Emerging Power
or Always the Bridesmaid?

As India heads into the next decade, it faces internal security challenges, an immediate region that is conflict-ridden, and the rise of China as a superpower that threatens to halt New Delhi's own rise to great power status and to constrain the country's economic development. On the other hand, the past two decades have witnessed a real change within India in terms of how business is done, in the outward orientation of the nation, and in the increasing confidence of the young population that makes up the majority of the country to successfully compete in the international arena. How India is able to marshal its internal resources to cope with the challenges of the internal and external environments will make for the future success of the country. The optimists see a vibrant India with a large middle class that goes up the value chain in production and creates broad-based domestic consumer demand. The same optimists also see an India that is likely to be far more proactive in international affairs by using its growing military capability to help maintain international order. There is also a pessimistic view on India that sees the country increasingly trapped within its domestic problems where caste, religious tensions, regional squabbles, and democratic gridlock force the nation to look inward and not convincingly ascend to the international stage. The truth, as is the case in any such discussion, lies somewhere in the middle.

Three major security challenges confront India in its quest to attain a more prominent role in the international arena: the challenge of domestic insurgencies, a chaotic region, and the rise of China. The first of these has been a challenge that India has faced since independence, and it led the observer Selig Harrison to write a book in 1960 titled, *India: The Most Dangerous Decades*. Harrison essentially saw India torn apart by centrifugal tendencies and headed possibly toward authoritarianism.[1] India has defied that logic and survived a series of challenges to its territorial integrity. In the 1940s, the Nehru government was able to put down a Communist uprising in Telangana and Nehru was able to persuade the Communists to participate in the electoral process—something that they have done with considerable success since the first national elections in 1952. After the uprising, Nehru banned the Indian Communist party in only two states, and once the Communist leadership accepted the legitimacy of the Indian state they were allowed to function freely and the party actually was the largest opposition group in parliament, with 30 seats after the 1952 elections.[2] Subsequent attempts by left-wing groups to stage a proletarian revolution—most notably the Naxalite revolts of the late 1960s and early 1970s—were also met with state repression, but the Indian government was careful to leave the door open for negotiations with the group, and once the Naxalite revolt was crushed in West Bengal the mainstream Communist parties in the state formed an alliance that remained in power for more than three decades by enacting significant land reforms and other social measures.

An insurgency in the Indian northeast began in the 1950s, largely due to the ineffectiveness of what was then the provincial government in Guwahati and the sense of alienation subsequently felt by the people of the region vis-à-vis New Delhi, because of the way that region was recreated into what some claim were artificial political entities.[3] India has by and large managed to contain these insurgencies, and given the lack of external interest in sustaining these insurgencies—despite Indian claims of Pakistan's ISI actively promoting them—they have been contained to the point that the only real active insurgency remains the one in Nagaland—even though on issues like the Armed Forces Special Powers Act (passed in 1958 and still used throughout the region), public opinion can become inflamed very quickly. Even in Nagaland, however, there is peace between the Indian state and the Indian Army on the one hand and the rebel groups on the other. The killing and violence is between rebel groups that seek to gain greater influence within the state.[4] The Naga groups have moved from the jungles to the towns to engage in urban criminality:

> The character of Naga insurgency has changed over the years. No longer [sic] the guerrillas contemplate a life in jungle hideouts. The scene of action has shifted to towns. In the early years the emphasis was on mass mobilisation and guerrilla tactics of hit and run. Now the emphasis is on extortion, kidnapping, arm-twisting and blackmail. The community is held to ransom by fear of militants who are running a parallel government. Every government employee including ministers pay a part of their salary to the underground as tax. So do professionals like doctors, traders and shop owners. For every contract, a commission is paid to one militant group or the other: The exchequer is part financing the insurgency.[5]

The fact of the matter is that the northeast is too far away from India's political heartland and the insurgencies are too small to effectively pose a challenge to the Indian state. A different situation exists in Kashmir.

In Kashmir, as in the northeast, the alienation of the people from the Indian government took place because of widespread corruption, the rigging of elections, and when the Kashmiri insurgency began in the 1980s, the resulting public backlash against the harsh measures used by the security forces to quell the rebellion. The Indian government has attempted negotiations with rebel groups and actually helped prop up the Hurriyat—an umbrella organization of 23 separatist groups—in order to continue a dialogue with the people of the region. There have also been elections to the state assembly, but the indigenous leadership that has emerged has done little to bring about the development of the people. Thus, alienation from the Indian government and its harsh policies, the lack of good and responsible representation, chronic underdevelopment, and corruption when combined with the large-scale support for jihadi organizations from Pakistan have led to a long and bloody conflict between rebel groups and the Indian state, with the Kashmiri civilian caught in the crosshairs.

Like other insurgencies in India, the Kashmiri one has reached a point of exhaustion, as more than 20 years of fighting have left the insurgents and the local population weary of the conflict. The other important turning point has been the increasing chaos in Pakistan and the violence that has ensued from it, making the Pakistani option a less attractive one for the Kashmiri people. Neither exhaustion nor the deteriorating security situation in Pakistan has worked, however, to shift the balances of political forces in favor of the Indian government. That will take a long concerted effort of confidence building, sustained economic development, and better governance on the part of the Indian government. At the same time, the Indian government and the general Indian public are not likely to make significant concessions as long as terrorist activities continue, particularly like the attack on Mumbai in 2008. There is also the fact that is usually ignored in the discussions on Kashmir that close to 40 percent of the population of the Indian part of the state is Hindu, Buddhist, Sikh, and Christian and the only voice that is heard in the international arena is that of the Kashmiri Muslim. In the 1990s, the ethnic cleansing of Srinagar took place when Kashmiri Hindus were forced to leave the city en masse.

The Indian government and Indian public opinion are more likely to work toward greater autonomy for Kashmir—the position for which there is considerable support in Indian circles—if there is a formal renunciation of violence and the link with jihadi elements in Pakistan, and with the Pakistani security forces, is disavowed. The option of an independent Kashmiri state or one where territorial adjustments are made to accommodate Pakistan's interests is not possible in the near future since the Indian government continues to fear that such accommodations would serve as the thin end of the wedge for the territorial disintegration of the Indian state. At the very least, it would result in large-scale transfers of population that would revive memories and fears of the partition of India in 1947. There is also the hardening of Indian public opinion post-Mumbai 2008 that is not willing to make concessions to Pakistan or to domestic groups because of being seen as cowing down to terrorism.

What is most likely though is that India will continue to maintain its current strategy in Kashmir, and if it can use the current level of exhaustion in Kashmir, which has led to a lull in the insurgency, to forge real political solutions, then there is hope for a long-lasting settlement in the state. Indian policymakers need to be cautious, however, in thinking that the current political turmoil in Pakistan can allow them to put Kashmir on the back burner. Once the United States has left Afghanistan, it will leave Islamabad free to pursue its traditional foreign policy agenda in Kashmir along with the jihadi activity that fuels it. In such circumstances, it is best to get a real peace process, significant investment in infrastructure, and a concrete development plan in place so that there can be a noticeable turnaround in the economic and political situation in the state.

THE SOUTH ASIAN REGION

The criticism made about India's drive to great power status is that unless it resolves the problems it has in the region it will remain locked in a series of disputes that drain its energies and do not enhance its capabilities. In the Indian case, this largely means the relationship with Pakistan, but one can make a similar argument for the relationship with Nepal and Bangladesh where Indian diffidence or lack of interest has led to two vital relationships not reaching their full potential. The Sheikh Hasina government in Bangladesh has made the normalization of relations with India a priority and it was expected that the summit meeting between the two countries in Dhaka, in September 2011, would bring the relationship to a higher level. Yet, Indian domestic politics led to a serious opportunity being wasted by the government in New Delhi. While the border dispute between the two countries was resolved, the sharing of the Teesta River waters was not due to domestic political wrangling in India. This in turn stalled the negotiations for opening up Bangladesh to transit trade from the Indian northeast.[6] As commentators point out, India lost a genuine opportunity to change the relationship with Bangladesh for the better and, not surprisingly, Dhaka has been making overtures to Beijing for increased trade connections and investments. This undermines India's game plan for keeping China out of the South Asian region.

Similarly, in Nepal, the Indian government has, due to its geographic proximity, been able to get the Communists to contest and, perhaps unexpectedly, win the elections. Yet, the Chinese have been the most proactive in providing aid and assistance to the new government, and this has again led to concerns in New Delhi about growing Chinese encirclement of the region. More fundamentally, the real problem is not so much of anti-Indian regimes in the nations of South Asia or, for that matter, of terrorist groups operating out of them. The issue is the long-term development of India, which essentially requires integrating the South

Asian region to avail of its full potential. The water resources of the region cannot be successfully harnessed unless there is cooperation between India, Nepal, Bhutan, and Bangladesh on the eastern flank of India. For Bangladesh, the bulk of its rivers dry up in the summer months and then overflow causing damaging floods in the monsoon. Similarly, when water levels are low in Nepal, electricity production drops sharply and the country depends on expensive diesel fuel to run generators and produce electricity. That this situation is causing economic deprivation and environmental degradation is obvious to all the states in the region. On the western flank, India and Pakistan have to work together to harness the resources of the Indus Valley system that is central to the agriculture of both nations. A water- and energy-starved Pakistan and an India that has a booming population with similar requirements will now have to cooperate and manage the water resources of the Indus far more efficiently in order to plan for future survival and potentially greater prosperity in the coming decades. Given the long lead times that will be required in all these countries to acquire financing, work to overcome opposition—either legal or grassroots based—to the acquisition and loss of land to hydroelectric projects, and the myriad treaties that will have to be worked out between the countries themselves, time may be running out on the nations of South Asia to achieve such developmental goals.

Pakistan provides a different set of challenges to India that range from terrorism, to nuclear and conventional war, to water resource issues. At the core of the dispute between the two countries is the issue of identity where Pakistan struggles with defining what kind of Islamic country it is and how it should distribute goods and services in a national setting to achieve some degree of egalitarianism. India has moved to become a nation that has a commitment to democracy and claims to try to bring about greater equality for its citizens. Part of this schism is the role of the military in both societies. In India, in spite of the occasional resort to legal measures, the Indian military has remained by and large apolitical and respected the civilian control of the military that is prescribed in the Indian Constitution. In contrast, Pakistan has become, as Stephen Cohen puts it, an army that owns a state (although one may now make the argument that it is an intelligence agency that controls an army that owns the state).[7] For the Pakistani military to retain its position of power and privilege, it has to be viewed by the Pakistani public as the defender against encroachments by Hindu India that seeks to either dismember Pakistan or, at the very least, make it a weak client state. While this rationale has lost its relevance in international circles where a shift is taking place toward worrying less about India and Kashmir and more about the domestic society and economy, it still has legs in Pakistan. Given this predicament, the Pakistani military cannot afford peace with India since it would almost certainly lead to serious questions being raised by the Pakistani intelligentsia and public about why so much money was being spent on propping up the nation's armed forces? Maintaining a level of tension with India therefore becomes a necessity for the survival of the Pakistani military, which hopes to continue receiving a generous share of the Pakistani budget. What complicates the India–Pakistan relationship is the fact that both nations have nuclear weapons and this has made both sides search for strategies with which to coerce each other and to maintain the nuclear balance.

The general argument is that after both nations achieved an overt nuclear capability in 1998 it permitted Pakistan to use coercive techniques at lower ends of the escalation ladder to try and resolve its outstanding disputes with India, most notably the Kashmir conflict. In actual fact, Pakistan, even before its acquisition of a nuclear capability, had trained Indian insurgents in Punjab during the 1980s. But its going covertly nuclear in 1987 coincided with the breakout of the insurgency in Indian Kashmir, and one can speculate that the acquisition of nuclear weapons encouraged Islamabad to train and arm the Kashmiri jihadis to wage war against India. For India, seeking ways to coerce a nuclear-armed Pakistan from backing the jihadis became a central concern.

The matter was driven home by the Kargil conflict of 1999 when India, worried about a limited conflict escalating into something more serious, scrupulously avoided crossing the international border with Pakistan for fear of making the conflict escalate into something far more serious. As a consequence, the Indian Army took significant casualties while taking back the mountain peaks from Pakistan. Had the Indian Air Force been allowed to cross the border, it could have interdicted Pakistani supply lines to the troops that had been placed on the peaks.

The limits of Indian conventional capability were once again brought out when the two countries almost went to war after the attack on the Indian parliament in December 2001. The Indian military was massed along the border, as was Pakistan's, and eventually the Indian government agreed to pull its troops back on Paksitani assurances that Islamabad would no longer support jihadi groups.

The inability to go across the border without potentially triggering a nuclear war led to the development of the Cold Start doctrine by India (discussed earlier in the chapter on Pakistan). The Cold Start doctrine was meant to provide India with the ability to strike targets within Pakistan without triggering a full-fledged nuclear attack in response. While the shortcomings of the doctrine were to become apparent, the unintended consequence was to get Pakistan to develop a range of short-range tactical nuclear weapons that could be used in such a contingency to deter an Indian attack and yet, at the same time, prevent escalation to a full nuclear conflict. Pakistani development of this range of weapons has left India with the same question of how to use military power to coerce Pakistan to deter from using jihadis against India.

Indian answers on countering terrorism are not encouraging, but what is working against Pakistan in using this strategy is the internal consequences of jihadi warfare and the growing opprobrium in the international community against such tactics. Internally, the jihadi strategy has spawned a whole set of violent groups that now challenge the existing power structure within Pakistan. Internationally, Pakistan's brand name has suffered a serious blow as it is seen in the world as the epicenter of international terrorism. The consequence of this has been the slow shrinking of Pakistan's international contacts and the increasing reluctance of foreign corporations to invest in Pakistan.

From an Indian perspective, as noted earlier, the nuclear arsenal limits how India can counter Pakistan's support to terrorist actions in India. So what India can do is to, first, develop a coherent and effective antiterrorism capability and, second, work with the international community to convince Islamabad that its long-term interests lie in delinking itself from jihadi groups and their terrorist activities. This may take a long time, but the most compelling argument to be made to Pakistan is that it is slowly but surely falling economically, technologically, and educationally behind India. For Pakistan, securing its internal society and opening itself up to foreign investments will be the way to regain socioeconomic parity with India. That may be aided by three facts.

First, there is the fact that India is no longer the country of the 1960s that feared Pakistan. Instead, there is a growing belief among young Indians that Pakistan is irrelevant to the future of India. Indians see China now as the natural competitor. This permits Indians, if not threatened by terrorism, to largely ignore Pakistan—a kind of security through neglect for Pakistani decision makers. Second, the Afghan war is drawing to an end, and if the regime in Kabul is sensitive to Pakistan's interests, then it will be more likely to rein in the jihadi elements it has used to supplement its foreign and security policy. Third, for the long-term development of Pakistan, there has to be economic cooperation with India, particularly in the area of water resources. The granting of most favored nation status to India in November 2011 is a small but positive step in this direction.[8]

In summary, India will continue to expect a poor to at best indifferent relationship with Pakistan in the short to medium term, but what it can do is to try and lower the inflammatory rhetoric that has further complicated the relationship between the two countries over the past few years. The media in both countries is quick to accuse the other side of bad faith and in the Indian case of ISI-sponsored attacks and machinations. While some of this is true and using the media to highlight it makes useful points to the international community, the atmosphere created by the media in both nations makes it difficult for their leadership to sit down and quietly and effectively work to reduce tensions.

At a more practical level, the Indian government can do two things: first, discuss with Pakistan what can be done jointly by the two countries and then approach the international community for funding to carry out these projects. The second is to revive the discussions that began under President Pervez Musharraf about a solution to the Kashmir dispute.

The international community has responded positively when India and Pakistan have come forward with joint projects that benefit both nations. Thus, the

World Bank bankrolled the Indus Waters Treaty, and the Iran–Pakistan–India natural gas pipeline as well as the Turkmenestan–Afghanistan–Pakistan–India pipeline would gain international financing if they ever come to fruition. These are the kinds of projects that would lead to broader development and integrate the two nations in a way that they end up in a situation of mutual dependence. While the present security situation and the continuing animosity between the two countries may prevent such projects gaining acceptance in the short term, discussing them leads to putting down proposals that may be rapidly implemented in the future.

But the most promising avenue to stabilizing the relationship may lie in reviving the back channel discussions that were meant to bring about a solution to the long-running Kashmir dispute.[9] The two countries agreed to a series of measures to resolve the Kashmir issue that included making the border irrelevant by allowing free movement of populations and increased autonomy for the Kashmiri people. Other proposals included in the nonpapers were putting an end to debilitating proxy wars and instead building a new regime "of free trade and political cooperation in the region from Central Asia to Bangladesh."[10] Pessimism exists in New Delhi and even Washington that these steps were just diversionary measures taken by Islamabad to buy time, but in a new environment where Islamabad is facing a poor relationship with the United States and China is unwilling to step in as a major economic contributor, rapprochement with India is perhaps the wisest short-term measure that Pakistan could take. In short, India can live with a failing Pakistan and even take the occasional terrorist hit. What it could not live with is a Pakistan lowering the threshold on nuclear war or one which faces total collapse. Working to ensure that neither worst-case scenario occurs is, therefore, India's major priority in its Pakistan policy.

CHINA

India's major concern in the next 10–15 years remains China. Four specific issues are seen as creating tensions within the India–China relationship. First, there is the continued inability to resolve the border dispute, which in recent years has acquired new undertones due to the Tibetan issue. Second, there is the fear that China is seeking to lock down energy supplies across the world and thus indirectly perhaps prevent India's own attempts to acquire energy to feed its developmental needs. Third, India worries about the growing Chinese presence in the Indian Ocean region and Beijing's efforts to move into South Asia and undermine India's role as a natural leader of the region. Finally, the continued Chinese resistance to supporting India's bid to be a permanent member of the United Nations Security Council, when every other permanent member has supported India's ambition, leads New Delhi to believe that China is unwilling to let India rise to its natural status as the other Asian superpower.

The concern about China is, however, tempered by the fact that Indian analysts recognize that China's strategic goals are global and focused against the United States rather than concentrated on the South Asian region and India. The Indian Sinologist Alka Acharya argues that China's primary objective is to become the world's number one trading state and until it achieves that objective it is likely to play within the current economic and power structure of the international system.[11] Similarly, Jabin T. Jacob makes the point that, "India has intimations of greatness and the Chinese are in no mood to acknowledge the one country that more than the US, they realize resembles them and therefore has a right to all that they dream of achieving themselves." He continues, "India is a democracy, China is not (yet) and both will increasingly try to export their model of governance to the outside world as the US/West gives way. That's when the differences between China and India will matter both for themselves and the world—and the boundary dispute continuing does not affect matters one way or the other. For the moment though, both China and India have an extremely difficult task trying to shore up the legitimacy of their governance systems at home."[12]

Chinese internal problems and its competition with the United States, therefore, may be the larger drivers than any problems in the India–China relationship. Coupled with these views of Chinese long-term ambitions is the fact that India and China have not had a shooting incident along the border since 1967, so both countries, despite the rhetoric, have been able to keep tensions from escalating along the border.[13] As a consequence, Indian militarization to counter China—the acquisition of nuclear submarines and the development of long-range missiles—has proceeded at a leisurely pace, making it the very much the "creeping weaponization" that Ashley Tellis has used to discuss the development of India's nuclear weapons program.

The India–China relationship is further complicated because China is the goose that lays the economic golden egg in Asia. If one looks at the data for China's major trading partners, it becomes clear that despite the new U.S. pivot in Asia and the multiple economic arrangements between Washington and its Asian allies, China has emerged as the largest trading partner for all these countries.

As the two tables show, the economic health of all the major Asian countries, including India and Australia, rests in having a strong economic relationship with China, and no one in the Asian continent wants to kill this economic relationship with China because of issues of power politics. This economic compulsion is felt in India as well for every time a target to raise bilateral trade has been set by the two countries they have exceeded it ahead of schedule. Thus, India and China hope to have trade to the tune of $100 billion by the middle of the decade and neither side views this target as a difficult one to meet. The unintended effect of this growing trading interdependence has been the rise of a pro-Chinese constituency in the Indian business community that is manifested in the burgeoning of India–China friendship societies across the country.[14] Thus, there is

Table 9.1 China's Top Trade Partners in 2009 ($ billion)

Rank	Country/region	Volume	% change over 2008
1	United States	298.3	−10.6
2	Japan	228.9	−14.2
3	Hong Kong	174.9	−14.1
4	South Korea	156.2	−16.0
5	Taiwan	106.2	−17.8
6	Germany	105.7	−8.1
7	Australia	60.1	0.7
8	Malaysia	52.0	−3.0
9	Singapore	47.9	−8.8
10	India	43.4	−16.3

Source: PRC General Administration of Customs, *China's Customs Statistics*

Table 9.2 China's Top Trade Partners in 2010 ($ billion)

Rank	Country/region	Volume	% change over 2009
1	United States	385.3	29.2
2	Japan	297.8	20.2
3	Hong Kong	230.6	30.8
4	South Korea	207.2	32.6
5	Taiwan	145.4	36.9
6	Germany	142.4	34.8
7	Australia	88.1	46.5
8	Malaysia	74.2	42.8
9	Brazil	62.5	47.5
10	India	61.8	42.4

Source: PRC General Administration of Customs, *China's Customs Statistics*

a small but influential group emerging in India that is not driven by the country's national security agenda and the memories of 1962 but instead by the belief that the growing economic connection between the two nations could lead to a win-win situation. Added to this is the fact that if the two nations are in the long term able to reach a free trade agreement then the political considerations that constrain the relationship would have to take a backseat to the economic agenda.

Indian analysts thus do not see a militarized conflict between the two countries in the near future, although Srikanth Kondapalli warns that a flashpoint could occur due to misperceptions or miscommunications and this is something that both sides are careful to avoid.[15] The key issue in this regard is likely to be the future role of the Dalai Lama and the exiled Tibetan community that lives in India. While India has agreed that is a historical part of China and thus removed the threat of any lingering territorial claims to that province, it has not been willing to burn its bridges with the Tibetan community and hand them over to Chinese authorities.

What is the most likely scenario to emerge, therefore, is one where India continues to build up its conventional and nuclear capabilities but does nothing to seriously aggravate China. At the same time, the economic linkages continue to grow as India sees the benefit of a Chinese economic connection. Along with these trends, however, India is likely to pursue tough diplomatic bargaining with China in areas that are of core interests to it. India has, for instance, asserted its territorial claims over the province of Arunachal Pradesh by not allowing the Chinese government to get away with not requiring visas for Indian citizens from that region who seek to visit China. In such circumstances, India and China are likely to continue economic cooperation within a framework of political tension. The one outlier of course is how the Tibetan issue is handled by both countries in the future.

INDIA IN ASIA

While India will be careful not to antagonize China, it will be increasingly willing to work to preserve order in the Indian Ocean and the Indo-Pacific region. Like the other nations of Asia, India recognizes the enormous economic potential that exists in the region, the natural connectivity between the countries of Asia in this regard, and the fact that regional security in an expanded region called the Indo-Pacific will underpin this growing economic enterprise. In effect, this will mean working with regional nations to deal with issues such as piracy and weapons of mass destruction and ensuring the freedom of the sea lanes. The concept of a strategic partnership works well in these areas. The Indian government is keen to do this since it solves several of its security concerns at the same time. Specifically, it means that the Indian Ocean area is less dependent on external powers for the maintenance of peace and order, something that India has seen as being central to its foreign policy efforts since the 1970s. It also does not convey the impression in the region that India is a regional bully willing to exercise power indiscriminately. Instead, it shows an India that is willing to work with other nations and is sensitive to their security concerns.

Piracy has become a major issue that unites the nations of the Indian Ocean region because of its debilitating effect on the freedom of navigation. The Indian

Navy, after reluctantly being given permission by the Government of India, has successfully engaged pirates in the ocean. As its maritime capabilities grow, particularly its maritime air surveillance capabilities, this role will only become more important for the Indian Navy and see it working more extensively with the other navies of the region. Similarly, the concern about the proliferation of weapons of mass destruction is equally important to the nations of the region. The Indian Navy had apprehended a North Korean vessel carrying missiles to an undisclosed location. This problem has been one that India has worked extensively to counter. One will, therefore, see India proactively seeking a convergence of nations to deal with this issue in the near future.

The more difficult problem will be how to deal with China in the broader Asian context. The Indian government has moved away from its usual caution on this matter and has begun to engage China in its own backyard. In the past, India watched worriedly, and helplessly, as China made economic and political moves into South Asia and the Indian Ocean region. Thus, the Chinese buildup of Pakistan as well as their willingness to economically develop Sri Lanka and Nepal did not get countered by India. In the last few years, however, India has decided to be a more active player in China's backyard. It has a bourgeoning relationship with Taiwan and has sent and received ambassador-level representatives to that country. Trade between the two nations has also increased and Taiwanese firms, driven out of China, have started to invest in India, where they are better protected by the rule of law.

India has also built up a strong relationship with Vietnam, somewhat to the displeasure of China. Indo-Vietnamese relations have been excellent since the 1970s when India decided to grant full diplomatic recognition to then North Vietnam. In the period since then, the two countries have established a strategic relationship, with Vietnam allowing Indian naval vessels the right to berth in its ports. More recently, India has been invited by Vietnam to engage in oil and natural gas exploration in the South China Sea. This led to Chinese protests and a rebuke by the Indian prime minister to the Chinese president at the 2011 East Asia Summit.

The other Chinese neighbor that India has sought to expand its relationship with is South Korea. In July 2011, the two countries signed a nuclear cooperation agreement that will permit South Korea to transfer nuclear technologies to India's civilian nuclear sector.[16] This will be complemented by increasing economic cooperation between the two countries in areas such as shipbuilding and road development. Most importantly, the two countries will see an increase in defense cooperation. South Korea would like to export weaponry to the booming Indian arms market. It was, in fact, a finalist for supplying a basic trainer aircraft for India and its objections were taken seriously enough to review the decision to give the contract to Pilatus of Switzerland.[17] The other area where cooperation is likely to take place is in antiterrorism training and military officer training. India, therefore, while not provoking China, has sought to make it clear that like Beijing it sees the broader Asia continent as its sphere of operations.

But the most important spheres of activity for India within Asia will remain the consolidation of economic and political partnerships that enhance its interests in the larger international system. Thus, India has worked to join more and more regional groupings, like the East Asia summit and the various ASEAN groupings, and has sought membership of the Shanghai Cooperation Organization. International groupings, like the BRICs and IBSA (India, Brazil, South Africa), also give India the influence to redraw international outcomes to its liking. In actual fact, given India's economic limitations in comparison with China's vast economic capability, India's role is more likely, in the short term, to be what Ian Hall calls that of a spoiler—as was seen in the 2009 climate summit in Copenhagen. There, Indian and Chinese protests led to a redrafting of the final statement to accommodate New Delhi and Beijing's interests.

To sum up, India, given its pressing economic needs, is likely to increase links with the Asian countries to extract technology and greater economic investments. This strategy is working as countries as varied as Singapore and South Korea seek to increase their market share of the Indian market. At the same time, India, like other Asian countries, is seeking to hedge its bets against China by talking about future power political situations in Asia and how to counter them. What India would like, as would all of China's neighbors, is a Beijing that plays by the rules of the established Asian order—free trade, respect for sovereignty, and the peaceful resolution of disputes—rather than be a country that is bellicose and belligerent in its external behavior. And the thinking is that the more countries that subscribe to this strategy, the more likely it is that Beijing will feel the pressure to be a status quo state.

INDIA AND THE UNITED STATES

Ultimately, however, Indian attempts to gain greater influence in the world will rest on its future links with the United States. The good news on this front is that many of the issues that over the years divided the two democracies have been resolved. The United States no longer hyphenates the two countries when it talks about South Asia and, instead, treats India and Pakistan as separate entities. The United States has also accepted the fact that the more spectacular terrorist activity in India emanates from Pakistan, most probably with governmental assistance. And, most importantly, the United States sees India not only as a future strategic partner in Asia but also as an emerging power. The decision to sign the nuclear agreement with India—which changed India's status in the nuclear world—as well as President Obama's decision to support India's candidacy for a permanent seat in the Security Council reflect this changed attitude. At the same time, irritants remain like the unwillingness of India to buy fighter aircraft from the United States because of fears of constraints on technology transfers and the real danger of a supply cutoff in case of a major conflict.

The latter point, while important, has been overblown as India in the next decade is likely to not only become a major importer of American hardware but also become a major partner of the United States because of such purchases. India's proposed purchases include C-17 and C-130 transport aircraft, naval surveillance aircraft, and attack helicopters. When one combines the Indian heavy lift and surveillance capabilities with those of the United States in Asia, it will provide an important back up and possibly interoperability with the United States in Asia. In the long run, such interoperability and redundancy of transport and surveillance capabilities would have far greater positive implications for American military actions in Asia rather than any that could have emerged from the Indian purchase of fighter aircraft whose limited range would make them more useful for the defense of Indian soil.

For this relationship to prosper in the long term, however, certain irritants have to be removed. While the United States and India have made considerable progress on moving beyond the Pakistan issue, it remains a crucial factor to enable the success of the future relationship. India would want the United States to come down harder on the government in Islamabad on the issue of terrorism and to help resolve the status quo by presumably legalizing the existing division of Kashmir. While the United States' ability to achieve such a solution is rather low, what is likely to happen is that the U.S.–Pakistan relationship is likely to be normalized in the coming decade. Post-September 2001, Pakistan assumed an important role in the war against terrorism and Islamabad received both U.S. military and economic largesse.

With the war in Afghanistan winding down and the opening up of the northern supply route, Pakistan's importance to the United States will start to decline. Additionally, the lack of trust between the two countries—engendered by Pakistani support to the Haqqani network, the unwillingness to take appropriate antiterrorist measures within Pakistan, and the cloud that settled over the U.S.–Pakistan relationship because of the bin Laden raid—will not be mended easily. Secretary Panetta probably summarized the mood in Washington well when in January 2012 he stated in an interview that he believed that some officials in Pakistan must have known about bin Laden's presence in the Abbotabad compound.[18] Given these facts, it is likely that once the Afghanistan war ends, the United States will accord lesser importance to Pakistan and seek to increase the strength of the relationship with India.

The other fear is about the continued restrictions on technology transfers to India. That one will only resolve itself as both countries engage in greater levels of trade and commerce and there is more comfort on both sides with doing business with the other. The most problematic irritant perhaps is the residual feeling in India that nonalignment has served the country as an effective foreign policy for more than 60 years, so the question is raised about what is the need for aligning India so closely with the United States and, consequently, losing considerable Indian autonomy in international affairs. This view has prevailed among certain Indian policy circles, most notably the various Communist parties, for nearly two decades, but one must make the counterargument that in the emerging international system India will require more rather than less help from the United States to achieve its strategic objectives.

India specifically needs four major inputs to make its foreign and economic policies successful in the coming decades. First, the country needs to continue on a trajectory of fairly rapid economic development in order to accommodate the huge youth bulge that is coming through in the next 10–15 years. Secondly, India will require greater access to technology to boost its productivity and competitiveness in the international system. Thirdly, the nation will require guaranteed energy supplies if it has to meet its developmental and population challenges. And, finally, India will have to work with other nations, most particularly the United States, to hedge against the rise of a potentially hostile China.

Rapid economic development rests on boosting agriculture (because the majority of Indians still live in villages), attracting foreign direct investment (FDI), and creating a brand name for the country that makes it attractive to other nations as an investment destination. Boosting agricultural performance will require assistance from the United States, which remains the largest exporter of agricultural products in the world. In fact, agricultural cooperation is one of the major goals that New Delhi seeks to achieve in its relationship with Washington. Attracting FDI is more problematic. India's record of rampant corruption and bureaucratic bottlenecks has forced many companies that were thinking of investing in India to do a doublethink on investing there. In 2010, FDI fell by about 31 percent even as investors actively sought markets in the non-Western world.[19] This has led the Indian finance minister, Pranab Mukherjee, to try and encourage corporations to invest in India. The finance minister has stated that foreign individuals will be allowed to invest directly in the Indian stock market. Specialty realtors like Gap and Nike will be allowed to open wholly owned stores in the country and even Walmart will be eventually allowed to enter the Indian market. There are also signs that foreign airlines will be allowed to buy up to 49 percent share of Indian airlines—most Indian aviation companies being heavily in debt.[20]

While some of these issues have to be resolved through internal policy measures, the role of the United States in facilitating international investment cannot be underestimated. In the 1990s, it was the push by the Clinton administration that led to the flow of FDI into China and the escalation of the Chinese economic miracle. A similar effort by the United States may push the Indian economy to the next stage in investments. This issue is particularly salient in the current economic climate because of the large-scale withdrawal of institutional investments in the non-Western world and their transfer to the U.S. economy, which is viewed as the least risky in an international system that is plagued with financial woes.

The other part of the economic puzzle lies in creating a successful brand name for the country. India since the early 2000s has used slogans like "Shining India" to project its international brand image. This branding has been dented by internal scandals and a lack of performance when compared to China. While the United States cannot help create India's brand, it can help prop it up through strong support for the Indian economy in the short to medium term.

On the energy front, India's pressing energy needs require external help in unlocking a tight energy market and sometimes reluctant suppliers who feel unable to provide India with its energy requirements for political reasons. India has banked on building up its nuclear sector as part of the answer to meeting its shortfall in electricity. One stumbling block, for instance, was the reluctance of Australia to supply uranium for Indian reactors. This was only resolved during President Obama's 2011 trip to Australia when, reportedly, the United States suggested that the Labor government, which has a strong commitment to nuclear disarmament, provide fuel to India. U.S. assistance may also be needed in getting alternative suppliers of oil to India. Indian dependence on Iranian oil, for example, cannot be reduced unless the United States is willing to put pressure on its allies to supply petroleum to New Delhi.

The United States as a counter to China adds an important dimension to India's foreign policy in Asia by bringing in the remaining superpower to balance the growing one in the region. For India, working with the United States on a strategic partnership in Asia complicates the Chinese security agenda in the continent and its surrounding oceans. It thereby gives India additional space to execute its own foreign policy objectives in the region. The danger for India lies, however, in not appreciating the opportunity provided by this new American commitment to the Indo-Pacific region. India will have to, first, work with the United States and others to lay out what it sees as the new order in the Indo-Pacific region, in other words the rules that guide the interaction between states in the area. Second, it will have to work with the United States and others to persuade China that working within such regional order is in Beijing's best political and economic interests. But doing so will involve recognizing that China and its interests, as what will soon be the world's largest economy, will have to be accommodated in any such regional order.

The solution for India may well lie in what the Australian security analyst Hugh White calls the Concert of Asia. Under this proposal, India, the United States, Japan, and China work together to maintain the order that has existed in the Asian region since the early 1970s when the United States established primacy in the region.[21]

White persuasively argues that it will be difficult for the United States to maintain primacy in the coming years because of China's growing economic and military strength. At the same time, it would be dangerous for China to attempt its own hegemony over the region since other nations would work to counterbalance it and it would endanger Chinese economic policies. White, therefore, calls for a great powers concert in Asia based on the United Nations Charter to maintain the order that has worked so well over the past 40 years.[22] Order would suit Indian interests, as it would those of other Asian nations, because it would allow both for economic engagement with China and for the political balancing of Beijing. The question is of course what price the Chinese would expect for entering into such an agreement? And no one is sure of that. But India's best chance of achieving this is to work with the other major powers in the region, which would be the United States and Japan.

In the end, however, India's development as a great power will depend on how well it is able to transform its domestic economy and polity to start to resemble that of a 21st-century nation. As things stand, the Indian economy has elements of the 19th, 20th, and 21st century in it, with the former two dragging down the overall economic performance. Agriculture in some parts of India has yet to enter the 20th, let alone the 21st, century and a successful transition will require the modernization of this sector of the economy. Industries in India are plagued by labor disputes, protectionism, and the lack of a strategic vision. Again, there will be the need for revamping labor laws, allowing foreign investment in the stagnating and failing sectors of the economy, and developing a 21st-century infrastructure that will allow for the more efficient and effective movement of goods and services. Twenty-first century industries like information technology, a range of service industries, and pharmaceuticals, while being world class and generating high profits, employ small numbers of people. Thus, a lot of the promise of the modern Indian economic revolution is restricted to a small number of people. It is not spreading to the vast numbers that still live in poverty or semi-poverty in India.

For a genuine, lasting, and widespread change to take place in India, several policy challenges will have to be resolved. First, economic policies will have to encourage foreign investment to create new jobs in the country, particularly in the manufacturing sector. Obsolete policies that are the leftovers from Socialism will have to be put aside to encourage such investment. This is easier said than done given India's coalitional politics and the tendency of regional politicians to hold narrow, local, and short-term interests over national ones (national policies which, incidentally, usually help the very states that subvert them). The refusal of West Bengal's chief minister, Mamata Banerjee, to sign an India–Bangladesh agreement, which would have eventually benefitted her state, is a case in point. The real danger is that if the policy drift continues then it will be increasingly difficult to move the nearly 35 percent of Indians who live below the poverty line, and this will only perpetuate the internal violence that challenges the Indian state.

Secondly, there has to be a concerted effort to seriously improve the country's energy requirements and its environmental climate. India will have to double its installed power generation capacity to 300GW by 2017—a target that is extremely ambitious and based on a series of optimistic projections.[23] Achieving this will require timely completion of domestic power generation projects—which have been held up for reasons ranging from legal disputes to the unavailability of fuel supplies—as well as continuing access to external sources of energy. India is caught in an unenviable situation in that it has to depend on energy supplies from the Middle East, particularly Iran, and has been outbid by China when it has sought to diversify into other regions. Yet, without a concerted and successful effort to gain access to new sources of energy, Indian developmental efforts are likely to be stalled.

Third, there is the challenge of building a 21st-century infrastructure so as to bring about a boom in trade and commerce as well as open up rural India to the economic revolution that is taking place in India's urban areas. In the period 2007–2012, India has planned to invest $320 billion[24] in infrastructure, but this is too modest an amount to bring about the transformation to a modern economy. More recent estimates state that more than a trillion dollars will have to be spent to achieve the kind of changes that will be needed both to promote higher growth and also to accommodate the needs of India's growing population.

Finally, there is the problem of educating Indians to fit them into the workforce of the 21st century. In effect, this will require raising the educational standards within the nation to allow more Indians to compete within the international system and to train for jobs that may come to India as the result of globalization. The other part of the puzzle lies in developing vocational education to meet the requirements for skilled and semiskilled labor in the country. The proliferation of private educational institutions in this context—both for learning English and for getting a better technical training—is heartening, but questions remain about how effective they are in developing high-caliber students?

The answer to all these policy challenges seems to be greater integration into the world economy to get both investments and markets. Doing this successfully will require creating a security environment that allows for cooperation in the Asian region and encourages confidence in investors to choose India. To do this, India will have to start to normalize relations in the South Asian region and manage the relationship with China in a manner that is mutually beneficial to New Delhi and Beijing. The real fear is that India may be overwhelmed by regional issues and find its relationship with China breaking down because of misperceptions or insecurities on either side.

NOTES

1. See Selig Harrison, *India: The Most Dangerous Decades* (Princeton, NJ: Princeton University Press, 1966).

2. Sisir Gupta, "India and Pakistan: A Comparison of Their Political Systems," in M.S. Rajan and Shivaji Ganguly (eds.), *Sisir Gupta: India and the International System—A Selection of the Major Writings of Sisir Gupta* (New Delhi: Vikas, 1981), pp. 114–15.

3. Rammathot Khongreiwot, "Understanding the Histories of Peoples on the Margins: A Critique of 'Northeast India's Durable Disorder,'" *Alternatives* 34 (2009): p. 443.

4. Charles Chasie and Sanjoy Hazarika, "The State Strikes Back: India and the Naga Insurgency," *Policy Studies* 52, East–West Center, Washington, DC, 2009, p. 26.

5. Brigadier S. P. Sinha, "Nagaland: The Beginning of the Insurgency II," *Indian Defence Review,* May 10, 2011, http://www.indiandefencereview.com/homeland%20security/Nagaland-The-Beginning-of-Insurgency—II.html.

6. Mahendra Ved "'Big Brother' India Loses Out in Dhaka," *New Strait Times,* September 12, 2011.

7. For a recent discussion of Cohen's views, see Stephen P. Cohen and others, *The Future of Pakistan* (Washington, DC: Brookings Institution Press, 2011), pp. 1–12.

8. Munir Ahmed, "Pakistan Grants India 'Most Favored Nation' Status," *The Christian Science Monitor,* November 2, 2011.

9. Steve Coll, "The Back Channel. India and Pakistan's Secret Kashmir Talks," *The New Yorker,* vol. 85, issue 3, March 2, 2009.

10. Ibid.

11. Alka Acharya, "Wither India–China Relations," *Economic and Political Weekly,* vol. XLIV, issue 45, November 7, 2009.

12. Interview with Jabin T. Jacob, assistant director, Institute for Chinese Studies Delhi, September 29, 2011.

13. Interview with Professor Srikanth Kondapalli, Center for East Asian Studies, Jawaharlal Nehru University, New Delhi, September 15, 2011.

14. Kingshuk Nag, "China's Protest against P.M.'s Visit to Arunachal Is Disgusting," *The Times of India,* October 13, 2009.

15. Interview with Professor Srikanth Kondapalli, Center for East Asian Studies, Jawaharlal Nehru University, New Delhi, September 15, 2011.

16. Jinwoog Kim, "On India–South Korea Relations," Institute for Peace and Conflict Studies, New Delhi, October 4, 2011, http://www.ipcs.org/article/india/on-india-south-korea-relations-3474.html.

17. "IAF Prefers Swiss Trainer PC-7 over Korean KT-1," *India Today,* December 14, 2011, http://indiatoday.intoday.in/story/iaf-swiss-trainer-jet-pc-7-vs-korean-trainer-jet-kt-1/1/164238.html.

18. Mark Mazetti, "Panetta Credits Pakistan Doctor in bin Laden Raid," *The New York Times,* January 28, 2012.

19. Vikas Bajaj, "Foreign Investment Ebbs in India," *The New York Times*, February 24, 2011.

20. Vikas Bajaj, "As Economy Slows, India Awakens to Need for Foreign Investment," *The New York Times,* February 7, 2012.

21. Hugh White, "Power Shift: Rethinking Australia's Place in the Asian Century," *Australian Journal of International Affairs,* 65, no. 1 (2011): pp. 86–87.

22. White, ibid., p. 86.

23. D. S Arora, et. al., "Indian Renewable Energy Status Report," NREL/TP-6A20-48948, October 2010, U.S. Department of Energy, Oakridge, Tennessee, October 2010, p. 1.

24. "Infrastructure Requirements Too Large for Budget Provision," *The Hindu,* March 12, 2007.

Bibliography

BOOKS AND MONGRAPHS

Ablett, Jonathan, et al. *The "Bird of Gold": The Rise of India's Consumer Market* (San Francisco, CA: Mckinsey Global Institute, May 2007).

Armitage, Richard L., R. Nicholas Burns, and Richard Fontaine. *Natural Allies: A Blueprint for the Future of U.S.–India Relations* (Washington, DC: Center for New American Security, 2010).

Broadman, Harry G. *Africa's Silk Road: China and India's Economic Frontier* (Washington, DC: International Bank for Reconstruction and Development, 2007).

Chari, P. R., Pervaiz Iqbal Cheema, Stephen P. Cohen. *Four Crises and a Peace Process: American Engagement in South Asia* (Washington, DC: Brookings Institution Press, 2007).Cohen, Stephen P., and others. *The Future of Pakistan* (Washington, DC: Brookings Institution Press, 2011).

Graham, Thomas, W. "India," in James Everett Katz (ed.), *Arms Production in the Third World* (Lexington: Lexington Books, 1984).

Guha, Ramchandra. *India after Gandhi: The History of the World's Largest Democracy* (New Delhi: Picador, 2007).

Gupta, Amit. *Building an Arsenal: The Evolution of Regional Power Force Structures* (London and Westport, CT: Praeger, 1997).

Gupta, Sisir. "India and Pakistan: A Comparison of Their Political Systems," in M. S. Rajan and Shivaji Ganguly (eds.), *Sisir Gupta: India and the International System—A Selection of the Major Writings of Sisir Gupta* (New Delhi: Vikas, 1981).

Harrison, Selig. *India: The Most Dangerous Decades* (Princeton, NJ: Princeton University Press, 1966).

Huntington, Samuel P. *Who Are We? The Challenges to America's National Security* (New York: Simon and Schuster, 2004).

Kaplan, Robert. *Monsoon: The Indian Ocean and the Future of American Power* (New York: Random House, 2011).

Khandelwal, Madhulika S. *Becoming American, Being Indian* (Ithaca, NY: Cornell University Press, 2002).

Kotkin, Joel. *Tribes* (New York: Random House, 1993).

Kux, Dennis. *Estranged Democracies: India and the United States* (Washington, DC: National Defense University Press, 1993).

Lanfranchi, Pierre, and Matthew Taylor. *Moving with the Ball: Migration of Professional Footballers* (New York: Berg Press, 2001).

Lieven, Anatol. *Pakistan: A Hard Country* (New York: Public Affairs, 2011).

Prashad, Vijay. *Uncle Swami: South Asians in America Today* (New York: The New Press, 2012).

Raja Mohan, C. *Impossible Allies: Nuclear India, the United States, and Global Order* (New Delhi: India Research Press, 2006).

Ramesh, Jairam. *Making Sense of Chindia: Reflections on China and India* (New Delhi: India Research Press, 2005).

Riedel, Bruce. *Deadly Embrace: Pakistan, America, and the Future of the Global Jihad* (Washington, DC: The Brookings Institution Press, 2011).

Rikhye, Ravi. *The Militarisation of Mother India* (New Delhi: Chanakya, 1990).

Schaffer, Teresita C. *India and the United States in the 21st Century: Reinventing Partnership* (Washington, DC: Center for Strategic and International Studies, 2009).

Shain, Yossi. *Marketing the American Creed Abroad: Diaspora in the U.S. and Their Homelands* (Cambridge and New York: Cambridge University Press, 1999).

Siddiqui, Aslam. *Pakistan Seeks Security* (Lahore: Longmans, Green and Co, 1960).

Sikri, Rajiv. *Challenge and Strategy: Rethinking India's Foreign Policy* (New Delhi: Sage, 2009).

Solomon, Steve. *Water: The Epic Struggle for Wealth, Power, and Civilization* (New York: HarperCollins, 2010).

Talbott, Strobe. *Engaging India: Diplomacy, Democracy, and the Bomb* (Washington, DC: Brookings Institution Press, 2004).

Tellis, Ashley J. *Dogfight! India's Medium Multi-Role Combat Aircraft Decision* (Washington, DC: Carnegie Endowment for International Peace, 2011).

Wildavsky, Ben. *The Great Brain Race: How Global Universities Are Reshaping the World* (Princeton, NJ: Princeton University Press, 2010).

Wolf Jr., Charles, et al. *China and India, 2025. A Comparative Assessment* (Santa Monica, CA: Rand Corporation, 2011).

Wolpert, Stanley. *Shameful Flight: The Last Years of British Rule in India* (New York: Oxford University Press, 2006).

Woodward, Bob. *Obama's Wars* (New York: Simon and Schuster, 2010).

ARTICLES AND REPORTS

Acharya, Alka. "Wither India–China Relations," *Economic and Political Weekly,* vol. XLIV, issue 45, November 7, 2009.

Ahmed, Munir. "Pakistan Grants India 'Most Favored Nation' Status," *The Christian Science Monitor,* November 2, 2011.

Aneja, Atul. "Oil Payment Row and India–Iran Ties," *The Hindu,* August 1, 2011.

Aris, Stephen "The Shanghai Cooperation Organisation: 'Tackling the Three Evils'. A Regional Response to Non-Traditional Security Challenges or an Anti-Western Bloc?," *Europe–Asia Studies* 61, no. 3 (2009).

Arora, D. S., et al. *Indian Renewable Energy Status Report,* NREL/TP-6A20-48948 October 2010, U.S. Department of Energy, Oakridge Tennessee, October 2010.

Arpi, Claude "China's Water War with India," *The Pioneer,* June 26, 2011.

Bahri, Deepika. "The Digital Diaspora: South Asians in the New Pax Electronica," in Makarand Paranjape (ed.) *IN Diaspora* (New Delhi: Indialog Publications, 2001).

Bajaj, Vikas. "As Economy Slows, India Awakens to Need for Foreign Investment," *The New York Times,* February 7, 2012.

Bajaj, Vikas. "Foreign Investment Ebbs in India," *The New York Times*, February 24, 2011.

Bajaj, Vikas. "India Approves Long Delayed Steel Mill Project," *The New York Times,* January 31, 2011.

Bakshi, Jyotsna. "India–Russia Defence Cooperation," *Strategic Analysis* 30, no. 2 (2006): pp. 453–54.

Baruah, Amit. "India, Russia May Invite China to Join Fighter Aircraft Project," *The Hindu,* June 27, 2004.

Baruah, Amit. "Multilateralism the Best Solution," *The Hindu,* October 11, 2004.

Bedi, Rahul. "India Finally Launches ATV," *Jane's Defence Weekly,* August 5, 2009.

Bedi, Rahul. "Klub-S Missile Snags Delay Delivery of Indian Sub," *Jane's Defence Weekly,* January 23, 2008.

Bedi, Rahul. "Moving Closer to Israel," *Frontline,* vol. 20, issue 4, February 15–28, 2003.

Bhushan, Ranjit. "Shock Therapy," *Outlook India,* December 24, 2001.

Borman, Matthew S. "NSSP: U.S., India Interests in Action," *The Hindu,* October 2, 2004.

Bose, Sumantra. "Kashmir, 1990–2000: Reflections on Individual Voices in a Dirty War," *Development* 43, no. 3 (September 2000).

Brulliard, Karen, and Debbie Wilgoren. "Failure to Discover bin Laden's Refuge Stirs Suspicion over Pakistan's role," *The Washington Post,* May 2, 2011.

Chasie, Charles, and Sanjoy Hazarika. "The State Strikes Back: India and the Naga Insurgency," *Policy Studies* 52, East–West Center, Washington, DC, 2009.

Chellany, Brahma. "Toward Asian Power Equilibrium," *The Hindu,* November 1, 2008.

Chellany, Brahma. "Troubled Times for Chinese–Indian Relations: Trade Isn't Enough to Build Goodwill between the Two Asian Giants," *The Washington Times,* January 3, 2011.

Chengappa, Raj. "LCA Project: A Testing Time," *India Today,* August 31, 1988.

Chenoy, Anuradha M. "A Defining Moment," *Frontline,* vol. 17, issue 21, October 14–27, 2000.

Cherian, John. "American Agenda," *Frontline,* vol. 27, issue 24, November 20–December 3, 2010.

Cherian, John. "Deals and Doubts," *Frontline,* vol. 22, issue 16, July 30–August 12, 2005.

Cherian, John. "The Defence Deals," *Frontline,* vol. 17, issue 21, October 14–27, 2000.

Clinton, Hillary Rodham. "America's Engagement in the Asia-Pacific, Remarks, Kahala Hotel," Honolulu, HI October 28, 2010, http://www.state.gov/secretary/rm/2010/10/150141.htm.

Coll, Steve "The Back Channel: Reporter at Large," *The New Yorker,* vol. 85, issue 3, March 2, 2009.

Crossette, Barbara. "The Elephant in the Room," *Foreign Policy,* January/February 2010.

D'Almeida, Kanya. "India's Stores on Big-Box Frontier," *Asia Times,* February 2, 2012.

Deshpande, Vinaya. "Curb Terrorism, Sarkozy Tells Pakistan," *The Hindu,* December 8, 2010.

Devraj, Ranjit. "India Fighting for a Less Corrupt Year," *Asia Times,* January 4, 2012.

Dikshit, Sandeep. "Let's Be Sensitive to Each Other's Concerns," *The Hindu,* December 17, 2010.

Dupont, Alan. "Unsheathing the Samurai Sword: Japan's Changing Security Policy," *Lowy Institute Paper* 03, 2004.

Dutt, Ela. "What the Results Mean for Indian American Interests," *News India Times,* November 22, 2002.

Duttagupta, Ishani. "Pravasi Bharatiya Divas 2012: Key Takeaways for Overseas Indians," *The Economic Times,* January 14, 2012.

Economic Survey, 2002–2003, Ministry of Finance and Company Affairs, Government of India, http://indiabudget.nic.in/es2002–03/chapt2003/chap612.pdf.

Einhorn, Bruce. "Chinese Companies Try to Solve Their India Problem," *Businessweek Bloomberg,* May 9, 2010, http://www.businessweek.com/blogs/eyeonasia/archives/2010/05/chinesecompaniestrytosolvetheirindiaproblem.html.

Ford, Peter "China Japan Territorial Spat over a Fishing Boat Flares," *The Christian Science Monitor,* September 10, 2010.

Freedman, Allison Marz. "USINPAC and the U.S.–India Nuclear Deal: Lasting Influence or One Shot Victory?" *CUREJ—College Undergraduate Research Electronic Journal,* August 2009.

Freedman, Samuel G. "Pride and Concern Follow Success of Indian-Americans," *The New York Times,* July 10, 2010.

Friedberg, Aaron L. "Hegemony with Chinese Characteristics," *The National Interest,* July/August 2011.

The Future of the Global Muslim Population, 2010–2030, Pew Templeton Global Religious Futures Project, Washington, DC, 2011.

Ghosh, Madhuchanda. "India and Japan's Growing Synergy: From a Political to a Strategic Focus," *Asian Survey* 48, no. 2 (2008).

Gidadhubli, R. G. "Refurbishing the Military Industrial Complex," *Economic and Political Weekly,* August 23, 2003.

Good, Chris. "Will Macaca Hurt George Allen in 2012?" http://www.theatlantic.com/politics/archive/2011/02/will-macaca-haunt-george-allen-in-2012/71513/.

Graham, Thomas, W. "India," in James Everett Katz (ed.), *Arms Production in the Third World* (Lexington: Lexington Books, 1984)

Grevatt, Jon. "India and Russia Sign Initial FGFA Design Contract," *Jane's Defence Weekly,* January 5, 2011.

Gupta, Amit. "Determining India's Force Structure and Military Doctrine: I Want My M-i-G." *Asian Survey* 35, no. 5 (1995).

Gupta, Amit. "India's Soft Power," *Indian Foreign Affairs Journal* 1, no. 1 (2006): p. 51.

Gupta, Sisir. "The Indus Waters Treaty 1960," *Foreign Affairs Report,* New Delhi, December 1960.

Gupta, Sisir. "India and Pakistan: A Comparison of Their Political Systems," in M. S. Rajan and Shivaji Ganguly (eds.), *Sisir Gupta: India and the International System—A Selection of the Major Writings of Sisir Gupta* (New Delhi: Vikas, 1981).

Hall, Ian. "The Other Exception?: India as a Rising Power," *The Australian Journal of International Affairs* 64, no. 5 (November 2010).

Haq, Noor ul. "Pakistan's Water Concerns," *IPRI Factfile* 127, October 2010.

Hate, Vibhuti. "India's Energy Dilemma," *South Asia Monitor,* vol. 98, September 7, 2006.

Hathaway, Robert. "Confrontation and Retreat: The U.S. Congress and the South Asian Nuclear Tests," *Arms Control Today,* January/February 2000.

Hathaway, Robert. "Unfinished Passage: India, Indian Americans, and the U.S. Congress," *The Washington Quarterly* 24, no. 2 (2001).

High Level Committee Report on the Indian Diaspora (New Delhi: Government of India, January 8, 2002).

Huang, Yasheng. "The Myth of Economic Complementarity in Sino-Indian Relations," *The Journal of International Affairs* 64, no. 2 (2011).

Hussain, Zakir. "India Woos GCC's Sovereign Wealth Fund: Policy, Scope and Precautions," IDSA Policy Brief, June 26, 2009, http://idsa.in/policybrief/IndiaWoosGCCsSovereignWealth Fundzhussain260609.

"The India Imperative: A Conversation with Robert D. Blackwill," *The National Interest* 80 (2005).

"The International Initiative for Justice in Gujarat," December 19, 2002, http://www.onli nevolunteers.org/gujarat/reports/iijg/.

Iyer-Mitra, Abhijit. "Debate: Is a Nuclear Iran Good for India?," *Article #3423, Institute for Peace and Conflict Studies,* New Delhi, July 11,2011, http://www.ipcs.org/article/india/debate-is-a-nuclear-iran-good-for-india-3423.html.

Jaffrelot, Christophe. "India's Look East Policy: An Asianist Strategy in Perspective," *India Review* 2, no. 2 (April 2003).

Jain, Purnendra. "Westward Ho! Japan Eyes India Strategically," *Japanese Studies* 28, no. 1 (2008).

Kanwal, Gurmeet. "Indo-Russian Partnership," *Deccan Herald,* 25 December, 2007.

Khanna, Vikram. "Merging Identity, Power and Space; Indian-American Author Parag Khanna Discusses the Importance of Diasporas in the Multipolar World of the 21st Century," *The Business Times,* Singapore, July 5, 2011.

Khongreiwot, Rammathot. "Understanding the Histories of Peoples on the Margins: A Critique of 'Northeast India's Durable Disorder,'" *Alternatives* 34 (2009).

Kim, Jinwoog. "On India–South Korea Relations," Institute for Peace and Conflict Studies, New Delhi, October 4, 2011, http://www.ipcs.org/article/india/on-india-south-korea-rela tions-3474.html.

Kinvall, Catarina, and Ted Svensson, "Hindu Nationalism, Diaspora Politics, and Nation-Building in India," *Australian Journal of International Affairs* 64, no. 3 (2010).

Kotkin, Joel, and Shashi Parulekar. "India Conquers the World; After a Long Eclipse, an Ancient Country Finally Returns As a Force in Global Business and Culture," *Newsweek,* August 8, 2011.

Krishna, Raj. "India and the Bomb," *India Quarterly* 21, no. 2 (April–June 1965).

Krishnan, Anantha. "Tank Buy, Missile Test Give Indian DRDO a Boost," *Aerospace Daily & Defense Report,* May 20, 2010.

Krishnaswami, Sridhar. "U.S. to Ease Curbs on Space, N-facilities," *The Hindu,* September 20, 2004.

Kronstadt, K. Alan. "India–U.S. Relations," *CRS Issue Brief for Congress,* July 29, 2004.

Kronstadt, K. Alan, and Kenneth Katzman. "India–Iran Relations and U.S. Interests," *CRS Report for Congress,* RS22486, August 6, 2007.

Kuchins, Andrew C. "Russia's Relations with China and India: Strategic Partnerships, Yes; Strategic Alliances, No," *Demokratizatsiya* 9, no. 2 (2001).

Kumar, Chethan. "Tejas Flies, but IAF Dithers," *Deccan Herald,* January 10, 2012.

Kumaraswamy, P. R. "Realism Replacing Rhetoric: Factors Shaping India's Middle East Policy," *The Round Table* 97, no. 397 (2008).

Kux, Dennis "India's Fine Balance," *Foreign Affairs* 81, no. 3 (2002).

Ladwig III, Walter C. "A Cold Start for Hot Wars: The Indian Army's New Limited War Doctrine," *International Security* 32, no. 3 (Winter 2007–2008).

Lakshman, Ganesh S. "American Jews Moot India–US–Israel Coalition against Terror," *The Hindustan Times,* September 14, 2002.

Lee, Chung Min. "China's Rise, Asia's Dilemma," *The National Interest,* Issue 81, Fall 2005.

Levi, Werner. "India Debates Foreign Policy," *Far Eastern Survey,* 20, no. 5 (1951).

Madan, Tanvi. "India," *The Brookings Foreign Policy Energy Security Studies,* Washington, DC, 2006.

Malgrem, Phillipa. "The China Temptation: Are Western Investors Being Foolhardy," *The International Political Economy,* 19, no. 2 (2005).

"Maoist Insurgents in India: More Bloody and Defiant," *The Economist,* July 22, 2010.

Masani, M. R. "The Communist Party of India," *Pacific Affairs,* 24, no. 1 (1951).

Mazetti, Mark. "Panetta Credits Pakistan Doctor in bin Laden Raid," *The New York Times,* January 28, 2012.

Medcalf, Rory. "Problems to Partnership: A Plan for Australia–India Strategic Ties," *Lowy Institute Policy Brief,* November 2009.

Mehta, Ashok K. "US Stumped by Europe," *Daily Pioneer,* May 11, 2011.

Menon, Narayan. "India Russia: Strategic Relations," *Indian Defence Review* 23, no. 1 (2008).

Mohapatra, Sankeet, Dilip Ratha, and Ani Silwal. "Outlook of Remittance Flows 2012–2014," The World Bank, *Migration and Development Brief 17,* December 1, 2011.

Murphy, Katharine. "Digging in on Uranium," *The Age,* Melbourne, November 17, 2011.

Mustafa, Seema. "Angry Russia Hikes Cost of Deals," *Asian Age,* November 19, 2007.

Nag, Kingshuk. "China's Protest against P.M.'s Visit to Arunachal Is Disgusting," *The Times of India,* October 13, 2009.

Nambath, Suresh. "When Modi Was Denied the Visa," *The Hindu,* March 22, 2011.

Nasr, Vali. "In Pakistan, No More Secrets," *The Washington Post,* May 5, 2011.

Nayar, K. P. "Why India Chose the Rafale," *The Telegraph,* Kolkata, India, February 6, 2012.

Nelson, Dean. "Afghanistan Is a Proxy War between India and Pakistan; When Afghanistan's President Hamid Karzai Visited New Delhi Earlier Last Month to Sign a Strategic Partnership Deal, He Quickly Reassured Islamabad It Remained Kabul's Most Important Partner," *The Telegraph,* November 2, 2011.

Nelson, Dean. "India Plans 'World's Most Dangerous Railroad' from Afghanistan to Iran," *The Telegraph,* November 2, 2011.

Nepal's Peace Process: The Endgame Nears, Asia Briefing No. 131, International Crisis Group, Brussels, December 13, 2011.

O'Hanlon, Michael. "U.S.–Pakistan: Bad Marriage, No Divorce," *Politico,* May 2, 2011, http://www.politico.com/news/stories/0511/54091.html.

Omvedt, Gail. "Dalits Mobilizing," *The Hindu,* May 27, 2003.

O'Neill, Jim. "The World, BRICs Dream and India," *Silicon India,* May 2006, p. 10.

Osnos, Evan. "The Next Incarnation," *New Yorker,* vol. 86, issue 30, October 4, 2010.

Panda, Rajaram, and Victoria Tuke, "India–Japan–US Trilateral Dialogue: A Promising Initiative," *IDSA Issue Brief,* November 22, 2011.

Pandit, Rajat. "With Own 5G Jet Plan India 'Rejects' U.S. Offer," *The Times of India,* January 30, 2011.

Pant, Harsh. "India's Relations with Iran: Much Ado about Nothing," *The Washington Quarterly,* 34, no. 1 (2011).

Pantucci, Raffaello, and Alexandros Petersen. "Russia's Eastern Anxieties," *The International Herald Tribune,* October 18, 2011.

Parashar, Sachin. "Drought Hit China to Divert Brahmaputra?" *The Times of India,* June 13, 2011.

Pattanaik, Smrutti S. "Bangladesh and the TATA Investment: Playing Politics with Economics," *IDSA COMMENT,* May 11, 2006, http://www.idsa.in/idsastrategiccomments/BangladeshandtheTATAInvestmentSSPattanaik110506.

Peer, Basharat. "Tear Gas over Batamaloo," *The National Interest,* November/December 2010.

Pei, Minxin. "Dangerous Misperceptions: Chinese Views of India's Rise," http://casi.ssc.upenn.edu/iit/pei.

Percival Wood, Sally. "So Where the Bloody Hell Are We? The Search for Substance in Australia–India Relations," *The Fearless Nadia Papers,* vol. 1, Winter 2011.

Perkovich, George. "Faulty Promises: The U.S.–India Nuclear," *Policy Outlook Carnegie Nonproliferation South Asia,* Carnegie Endowment for International Peace, Washington, DC, September 2005.

Perkovich, George. "Global Implications of the US–India Deal," *Daedalus,* Winter 2010.

Posen, Barry R. "Command of the Commons: The Military Foundations of U.S. Hegemony," *International Security,* 28, no. 1 (2003).

Prabhu, Rajendra. "Misgivings over LCA Plan Changes," *The Hindustan Times,* January 24, 1987.

Pradhan, Samir. "India's Economic and Political Presence in the Gulf: A Gulf Perspective," *India's Growing Role in the Gulf: Implications for the United States,* Gulf Research Center Dubai, 2009.

Quek, Tracey. "U.S. Exempts India from Iran Sanctions; Strategic Move Ahead of Talks Follow Cuts by India in Iranian Oil Purchases," *The Straits Times,* June 13, 2012.

Raghuvanshi, V. "Report Urges India to Widen Contracting Process," *Defense News,* April 30, 2001.

Rai, Archana. "Thriving Economy Lures NRIs Back to India," *The Economic Times,* April 29, 2011.

Raja Mohan, C. "Ending Our Nuclear Winter," *The Indian Express,* July 26, 2005.

Raja Mohan, C. "India's Strategic Challenges in the Indian Ocean and the Gulf," *India's Growing Role in the Gulf: Implications for the United States,* Gulf Research Center Dubai, 2009.

Raja Mohan, C. "Indo-Pacific Naval Cooperation Open to India and Canberra," *The Australian,* November 2, 2011.

Ramachandran, R. "India, U.S. & Trade in Technology," *The Hindu,* September 27, 2004.

Ramachandran, R. "Just a Promise," *Frontline,* vol. 27, issue 24 November 20–December 3, 2010.

Ramachandran, Sudha. "India–Iran Relations at Nadir," *Asia Times,* December 4, 2010.

Ramachandran, Sudha. "India, Russia Still Brothers in Arms," *Asia Times,* October 27, 2007.

Rao, Radhakrishna. "Boosting India's Defense Production Base," *Military Technology,* November 2010.

RBI Monthly Bulletin. "Remittances from Overseas Indians: Modes of Transfer; Transaction Cost and Time Taken," April 2010.

Reconciliation in Sri Lanka: Harder than Ever, Asia Report No. 209, International Crisis Group, Brussels, 18 July, 2011.

Reddy, C. Manmohan. "Making Haste, Slowly," *The Hindu,* December 26, 2002.

Reddy, B. Muralidhar. "Pak. Rejects Sinha's 'Talk of Preemption,'" *The Hindu,* April 4, 2003.

Riedel, Bruce. "American Diplomacy and the 1999 Kargil Summit at Blair House," *Policy Paper Series 2002,* Center for the Advanced Study of India.

Riedel, Bruce. "Pakistan Plays Hardball: Relations with Washington Are on the Skids," *Newsweek,* April 25, 2011.

Rodriguez, Alex, and Mark Magnier. "Pakistan–India Tensions Ease Amid New Concerns; Islamabad, Worried about Afghanistan, Makes a Trade Overture," *Los Angeles Times,* November 7, 2011.

Rowley, Anthony. "Japan MPs Okay 4 Nuke Deals," *The Business Times,* Singapore, December 10, 2011.

Sachar Committee Report, *Social, Economic, and Educational Status of the Muslim Community in India,* Prime Minister's High Level Committee, Government of India, New Delhi, November 2006.

Sachdev, Gulshan. "Reviving Economic Interests," *Frontline,* vol. 17, issue 21, October 14–27, 2000.

Sadeqi, Hadi. "Asian Triangle Will Emerge!" *Daily Afghanistan,* December 18, 2011.

Sahkuja, Vijay. "Huawei Points Way into India," *Asia Times,* January 27, 2010.

Sarkar, Runa. "Overview of the Report," in Nirmal Mohanty, Runa Sarkar, and Ajay Pandey (eds.), *India Infrastructure Report 2009* (New Delhi: Oxford University Press, 2009).

Saxenian, Anna Lee. "Silicon Valley's New Immigrant Entrepreneurs," Working Paper 15, The Center for Comparative Immigration Studies, University of California San Diego, May 2000.

Sheridan, Greg, and Imre Salusinszky. "PM's Uranium Backflip Opens US Door to Delhi. PLAN TO END INDIAN EXPORT BAN OPENS RIFTS IN LABOR," *The Australian,* November 16, 2011.

Sikri, Rajiv "India's 'Look East' Policy," *Asia-Pacific Review,* 16, no. 1 (2009).

Singh, Rahul, and Pramit Pal Chaudhuri. "Can India Pull Off a Covert Strike?" *The Hindustan Times,* May 6, 2011.

Sinha, S. P. "Nagaland: The Beginning of the Insurgency II," *Indian Defence Review,* May 10, 2011, http://www.indiandefencereview.com/homeland%20security/Nagaland-The-Beginning-of-Insurgency—II.html.

Slevin, Peter, and Bradley Graham. "Indian Arms Plan Worries State Dept.," *The Washington Post,* July 23, 2002.

Springer, Richard. "Indian Americans Number 2.8 Million," *India West* XXXVI, no. 28 (2011).

Srivastava, Anupam. "Positive-Sum Game Accruals in US–India Relations," *Bharat Rakshak Monitor,* vol. 51, July–September, 2002, http://www.bharatrakshak.com/MONITOR/ISSUE5-1/anupam.html.

Subrahmanyam, K. "Narasimha Rao and the Bomb," *Strategic Analysis* 28, no. 4 (2004).

Talbott, Strobe. "Dealing with the Bomb in South Asia," *Foreign Affairs* 78, no. 2 (1999).

Tavan, Gwenda. "The Dismantling of the White Australia Policy: Elite Conspiracy or Will of the Australian People?" *Australian Journal of Political Science* 39, no. 1 (March 2004).

Tellis, Ashley. "The Strategic Consequences of a Nuclear India," *Orbis* 46, no. 1 (Winter 2002).

Tellis, Ashley. *India as a Global Player: An Action Agenda for the United States* (Washington, DC: Carnegie Endowment for International Peace, July 2005).

Tellis, Ashley. "Obama in India. Building a Global Partnership: Challenges, Risks, and Opportunities," *Policy Outlook,* Carnegie Endowment for International Peace, October 28, 2010.

Tellis, Ashley "What Should We Expect from India As a Strategic Partner," in Henry D. Sokolski (ed.), *Gauging U.S.–Indian Strategic Cooperation* (Carlisle, PA: Strategic Studies Institute, Army War College, 2007).

Thomas, Raju G. C. "U.S. Transfers of 'Dual-Use' Technologies to India," *Asian Survey* XXX, no. 9 (1990).

Thompson, Krissah. "Indian Americans Take Next Step in Political Ascent; Record Number Seek Office Moving from the Sidelines to Candidacy," *The Washington Post,* July 6, 2010.

Unnithan, Sandeep. "Battle over Gorshkov," *India Today,* December 7, 2007.

Varadarajan, Siddharth. "Joint Statement Flowed from Meeting of Prime Ministers," *The Hindu,* July 17, 2009.

Ved, Mahendra. "'Big Brother' India Loses Out in Dhaka," *New Strait Times,* September 12, 2011.

Velloor, Ravi. "India Extends Reach with N-Sub Launch," *The Straits Times,* July 27, 2009.

Vishwanath, Rohit. "It's Smart Diplomacy," *The Times of India,* May 10, 2011.

Wade, Matt. "Primed and Ready: One Misbeat from Nuclear War," *Sydney Morning Herald,* December 2, 2010.

Watt, Nicholas, and Vikram Dodd. "Cameron Sparks Diplomatic Row with Pakistan after 'Export of Terror' Remarks," *The Guardian,* July 28, 2010.

White, Hugh. "The Limits to Optimism: Australia and the Rise of China," *Australian Journal of International Affairs* 59, no. 4 (2005).

White, Hugh. "Power Shift: Rethinking Australia's Place in the Asian Century," *Australian Journal of International Affairs* 65, no. 1 (2011).

Witte, Griff. "Pakistan Courts China as U.S. Sour," *The Washington Post,* June 23, 2011.

World Population Prospects: The 2010 Revision, http://esa.un.org/wpp/Excel-Data/population.htm.

Yardley, Jim. "India's Diplomatic Balancing Act; with Iranian Delegation in Delhi, Clinton Seeks to Isolate Tehran Further," *International Herald Tribune,* May 9, 2012.

Yaskina, Galina. "Russia–China–India: Prospects for Trilateral Cooperation," *Far Eastern Affairs,* 31, no. 1 (2003).

Yong, Tan Tai, and See Chak Mun. "The Evolution of India–ASEAN Relations," *India Review,* 8, no. 1 (2009).

Yuan, Jing-Dong. "China's Role in Establishing and Building the Shanghai Cooperation Organization (SCO)," *Journal of Contemporary China* 19, no. 67 (2010).

Index

About the Author

AMIT GUPTA is an associate professor in the Department of International Security Studies at the United States Air Force Air War College, Maxwell AFB, Alabama. His work has focused on South Asian and Australian security issues, globalization, and the link between sports and politics.